Los Secretos Mejor Guardados de España

Best Kept Secrets of Spain

Los Secretos Mejor Guardados de España

Siete Destinos Inexplorados

Un Libro Bilingüe

Best Kept Secrets of Spain

Seven Destinations Off The Beaten Track

A Bilingual Book

Por/By : Catalina Ibáñez

Galicia · Asturias · Cantabria · País Vasco · Navarra · Castilla y León · La Rioja · Aragón · Cataluña · Madrid · Extremadura · Castilla-La Mancha · Comunidad Valenciana · Islas Baleares · Murcia · Andalucía · Islas Canarias

España

Los Secretos Mejor Guardados de España/ Spain's Best Kept Secrets offers the joy of mastering a foreign language together with the pleasure of exploring an enticing culture. This bilingual book, especially designed for language learners, will transport you to Spain, as some of the country's most stunning destinations are revealed.

Discover the history, architecture, cuisine and natural beauty of this country's hidden gems as you perfect your Spanish. Miss a word while you're reading in Spanish? Don't worry - the English version is right beside you on the opposite page.

Whether you're looking to perfect your Spanish, explore Spain's alluring culture or plan your next holiday (or perhaps all three!) *Los Secretos Mejor Guardados de España/ Spain's Best Kept Secrets* is your ticket to Spain. Let's go!

Oviedo

Cañón del Sil

Islas Cíes

Laguardia

Castillo de Loarre

Albarracín

Trujillo

España

ÍNDICE

INTRODUCCIÓN

Cuando la gente piensa en España, a menudo imagina cielos despejados sin fin, playas espléndidas, jarras de sangría y noches de fiesta. Aunque la mayoría de los turistas extranjeros visitan destinos populares como Barcelona, Madrid, Granada y las costas del sur, parecen haber olvidado toda una zona de España, en su mayoría virgen. Ideal para aquellos que quieren vivir la emocionante experiencia de descubrir tesoros en caminos apartados, existen gemas en regiones como **Aragón, Asturias, País Vasco, Extremadura** y **Galicia** que permanecen tan inexploradas, que algunos visitantes ni siquiera pueden encontrarlas en un mapa. Sin embargo, con estos tesoros aislados en estas regiones, es difícil imaginar que permanecerán en secreto durante mucho más tiempo.

España esconde dos de sus secretos tan bien, que encontrarlos requiere un gran esfuerzo. El **Castillo de Loarre** y el pueblo de **Albarracín** están enclavados en **Aragón**, una región con esplendor de fama medieval que, a día de hoy, es una de las menos habitadas del país. Dividido en tres áreas geológicas muy distintas, con picos nevados hacia el este, exquisitos valles verdes hacia el oeste y colinas desoladas y áridas hacia el sur, Aragón ofrece ejemplos excepcionales de

INTRODUCTION

When people think of Spain, they often imagine endless sunny skies, glorious beaches, jugs of sangría and party nights. Whilst most foreign tourists visit popular destinations like Barcelona, Madrid, Granada and the southern coasts, they seem to have left a whole side of Spain largely undisturbed. Ideal for those who want to have the exhilarating experience of discovering off-the-beaten-path treasures, gems in regions like **Aragón, Asturias, Basque Country, Extremadura** and **Galicia** remain so unexplored that some visitors couldn't even find them on a map. However, with the treasures tucked away in these regions, it is hard to imagine they will remain secrets for much longer.

Spain hides two of its secrets so well that finding them requires a great deal of effort. **Loarre Castle** and the town of **Albarracín** are nestled in **Aragón**, a splendour of medieval fame that today is one of the least densely populated regions of the country. Divided into three very distinct geological areas, with snow capped peaks to the east, luscious, green valleys to the west and desolate, arid hills to the south, Aragón offers exceptional examples of

pueblos medievales con encanto, así como arquitectura románica y mudéjar: la deslumbrante mezcla gótico-islámica por la que España es conocida.

Una vez descrita por el director Woody Allen como "de cuento de hadas", la ciudad de **Oviedo** es la capital de **Asturias**. Todo acerca de esta ciudad tan especial confirma el dicho local: *"Asturias es España y lo demás, tierra conquistada".* Entra en el antiguo centro de la ciudad, y te transportarás al pasado. Aventúrate fuera de Oviedo, donde la espectacular belleza natural de Asturias te espera: los elevados Picos de Europa, las imponentes playas de la Costa Verde y los exuberantes bosques que rodean las cuencas de los ríos y los lagos de montaña.

Lugar del vino de primera categoría, cocina deliciosa y arquitectura fenomenal, **Laguardia** "se esconde" de lleno en el **País Vasco**. Siendo uno de los pueblos amuralla-dos medievales más encantadores y mejor preservados de España, Laguardia está rodeado por los famosos viñedos de La Rioja, aunque permanece como un tesoro sin descubrir.

Trujillo, un pueblo lleno de historia y costumbres antiguas, te hará sentir como si hubieras viajado al pasado. Ubicado en **Extremadura** (la verdadera esquina "extrema" del oeste de España), es un lugar perfecto para aquellos que quieren disfrutar de las atracciones en vez de ver autobuses turísticos. Este lugar ha sido hogar de los más famosos e infames conquistadores del país, Trujillo y Extremadura definitivamente conquistarán tu alma.

charming medieval villages, as well as Romanesque architecture and Mudéjar architecture - the stunning Gothic and Islamic mix for which Spain is renowned.

Once described by director Woody Allen as a "fairytale", the city of **Oviedo** is the capital of **Asturias.** Everything about this special city confirms the local saying: "Asturias is Spain, and the rest is conquered land". Enter its old town centre, and you will step back in time. Venture outside Oviedo where the spectacular natural beauty of Asturias awaits you: the towering Picos de Europa, the stunning beaches of the Costa Verde and the lush forests surrounding river valleys and mountain lakes.

A place of world class wine, delicious cuisine and phenomenal architecture, **Laguardia** "hides" deep within **Basque Country**. One of the most enchanting and best preserved medieval walled towns in Spain, Laguardia is surrounded by the famed vineyards of La Rioja, but this town remains an undiscovered treasure.

Trujillo, a town full of history and ancient customs, will make you feel like you have travelled back in time. Located in **Extremadura** (the real "extreme" western corner of Spain), this is a perfect place for those who want to see sights instead of tour buses. Home to some of the country's most famous and infamous conquistadors, Trujillo and Extremadura will definitely conquer your soul.

El **Cañón del Sil** en **Galicia** es para aquellos que prefieren perderse en la madre naturaleza, en vez de en inmensas muchedumbres de turistas. Aferrados firmemente a empinadas pendientes de montaña, los viñedos aquí han prosperado desde tiempos antiguos. Las mezclas de vinos de Calidad Certificada, ya de fama internacional, se cultivan empleando algunos de los mismos métodos que utilizaban los antiguos romanos. Galicia es absolutamente espléndida en sus contrastes místicos: desde algunos de los más espectaculares cañones en Europa, a destellantes trechos de playas inmaculadas a lo largo de la costa Atlántica. Las aguas turquesas y las costas impolutas de las **Islas Cíes** han situado este parque nacional gallego en las listas de las mejores playas del mundo.

Pero espera, hay más…

Esta estupenda guía de los **secretos mejor guardados de España** no es de ningún modo exhaustiva. Escoger sólo un puñado de destinos "escondidos" ha sido un reto, ya que el país presume de una larga lista de lugares maravillosos que aún esperan ser descubiertos. Si crees que hay algún lugar especial o notable de España que deberíamos incluir en nuestra próxima edición, visita nuestra web www.SecretosDeEspana.com y ¡háblanos de él!

Cañón del Sil in **Galicia** is for those who prefer to get lost in Mother Nature, instead of in immense tourist crowds. Clinging firmly to steep mountain slopes, the vineyards here have been thriving since ancient times. The quality-certified blends of wine, now of international fame, are grown using some of same methods that the ancient Romans used. Galicia is absolutely splendid in its mystical contrasts: from some of the most spectacular canyons in Europe to sparkling stretches of unspoiled beaches along the Atlantic coast. The turquoise waters and pristine coasts of the **Islas Cíes** have put this Galician national park on lists of the world's best beaches.

But wait, there's more...

This great guide of **Spain's best kept secrets** is by no means exhaustive. Choosing only a handful of "hidden" destinations has been a challenge, as the country boasts a long list of marvellous places still waiting to be discovered. If you think there is a special or remarkable place in Spain that we should include in our next edition, visit our website www.SecretosDeEspana.com and tell us about it!

ALBARRACÍN

ALBARRACÍN

Albarracín

No es difícil imaginar por qué España es el cuarto destino vacacional más popular. Su magnífico clima, paisajes variados, deliciosa gastronomía y lugares históricos actúan como imanes para millones de visitantes cada año. Lo que sí *es* bastante desconcertante es que, tras siglos de turismo, sigamos descubriendo preciosos rincones escondidos en uno de los países más populares del mundo. Albarracín es uno de estos tesoros. El pueblo entero ha sido **monumento nacional** de España desde 1961. Es probable que la UNESCO prefiera añadirlo a su lista de lugares…ojalá puedan encontrar la forma de llegar.

Albarracín es uno de los pueblos más remotos en uno de los rincones más remotos de España, si no de Europa. Situado a una altitud de más de 1100 metros, colocado en lo alto de la cima de una montaña y enmarcado por un río espléndido, Albarracín parece estar perdido en su propio universo, en un lugar donde el tiempo se ha detenido. Preservado en toda su belleza por los **Montes Universales**, este pueblo en la región noroeste española de Aragón ofrece una mezcla exótica de arquitectura medieval e islámica, la cual le proporciona un encanto único.

UN PASO ATRÁS EN EL TIEMPO

Durante la ocupación musulmana de la Península Ibérica, la familia del bereber Banu Razin reinó sobre la región y le dio al Albarracín actual su nombre original "Al Banu Razin". Este pasado morisco dotó a Albarracín de una arquitectura espléndida, que es aún más significativa

It's not hard to imagine why Spain is the fourth most popular holiday destination. Its superb climate, varied landscape, delicious cuisine and historic sites act as magnets for millions of visitors each year. What *is* rather puzzling is that after centuries of tourism, we keep discovering gorgeous hidden nooks in one of the most popular countries in the world. Albarracín is one such treasure. The whole town has been a **national monument** of Spain since 1961. It's likely that UNESCO prefers to add it to its list of sites…if only they could find a way to get here.

Albarracín is one of the most remote towns in one of the most remote corners of Spain, if not Europe. Situated at an altitude of over 1,100 meters, perched high on a mountaintop and framed by a splendid river, Albarracín seems to be lost in its own universe, in a place where time stands still. Preserved in all its beauty by the **Montes Universales**, this town in the Aragón region of northeast Spain offers an exotic mix of medieval and Islamic architecture, which gives it a unique charm.

A STEP BACK IN TIME

During the Muslim occupation of the Iberian Peninsula, the Berber Banu Razin family reigned over the region and gave modern day Albarracín its original name "Al Banu Razin". This Moorish past endowed Albarracín with splendid architecture, which is even more significant

porque el clima seco y árido y su relativa lejanía han preservado el centro histórico en un estado casi perfecto.

No fue hasta el siglo XII cuando la dominación cristiana del área prevaleció. Albarracín fue tomado bajo el reinado de Azagra, la familia regente que se encontró destituida dos siglos después, cuando Albarracín se unió al Reino de Aragón.

ALBARRACÍN EN EL DÍA DE HOY

El Albarracín de hoy, con una población de apenas más de 1000 personas, pertenece a la provincia de **Teruel**, un lugar tan empeñado en obtener más reconocimiento que emprendió la campaña "Teruel existe" a finales de los años 90 en un intento de atraer inversión y turismo a esta región aislada. En consecuencia, Teruel ha mejorado sus conexiones de autopistas, pero aún no hay un tren directo a Madrid. Aunque esto es frustrante para los propietarios de negocios locales, es bastante adorable desde el punto de vista del visitante. Desde Teruel, un destino que en sí mismo que merece una visita por los exquisitos ejemplos de arquitectura mudéjar, hay un trayecto de media hora en coche a Albarracín, por un trecho de carretera increíblemente pintoresco. Conducir a lo largo del **Río Guadalaviar** y junto a los restos de antiguos acueductos romanos, mientras evitas a ocasionales ovejas o burros sueltos de la granja de al lado, proporciona una introducción fenomenal al pueblo. Cuando ves Albarracín por primera vez, en la cima de una montaña y rodeado por el Guadalaviar, el cual siempre ha actuado como

because the dry, arid climate and relative obscurity have preserved the historic centre in a nearly perfect state.

It wasn't until the 12th century that Christian dominance of the area prevailed. Albarracín was seized under the Kingdom of Azagra, whose ruling family found itself deposed two centuries later when Albarracín joined the Kingdom of Aragón.

MODERN DAY ALBARRACÍN

Today's Albarracín, with a population of just over 1,000 people, belongs to the province of **Teruel**, a place so intent on gaining more recognition that it undertook the "*Teruel existe*" ("Teruel exists") campaign at the end of the 90's in an effort to attract investment and tourism to the isolated region. As a result, Teruel has improved highway connections, but there is still no direct train to Madrid. Although this is frustrating to local business owners, it is quite endearing from a visitor's point of view. From Teruel, a destination which itself merits a visit for the exquisite examples of Mudéjar architecture, it is a half an hour journey by car to Albarracín, on an incredibly scenic stretch of road. Driving alongside the **Guadalaviar River** and beside the remains of ancient Roman aqueducts, while dodging the odd sheep or donkey on the loose from a neighbouring farm, provides a brilliant introduction to the town. When you first spot Albarracín, atop a mountain and surrounded by the Guadalaviar, which has always acted as

Albarracín

una fosa natural, entiendes cuán estratégica era en realidad su ubicación.

EL CASCO ANTIGUO DE ALBARRACÍN

Dentro del **barrio histórico**, encontrarás una colección de caminos sinuosos, casas e iglesias con siglos de antigüedad, todos ellos reunidos dentro de una antigua muralla. A medida que exploras las estrechas calles empinadas y las murallas fortificadas, los siglos de historia cobran vida. Perderse aquí no es tan sólo inevitable, ¡es también una forma divertida e intrínseca de explorar el pueblo!

Las altas **casas históricas** están adornadas con preciosos balcones de madera y decorados con los escudos de armas de

Albarracín

a natural moat, you then understand how strategic its location really was.

ALBARRACÍN'S CASCO ANTIGUO

Inside the **historic quarter**, you'll find a collection of winding lanes, centuries-old houses and churches, all encompassed in an ancient city wall. As you explore the town's steep, narrow streets and fortified walls, the centuries of history come to life. Getting lost here is not only inevitable, but also fun and an intrinsic way of exploring the town!

The tall, **historic houses** are adorned with beautiful wooden balconies and decorated with the coats of arms of

las familias aristocráticas de Albarracín. Como algunas de las calles son muy estrechas, ¡los balcones opuestos a menudo están sólo a un paso los unos de los otros! Una de las escenas más encantadoras aquí es observar a los lugareños charlar e interactuar unos con otros de un balcón a otro.

Muchas de estas casas tienen rejas decorativas de hierro forjado que protegen las ventanas, y algunas piezas bastante interesantes e inusuales vigilando las entradas. Las sólidas puertas de madera de las casas color siena de Albarracín están adornadas con aldabas y pomos tallados intrincadamente: verdaderas obras de arte en sí mismas. Estas **estatuillas de hierro fundido**, que representan flores, serpientes, lagartos y dragones, son algunos de los emblemas más singulares de Albarracín.

No importa lo perdido que estés en el centro, de una forma u otra al final te encontrarás con la plaza del pueblo: la **Plaza Mayor**. Como en muchos pueblos españoles, la Plaza Mayor es el lugar de encuentro principal. Aunque bastante pequeña, desde luego aprovecha su espacio compacto. Los lugareños se congregan en la acogedora taberna para beber cerveza, charlar, comer tapas y jugar a las cartas.

El **Ayuntamiento** medieval, con preciosos arcos, pórticos y balcones, data del siglo XVI. No te pierdas la oportunidad de disfrutar de increíbles vistas desde el segundo piso, desde el que sin duda verás el escudo de Albarracín decorando el balcón a lo largo del trío de banderas: las de España, Aragón y Albarracín.

Albarracín's aristocratic families. Since some of the streets are very narrow, opposing balconies are often only a step away from each other! One of the loveliest scenes here is watching locals talk and interact with each other from one balcony to another.

Many of these homes have decorative wrought iron railings protecting the windows, and some rather interesting and unusual pieces guarding the entrances. The solid wooden doors of Albarracín's sienna-coloured homes are adorned with intricately carved door knockers and handles - true works of art in themselves. These **cast iron figurines**, that depict flowers, snakes, lizards and dragons, are some of Albarracín's most unique emblems.

No matter how lost you are in the centre, in one way or another you will eventually come upon the main town square: the **Plaza Mayor**. As in most Spanish towns, the Plaza Mayor is the principal gathering place. Although rather small, it certainly makes the most of its compact space. Locals congregate in the cozy taberna to drink cerveza, chat, eat tapas and play cards.

The medieval **Ayuntamiento**, with beautiful archways, porticoes and balconies, dates from the 16th century. Don't miss the chance to enjoy great views from the second floor, where you'll no doubt notice Albarracín's shield decorating the balcony along with the trio of flags: those of Spain, Aragón and Albarracín.

Albarracín

A mediados de septiembre pasa a su "modalidad de celebración" ya que a la santa patrona, Santa María, se le celebra una animada fiesta. Albarracín organiza su propio encierro de toros por la Plaza Mayor y por las estrechas calles adoquinadas. ¡El tumulto de este evento hace que sea muy interesante observarlo!

Cuando dejes la plaza principal, continúa tu ascenso a la llamativa **Catedral de El Salvador**, construida en el siglo XIII, completamente reconstruida en el siglo XVI, y renovada durante el siglo XVIII. Con una seductora mezcla de elementos góticos y renacentistas, la catedral es una joya de la arquitectura y presume de un campanario decorado con llamativas baldosas. No te pierdas el mirador al lado de la catedral: las vistas de gran alcance del pueblo y el campo desde aquí son increíbles.

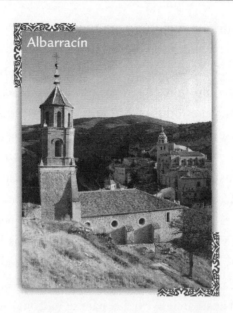

Albarracín

In mid-September it goes into full celebration mode as the patron saint, Santa María, is given a lively fiesta. Albarracín organizes its own running of the bulls around the Plaza Mayor and through the narrow cobblestone streets. The mayhem of this event makes it quite exciting to watch!

When you leave the main plaza, continue your ascent to the striking **Catedral de El Salvador**, built in the 13th century, completely refurbished in the 16th century, and renovated during the 18th century. With an enticing mix of Gothic and Renaissance elements, the cathedral is an architectural gem and boasts a bell tower decorated with bright tiles. Don't miss the lookout point next to the cathedral - the sweeping town and countryside views from here are amazing.

¿Buscas más miradores espectaculares? Pues entonces dirígete a la **fortaleza en la cima de Albarracín**. De camino a esta fortaleza del siglo X, encontrarás un pequeño y casi escondido quiosquito que sirve una pequeña selección de tapas. Llena el estómago con algunas delicias locales antes de dirigirte al lugar del pueblo con las mejores vistas: las **murallas**. Varias secciones de esta muralla antigua han sido reconstruidas a lo largo de los años, pero la sensación de antigüedad permanece. La caminata al punto más alto de la muralla puede que sea un poco dura, ¡pero la recompensa vale la pena! Estas enormes murallas bajan por las colinas que rodean el pueblo y ofrecen increíbles vistas panorámicas, las cuales incorporan el precioso campanario de la catedral, el río y el parque nacional adyacente.

Si hay una atracción favorita aquí, tienen que ser las **puestas de sol**. Los magníficos tonos terrosos de los edificios del pueblo casi hacen que Albarracín parezca estar en llamas cuando los últimos rayos de sol del día proyectan su resplandor. Encuentra un punto perfecto para admirar el espectáculo y disfruta del fulgor único que exuda Albarracín.

LA BELLEZA NATURAL DE ALBARRACÍN

Los alrededores de Albarracín son un verdadero paraíso natural, conocido por su excelente **escalada de montaña**, **montañismo** y **pesca**. Abundan en esta área las **cascadas bravas**, los **arroyos naturales** y la bonita **flora y fauna**, y también presume de unos de los mejores ríos para la pesca de truchas en España: el Guadalaviar.

Looking for more spectacular viewpoints? Then head up to **Albarracín's hilltop fortress**. On your way to this 10th century fortress, you'll find a small, almost hidden little kiosk that serves a small selection of tapas. Fill your belly with some local delights before heading to the place with the best view in town: the **city walls**. Several sections of this ancient wall have been rebuilt over the centuries, but the feeling of antiquity remains. The trek to the wall's highest point may be a bit taxing, but the hard work certainly pays off! These massive walls cascade down the hills that surround the town and provide unbelievable panoramic views, which incorporate the gorgeous cathedral bell tower, the river and adjacent national park.

If there is one favourite attraction here, it has to be the **sunsets**. The wonderful earthy tones of the town's buildings almost make Albarracín look as if it was ablaze when the day's last rays of sun cast their glow. Find a perfect spot to admire the spectacle and bask in the unique radiance Albarracín exudes.

ALBARRACÍN'S NATURAL BEAUTY

Albarracín's surroundings are a true natural paradise, renowned for its excellent **mountain climbing**, **hiking** and **fishing**. **Wild waterfalls**, **natural springs** and beautiful **flora and fauna** abound in this area, which also boasts one of the premier trout fishing rivers in Spain: the Guadalaviar.

CASTILLO DE LOARRE

San Juan de la Peña

Castillo de Loarre

Huesca

Zaragoza

Teruel

Aragón

CASTILLO DE LOARRE

Castillo de Loarre

Austero, colosal, orgulloso y solitario…estos son los adjetivos más comunes que la gente utiliza para describir el Castillo de Loarre. En un país con más de 2000 castillos, Loarre es verdaderamente excepcional. Descansa majestuosamente en una prominencia rocosa a lo largo de los bordes de los Pirineos y preside los vastos planos de Aragón. Considerado como el castillo románico mejor preservado de Europa, Loarre también presume de uno de los mejores **miradores** de Aragón. El hecho de que encontrarlo, para empezar, no sea exactamente fácil, simplemente lo hace más misterioso. Una única carretera llena de giros conduce aquí, de lleno al corazón de lo que fue una vez la línea divisoria absoluta entre los reinos cristianos y musulmanes.

El castillo ha sido escenario de muchas películas, la más notable *El reino de los cielos*, 2005 de Ridley Scott. Su ambiente etéreo y su marco de cuento de hadas te hacen sentir como si estuvieras viajando hacia el pasado cuando subes por los escalones de piedra que se alejan de la entrada del castillo. Mientras que la restauración de muchas otras fortalezas históricas las han dejado apenas reconocibles, el Castillo de Loarre no ha visto cambios en casi un milenio. Obsérvalo hoy como era hace 1000 años, y no podrás evitar sentirte abrumado por su **grandiosa presencia**.

Hoy en día, la **altura** del castillo brinda vistas imponentes de los bosques de pinos y los olivos circundantes. Sin embargo, en los tiempos de los conflictos medievales, cuando los reinos de España estaban en guerra (no sólo entre ellos, sino también

Austere, colossal, proud and solitary...these are the most common adjectives people use to describe Loarre Castle. In a country with more than 2,000 castles, Loarre is truly exceptional. It rests majestically on a rocky protrusion along the fringes of the Pyrenees and presides over the vast Aragón plains. Considered the best preserved Romanesque castle in Europe, Loarre also boasts one of the best **lookout points** in Aragón. The fact that locating it in the first place isn't exactly easy simply makes it more intriguing. A single lane road full of twists and turns leads here, deep in the heart of what was once the absolute dividing line between the Christian and Muslim kingdoms.

The castle has provided the setting for many films, most notably Ridley Scott's 2005 movie: *Kingdom of Heaven*. Its ethereal ambience and fairytale setting make you feel like you are travelling back in time when you climb the stone steps that lead up and away from the castle's entrance. While restoration of many other historic fortresses has rendered them barely recognizable, Loarre Castle has not seen changes for almost a millennium. View it today as it was 1,000 years ago, and you can't help feeling over-whelmed by its **grandiose presence**.

Nowadays, the castle's **elevation** provides stunning views of the surrounding pine forests and olive trees. However, back in the days of medieval unrest, when the kingdoms of Spain were at war (not just with each other, but also

con los moros), esta suprema ubicación posibilitó a los reyes a proteger mejor sus preciados imperios.

LA CONSTRUCCIÓN DE UNA LEYENDA

El Castillo de Loarre se construyó en el siglo XI, cuando el estilo de arquitectura **románica** estaba en la cima de su popularidad. Utilizado extensamente entre los siglos VI y XII, el estilo incorpora grandes torres de vigilancia, muros anchos, arcadas y arcos. Las estructuras románicas como el Castillo de Loarre son reconocidas por ser particularmente simplistas, pero aun así son enormes y brutalmente fuertes.

Aunque fue el rey Sancho III de Navarra quien puso las fundaciones de la estructura que vemos hoy, una fortaleza de algún tipo se levantaba en esta ubicación estratégica desde antes de los tiempos de Jesucristo. Los historiadores especulan que los romanos primero construyeron *Calagurris Fibulariensis* en este mismo lugar, un fuerte que perdieron frente a los bárbaros visigodos invasores durante la Edad Oscura, los cuales también lo perdieron frente a los musulmanes en el siglo VIII. Para cuando Sancho III llegó y anexó el fuerte de los musulmanes, Sancho, o se dio cuenta de la importancia de tener una fortaleza protectora aquí, o disfrutaba de tantas puestas de sol románticas que ¡decidió que debería construir su propio castillo! Los arqueólogos han descubierto en este lugar artefactos que datan de los antiguos romanos, incluyendo monedas, pero la historia del fuerte romano aun está por verificar y sigue siendo un misterio.

with the Moors), this prime location enabled kings to better protect their prized empires.

THE BUILDING OF A LEGEND

Loarre Castle was built in the 11th century, when the **Romanesque** style of architecture was at the height of its popularity. Used widely between the 6th and 12th centuries, the style incorporates large watch towers, thick walls, arcades and arches. Romanesque structures like Loarre Castle are renowned for being particularly simplistic yet massive and brutally strong.

Whilst King Sancho III of Navarra laid the foundations of the structure we see today, a fortress of some form stood on this strategic location since before the time of Christ. Historians speculate that the Romans first built *Calagurris Fibulariensis* at this same location, a fort they lost to the invading barbarian Visigoths during the Dark Ages, who in turn lost it to the Muslims in the 8th century. By the time Sancho III arrived and annexed the fort from the Muslims, he either realized the importance of having a protective fortress here, or he enjoyed so many romantic sunsets that he decided he should build his own castle! Archaeologists have discovered on this site artefacts dating back to the ancient Romans, including coins, yet the story of the Roman fort is still unverified and remains a mystery.

Castillo de Loarre

Como prueba de que ni siquiera *esta* ubicación estratégica garantizaba la seguridad, los moros liberaron a Sancho III de su reinado en 1062 y mantuvieron el área durante los siguientes siete años. Cuando el nieto de Sancho III, rey Sancho Ramírez, retomó el control de Loarre en 1070, emprendió un gran periodo de "arreglos caseros". Mucho de lo que vemos hoy fue construido durante este segundo gran periodo de construcción, incluyendo la imponente Iglesia de San Pedro y el monasterio del castillo.

Mientras la enemistad continuada entre cristianos y musulmanes se movía más hacia el sur de España, la importancia y prominencia de Loarre disminuyó mucho. A principios del siglo XII, el Castillo de Loarre ya no servía como fortaleza militar. Esto resultó ser una bendición. El

San Juan
de la Peña

As proof that not even *this* strategic location guaranteed
safety, the Moors relieved Sancho III of his reign in 1062
and held the area for the next seven years. When the
grandson of Sancho III, King Sancho Ramírez, retook
control of Loarre in 1070, he undertook a major period
of "home improvements". Much of what we see today
was built during this second major period of construction, including the stunning Iglesia de San Pedro and the
castle's monastery.

As the continuing feud between Christians and Muslims
moved further south in Spain, the importance and prominence of Loarre greatly diminished. By the beginning
of the 12th century, Loarre Castle no longer served as a
military fortress. This turned out to be a blessing. The

castillo disfrutó de su "jubilación" como sede de goberna-
dores y vivió en relativa tranquilidad y paz, con vistas de
las **puestas de sol aragonesas**.

EXPLORAR EL CASTILLO

El **interior** de Loarre es una maravilla absoluta para
explorar, particularmente por su accesibilidad, aunque
se necesita una linterna para sus esquinas más oscuras e
inquietantes. A diferencia de los castillos más prominentes, apenas nada está acordonado. Pasar el día entero aquí,
interpretando el rol de un rey o de un soldado, es una
actividad maravillosa. Hay túneles oscuros por los que
pasear, así como pasadizos, criptas y mazmorras esperando
a ser explorados. Encuentra una buena mazmorra oscura,
huele las piedras cubiertas de moho y absorbe la atmósfera.
Entonces, sólo por un momento, apaga la linterna. El
siglo XXI parece desaparecer al instante en la oscuridad.

Hay que decir que el rey eligió realmente un lugar encantador para la **Iglesia de San Pedro**. En un día despejado,
la cúpula de 26 metros de altura, empapada de la luz
del sol, irradia una sensación casi espiritual dentro de
la iglesia. Más de 80 columnas, muchas talladas de
forma compleja con representaciones de plantas, flores
y animales, soportan esta estructura impresionante. El
ábside de la iglesia tiene 14 columnas, cada una adornada
con su propia escultura única que, cuando se ven juntas,
cuentan la historia de Adán y Eva.

castle enjoyed its "retirement" as the seat of governors and lived in relative peace and quiet, with views of **Aragón's sunsets**.

EXPLORING THE CASTLE

Loarre's **interior** is an absolute wonder to explore, particularly because of its accessibility, although you need a flashlight in its darkest and most eerie corners. Unlike most prominent castles, hardly any of it is cordoned off. Spending an entire day here, playing the role of a king or a soldier, is a wonderful activity. There are dark tunnels to walk through, along with corridors, crypts and dungeons waiting to be explored. Find a nice dark dungeon, smell the mould covered stones and absorb the atmosphere. Then, for just a moment, turn the flashlight off. The 21st century seems to instantly disappear into the darkness.

It must be said that the king really chose a lovely spot for the **Iglesia de San Pedro**. On a clear day the 26-metre high dome, drenched in sunlight, radiates an almost spiritual feel inside the church. More than 80 columns, many intricately carved with depictions of plants, flowers and animals, support this impressive structure. The church's apse has 14 columns each adorned with its own unique sculpture that, when seen together, tell the story of Adam and Eve.

Los **muros exteriores** son colosales, casi de dos metros de grosor en algunas partes, con 11 torres fortificadas. Este muro no se construyó hasta el siglo XIII, cuando se desarrolló un pueblo alrededor del castillo y emergió la necesidad de semejante estructura. El perímetro de casi 200 metros es testamento de las habilidades de construcción en la Edad Media.

UN TESORO CERCANO: SAN JUAN DE LA PEÑA

Sólo a una hora de Loarre, después de un trayecto en coche por el campo aragonés con los elevados Pirineos en la distancia, se alza el **Monasterio de San Juan de la Peña**, una de las estructuras religiosas más impresionantes de España. El clásico diseño románico es precioso, pero el hecho de que el monasterio esté casi dentro de una peña hace que sea una vista extraordinaria.

La mayoría de recuentos afirman que la construcción inicial del monasterio data del siglo X, pero la parte más impactante de la estructura sigue siendo el claustro de piedra del siglo XII, completo con ornados capitolios decorados con imágenes de santos y escenas de la Biblia. La enorme peña se cierne a lo alto y sirve como el "techo" del claustro. La leyenda cuenta que fue aquí donde los monjes de San Juan escondieron el Santo Grial, protegiéndolo de los moros. Dentro del panteón real yace la tumba del rey Sancho Ramírez, soberano de Aragón, y el rey más famoso del Castillo de Loarre.

The **exterior walls** are colossal, almost two meters thick in some parts, with 11 fortified towers. This wall was not built until the 13th century, when a small village developed around the castle and the need for such a structure emerged. The almost 200-meter perimeter stands as a testament to construction skills in the Middle Ages.

SURROUNDING TREASURE: SAN JUAN DE LA PEÑA

Just an hour away from Loarre, after a drive through the Aragón countryside with the towering Pyrenees in the distance, stands the **Monasterio de San Juan de la Peña**, one of Spain's most breathtaking religious structures. The classic Romanesque design is beautiful, but the fact that the monastery is almost tucked inside a huge boulder makes it an astounding sight.

Most accounts have the monastery's initial construction dating from the 10th century, but the most striking part of the structure remains the 12th century stone **cloister**, complete with ornate capitals decorated with images of saints and scenes from the Bible. The massive boulder hovers above and serves as the cloister's "ceiling". Legend has it that it was here that the monks of San Juan hid the Holy Grail, protecting it from the Moors. Inside the royal pantheon lies the tomb of King Sancho Ramírez, ruler of Aragón, and Loarre Castle's most famous king.

OVIEDO

Costa Verde

Cudillero   Avilés   Gijón

Picos de Europa

★
Oviedo

Asturias

OVIEDO

Oviedo

Los turistas extranjeros, que van en manada a los destinos más populares de las costas sureñas, a menudo pasan por alto la región de Asturias en el norte de España. La capital de la región, Oviedo, es un tesoro "de postal" de increíble arquitectura, exquisitos paisajes y cultura cautivadora. El famoso director de cine Woody Allen (algunas escenas de su famosa película *Vicky Christina Barcelona* se rodaron aquí) dijo una vez que Oviedo es una "ciudad deliciosa, exótica, preciosa...como un cuento de hadas". Un lugar que ofrece tanta historia, tantos obsequios deleitables y la oportunidad de descubrir las maravillas naturales de toda la región de Asturias tiene que ser verdaderamente un destino de cuento.

HISTORIA Y PATRIMONIO

Originariamente fundado por el rey Fruela I de Asturias en el siglo VIII, Oviedo en realidad le debe su existencia al hijo del rey, Alfonso II, el cual consolidó la prominencia de la ciudad declarándola la capital de su reino. Los asturianos son gente orgullosa, que presumen de que **"Asturias es España y lo demás es tierra conquistada"**, refiriéndose al hecho de que los moros, que invadieron España en el siglo VIII, nunca fueron capaces de conquistar el reino de Asturias. Gracias al terreno traicionero de los elevados Picos de Europa, Asturias permaneció protegida e aislada durante siglos. Este aislamiento contribuyó a la diversidad que hace que esta zona sea un lugar tan interesante de explorar. Tiene un ambiente distintivamente diferente al resto del país, algo que sólo lo hace aún más encantador.

oreign tourists, flocking instead to the more popular destinations on the southern coasts, often overlook the region of Asturias in northern Spain. The region's capital, Oviedo, is a picture-perfect treasure of incredible architecture, luscious landscapes and captivating culture. Famed movie director Woody Allen (scenes from his famous film *Vicky Christina Barcelona* were filmed here) once said that Oviedo is a "delicious city, exotic, beautiful...like a fairytale". A place offering so much history, so many delectable treats and the opportunity to discover the natural wonders of the entire Asturias region has to be a fairytale destination indeed.

HISTORY AND HERITAGE

Originally founded by King Fruela I of Asturias in the 8th century, Oviedo actually owes its existence to the king's son, Alfonso II, who cemented the city's prominence by declaring it the capital of his kingdom. Asturians are a proud people, boasting that **"Asturias is Spain and the rest is conquered land"**, referring to the fact that the Moors, who invaded Spain in the 8th century, were never able to conquer the kingdom of Asturias. Thanks to the treacherous terrain of the towering Picos de Europa, Asturias remained protected and isolated for centuries. This isolation contributed to the diversity that makes this area such an interesting place to explore. It feels distinctively different from the rest of the country, something which only makes it more charming.

EL CASCO ANTIGUO DE OVIEDO

Pon un pie en Oviedo y posiblemente pensarás que has llegado a una ciudad bulliciosa. Sin embargo, si entras dentro del centro histórico, el **Casco Antiguo**, te adentras en otro mundo; un mundo lleno de edificios hermosamente preservados, plazas pintorescas y calles adoquinadas. El centro de Oviedo está casi totalmente libre de coches, lo que lo convierte en un sueño para el turismo. Aunque que Oviedo sirve como un lugar famoso para los peregrinos que completan el Camino de Santiago, no necesitas ser un alma demasiado pía para disfrutar de las increíbles atracciones que ofrece la ciudad. Aun así, ayuda el tener un interés por la historia y la arquitectura. Abundan las iglesias, mansiones, monasterios y conventos, algunos de más de hace 1000 años.

CATEDRAL DE SAN SALVADOR

Esta magnífica y ornamentada iglesia, construida en el siglo XIV, es por mucho una de las estructuras más impresionantes de Casco Antiguo. La prominente torre de aguja, la fachada adornada de forma opulenta, junto con la mezcla de elementos románicos, góticos, renacentistas y barrocos, hacen de esta catedral todo un espectáculo. Dentro de la iglesia, uno encuentra un amplio abanico de importantes reliquias cristianas. La iglesia alberga una reliquia que sólo se muestra unas veces al año, el *Sudarium*, un trapo manchado de sangre que se cree que fue parte del sudario de Turín, el paño que se colocó sobre la cabeza de Jesús tras su muerte.

OVIEDO'S CASCO ANTIGUO

Set one foot in Oviedo and you are likely to think that you've reached a bustling city. Yet step inside the historic centre, the **Casco Antiguo**, and you step into another world - a world filled with beautifully-preserved buildings, picturesque plazas and cobblestone streets. Oviedo's centre is almost entirely car-free, making it a sightseeing dream. Whilst Oviedo serves as a renowned site for pilgrims completing the Camino de Santiago, you need not be an overly pious soul to enjoy the stunning attractions that the city offers. Yet it does help to be interested in history and architecture. Churches, mansions, monasteries and convents abound, some dating from over 1,000 years ago.

CATEDRAL DE SAN SALVADOR

This magnificent and ornate Gothic church, built in the 14th century, is by far the most impressive structure in Casco Antiguo. The prominent spire, the opulently adorned façade, together with the mix of Romanesque, Gothic, Renaissance and Baroque elements, make this cathedral quite a sight. Inside the church, one finds a vast array of important Christian relics. The church houses a relic displayed only a few times a year - the *Sudarium*, a bloodstained cloth believed to be a part of the famed Shroud of Turin, the cloth placed on Jesus' head after his death.

En la **Cámara Santa** de la catedral hay algunas joyas y reliquias espectaculares, de las cuales la más impresionante es la **Cruz de la Victoria**, que se cree que ayudó a los asturianos en su derrota contra los moros. La mayoría de visitantes, lo suficientemente intrigados por las joyas, pueden pasar por alto las tallas sobre la entrada de la cámara, que se merecen un vistazo más de cerca. Si miras hacia arriba, verás una interesante y, de algún modo, peculiar atracción. Sobre el portal yacen piedras con tallas de lo que parecen ser las cabezas incorpóreas de María, José y Jesús. Encantador, ¿verdad?

IGLESIA DE SAN JULIÁN DE LOS PRADOS

No permitas que la ubicación de esta increíble iglesia, San Julián de los Prados, te disuada de visitarla. Puede que se alce cerca de una autopista y parezca bastante ordinaria desde fuera, pero dentro esta iglesia esconde un tesoro: preciosos frescos que cubren las paredes, arcos y cornisas del llamativo interior. Originariamente construida en la primera mitad del siglo IX, esta basílica exhibe espectaculares murales, que recuerdan a frescos antiguos que normalmente datan de hace miles de años.

ESTATUAS DE OVIEDO

Uno podría pasar un día entero intentando encontrar todas las esculturas y estatuas al aire libre de la ciudad. ¡Hay más de cien! Desde el viajero con maleta, hasta el gitano,

In the cathedral's **Camara Santa** are some spectacular jewels and relics, the most impressive of which is the **Victory Cross**, believed to have helped Asturians in their defeat of the Moors. Most visitors, intrigued enough by the jewels, may miss the carvings above the chamber's entrance which merit a closer look. If you look up, you will see an interesting and somewhat peculiar attraction. Above the doorway lay stones with carvings of what seem to be the disembodied heads of Mary, Joseph and Jesus. Charming, no?

IGLESIA DE SAN JULIÁN DE LOS PRADOS

Don't let the location of this incredible church, San Julián de los Prados, deter you from visiting. It may stand near a highway and look rather ordinary from the outside, but inside, this church hides a treasure - beautiful frescoes covering the walls, arches, and cornices of the striking interior. Originally built in the first half of the 9th century, this basilica showcases outstanding murals, reminiscent of ancient frescoes normally dating back thousands of years.

OVIEDO STATUES

One could spend an entire day trying to find all of the city's outdoor sculptures and statues. There are over one hundred! From the suitcase-wielding traveller to the gypsy,

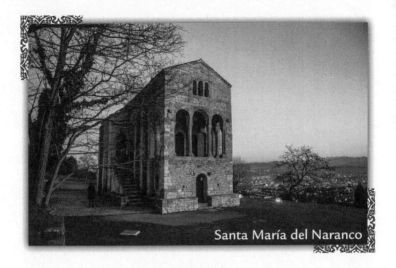
Santa María del Naranco

el burro e incluso Woody Allen, estas esculturas añaden un estilo artístico a la ciudad.

COMIDA Y BEBIDA

¡Tienes que amar una ciudad que tiene toda una calle dedicada a su bebida favorita! El Bulevar de la Sidra es la sede central de las casas de sidra de la ciudad, y **la sidra asturiana** es tan conocida como deleitable y un obsequio para quitar la sed. La tradición de la sidra tiene tanto que ver con la forma en que se sirve, como con la bebida en sí. Los hábiles camareros sostienen las jarras de sidra por encima de la cabeza, y los vasos bajo las caderas, asegurándose de que se atrapa una buena cantidad de aire en la bebida cuando va de la jarra al vaso. Esta forma amena de servir, no sólo hace que la sidra sepa mejor, sino que es una de las mejores experiencias de Oviedo.

San Miguel de Lillo

the donkey and even Woody Allen, these sculptures add an artistic flair to the city.

FOOD AND DRINK

You've got to love a city that has an entire street dedicated to its favourite drink! The Bulevar de la Sidra is the headquarters of the city's cider houses, and **Asturian cider** is renowned as a delectable and thirst quenching treat. The tradition of cider has as much to do with the way it is served as with the drink itself. Skilled waiters hold cider jugs above their heads, and the glasses below their hips, ensuring that a good deal of air is trapped in the drink as it travels from the jug to the glass. This entertaining way to pour not only makes the cider taste better - it is one of the best experiences in Oviedo.

No te olvides de la deleitable cocina de Oviedo: **marisco** fresco traído a diario desde los cercanos pueblos pesqueros como Cudillero, Gijón y Avilés, así como la sustanciosa comida por la que Asturias es famosa. La **fabada asturiana**, un estofado hecho de habas blancas y diferentes partes del cerdo, es el plato más icónico de la ciudad. El **Cabrales**, un queso azul agrio y totalmente adictivo, combina perfectamente con un vaso de sidra asturiana.

TESOROS CIRCUNDANTES

Dos iglesias prominentes, ambas Patrimonio de la Humanidad por la UNESCO, descansan sólo a unos kilómetros a las afueras de Oviedo. **Santa María del Naranco** y **San Miguel de Lillo** pueden parecer pintorescas a primera vista, pero de hecho son conocidas por su importancia histórica y su diversidad arquitectónica. Construidas en el siglo IX, las iglesias presumen de un estilo arquitectónico único de Asturias. Este estilo combina elementos de la arquitectura románica junto con estilos visigodos y bizantinos que crean un resultado único y bastante impactante.

Santa María del Naranco, un edificio rectangular de dos pisos, es considerado por algunos el palacio más antiguo de Europa. El rey Ramiro I, ordenó la construcción de Santa María en el año 848 en el Monte Naranco, para que sirviera como su residencia. Tras más de mil años, el edificio permanece en excelente condición. Evocador de arquitectura que a menudo se encuentra en lugares como Siria o Turquía, el interior de Santa María presume de techos y muros opulentamente decorados.

Don't forget Oviedo's delectable cuisine: fresh **seafood** brought in daily from nearby fishing villages like Cudillero, Gijón and Avilés as well as the heartier fare for which Asturias is famous. **Fabada Asturiana**, a stew made of white beans and different cuts of pork, is the city's most iconic dish. **Cabrales**, a tangy and totally addictive blue cheese, goes perfectly with a glass of Asturian cider.

SURROUNDING TREASURES

Two outstanding churches, both UNESCO World Heritage sites, rest just a few kilometres outside of Oviedo. **Santa María del Naranco** and **San Miguel de Lillo** may seem quaint at first, but they are actually renowned for their historical importance and architectural diversity. Built in the 9th century, the churches boast an architectural style unique to Asturias. This style blends elements of Romanesque architecture together with Visigoth and Byzantine styles for an utterly unique and quite astounding result.

Santa María del Naranco, a two storey rectangular building, is considered by some to be the oldest palace in Europe. King Ramiro I ordered Santa María built in 848 on Mount Naranco to serve as his residence. After more than one thousand years, the building remains in excellent condition. Reminiscent of architecture often found in places like Syria and Turkey, Santa María's interior boasts richly decorated ceilings and walls.

San Miguel de Lillo se construyó al lado de Santa María para complementar la mansión y, claro está, para que actuara como iglesia real. Hoy en día tan sólo un tercio permanece intacto; aun así lo que queda es tan espectacular que la UNESCO lo ha listado como hito protegido. La puerta enrejada fue tallada de una única piedra, y la ventana misma ofrece vistas de gran alcance de Oviedo.

LA BELLEZA NATURAL DE ASTURIAS

Oviedo sirve como base perfecta para descubrir toda la belleza natural que ofrece la región de Asturias. Si Asturias tuviera que ser descrito con un único color, tendría que ser un verde brillante. La **Costa Verde** (que es como se conoce a la costa Atlántica de Asturias) posee una deslumbrante diversidad: desde las tranquilas calas rodeadas de impresionantes acantilados, hasta los largos trechos de arena polvorienta bordeados por bosques de pinos. El área entera brinda una oportunidad verdaderamente única de nadar en las aguas brillantes de la Costa Verde por la mañana y caminar por partes de los espectaculares **Picos de Europa** por la tarde. Ríos bravos, lagos glaciales, exquisitos bosques alpinos y pastos verdes sin fin, son sólo una parte del paisaje increíble que te espera.

San Miguel de Lillo was built alongside Santa María to complement the mansion and, of course, to act as a royal church. Today only about a third of it remains intact; yet what does remain is so outstanding that UNESCO has listed it as a protected landmark. The latticed window was carved from a single stone, and the window itself offers sweeping views over Oviedo.

THE NATURAL BEAUTY OF ASTURIAS

Oviedo serves as a perfect base for discovering all the natural beauty that the region of Asturias has to offer. If Asturias were to be described in just one single colour, it would have to be brilliant green. The **Costa Verde** (as the Atlantic coast of Asturias is known) has stunning diversity: from quiet coves surrounded by dramatic cliffs to long stretches of powdery sand bordered by pine tree forests. The whole area provides a truly unique chance to swim in the sparkly waters of the Costa Verde in the morning and hike parts of the dramatic **Picos de Europa** in the afternoon. Raging rivers, glacial lakes, luscious alpine forests and endless green pastures are just some of the amazing scenery that awaits you.

Laguardia

LAGUARDIA

Laguardia

Enclavado de lleno en el corazón de la región vinícola española de La Rioja, asentado orgullosamente encima de una colina rocosa, está Laguardia, uno de los municipios más pintorescos e históricos del norte de España. En medio de mares de viñedos y verdes colinas, con las montañas Cantábricas a lo lejos, este municipio histórico amurallado es verdaderamente una de las joyas escondidas de España. A una hora de trayecto en coche desde la capital regional de Vitoria, Laguardia tiene raíces en tres regiones diferentes: está políticamente ligado al País Vasco, situado en la región vinícola de La Rioja y debe su existencia a la región vecina de Navarra. Laguardia puede que sea pequeño en tamaño, pero presume de una maravillosa combinación de paisajes soberbios, fantástico vino y deliciosa gastronomía.

Si entras en el pueblo por su estrecho arco de piedra, la **Puerta de San Juan**, serás recibido por una encantadora **placa** que dice: "Paz a los que llegan. Salud a los que habitan. Felicidad a los que marchan". El lema de Laguardia resume perfectamente su esencia verdadera: un destino relajante, seductor y totalmente absorbente. Su vino, comida e historia hechizan a todos los que entran en su reino, y se aseguran de que lo único que se lleven sus visitantes sea el ardiente deseo de volver algún día…y unas cuantas botellas de vino en su maleta.

UN PASO ATRÁS EN EL TIEMPO

Aquí se construyó un castillo en la cima de una colina en el año 908 como puesto de vigilancia fronterizo para la región de Navarra. El rey Sancho Abarca,

Nestled deep within the heart of Spain's La Rioja wine region, sitting proudly atop a rocky hill, is Laguardia, one of the most picturesque and historic towns in northern Spain. Amidst the oceans of vineyards and verdant hills, with the Cantabria Mountains in the distance, this historic walled town is truly one of Spain's hidden gems. An hour's drive from the regional capital of Vitoria, Laguardia has roots in three different regions: it's politically tied to the Basque Country, rests in La Rioja wine country and owes its existence to the neighbouring Navarra region. Laguardia may be small in size, but it boasts a marvellous combination of superb scenery, fantastic wine and delectable cuisine.

If you enter the town through its narrow stone archway, the **Puerta de San Juan**, you are greeted by a charming **plaque** that reads, "*Peace to those who arrive. Health to those who live here. Happiness to those who depart*". Laguardia's motto perfectly encapsulates its true essence – a relaxing, enticing and totally engrossing destination. Her wine, food and history cast a spell on all those who enter her realm, and ensure that the only things its visitors leave with are a fervent desire to one day return…and with a few bottles of wine in their suitcase.

A STEP BACK IN TIME

A hilltop castle was initially built here in 908 as a frontier guard post for the Navarra region. King Sancho Abarca,

preocupado sobre la posible invasión por parte de vecinos hostiles, decidió que este era el sitio ideal para vigilar su preciado reino. Dos siglos más tarde, el rey Sancho VI fundó el municipio de Laguardia. Aunque el castillo fue trágicamente demolido en el siglo XIX, el pueblo medieval de Laguardia permanece en pie, aún vigilando Navarra y los gloriosos viñedos de La Rioja y aún rodeado por murallas del siglo XIII. Laguardia, un pueblo medieval maravillosamente preservado, incluso presume de unos cuantos tesoros escondidos que datan de la Edad Media.

Había una vez, hace siglos, un pueblo casi entero bajo tierra, justo debajo del Laguardia actual. Esculpido inicialmente durante la Edad Media,

Laguardia

concerned about a possible invasion from unfriendly neighbours, decided this was the ideal spot to guard his precious kingdom. Two centuries later, King Sancho VI founded the town of Laguardia. Whilst the castle was tragically demolished in the 1800s, the medieval town of Laguardia remains standing, still guarding Navarra and La Rioja's glorious vineyards and still surrounded by 13th century walls. Laguardia, a wonderfully preserved medieval town, even boasts a few hidden treasures that date back to the Middle Ages.

There was once, centuries ago, almost an entire village underground, right below present day Laguardia. Initially carved during the Middle Ages,

se fue creando como un complejo sistema de túneles para mantener a los habitantes protegidos de los invasores, y como forma de asegurar el suministro de alimentos del pueblo. Con el paso del tiempo, y con el desarrollo de la industria de cultivo de la uva, el laberinto de túneles subterráneos de Laguardia empezó a servir como lugar de almacenamiento para las reservas de vino del pueblo y como sitio ideal para hacer vino.

LAGUARDIA EN EL DÍA DE HOY

Los **túneles** que existen aún hoy son tan extensos y tan profundos que, por razones de seguridad, no se permite a los coches circular dentro de las fronteras de la ciudad. Actualmente sólo algunas bodegas hacen todavía su vino bajo tierra, ya que el nivel ideal de humedad y la temperatura de los túneles son fácilmente replicables sobre tierra. La necesidad de cargar las uvas bajo tierra a espaldas de los hombres ha resultado demasiado difícil y caro, además de llevar demasiado tiempo, así que la mayoría de la producción vinícola de Laguardia se realiza sobre tierra. Aún es posible visitar algunas secciones de los túneles, y participar en un recorrido de una bodega subterránea es una de las cosas más cautivadoras que puedes hacer.

Por encima del subsuelo descubrirás **un mundo vinícola** incluso mejor. Muy alabado por sus destacados vinos rojos Garnacha, Tempranillo y Mazuelo, Laguardia está rodeado por más de una docena de bodegas, todas de primera categoría y todas complementadas por comida igualmente deleitable. ¡Vaya combinación!

a complex system of tunnels was created to keep inhabitants protected from invaders, and as a way to secure the town's food supply. With the passage of time, and with the development of the grape growing industry, Laguardia's maze of underground tunnels started serving as storage spots for the town's wine stocks and as ideal places to make wine.

MODERN DAY LAGUARDIA

The **tunnels** still in existence today are so vast and so deep that for safety purposes cars are not allowed to drive within the city boundaries. Today only a few bodegas still make their wine underground, as the ideal humidity level and temperature of the tunnels are easily replicated above ground. The need for the grapes to be carried underground on men's backs has proven too difficult, costly and time consuming, so the majority of Laguardia's wine production is above ground. It is still possible to visit some sections of the tunnels, and taking an underground bodega tour is one of the most enchanting things you can do.

Above ground you will discover an even greater **world of wine**. Highly revered for its outstanding Garnacha, Tempranillo and Mazuelo red wines, Laguardia is surrounded by over a dozen bodegas, all world class and all complemented by equally delectable food. What a combination!

Desde el chorizo picante hasta el suculento cordero y los pimientos del piquillo, la **gastronomía** en esta región es tan excepcional como su vino. El producto fresco abunda en estas tierras fértiles y por suerte para todos los que las visitan, los lugareños de Laguardia han desarrollado un espectacular paladar para el vino y la comida. Los lugareños a menudo dicen que lo que más les gusta en la vida es comer y beber.

DENTRO DE LAS MURALLAS MEDIEVALES

El corazón de Laguardia es la **Plaza Mayor**, su plaza central, donde el escudo de armas del rey Carlos V adorna la fachada del Ayuntamiento del siglo XV. Cuando la visites, no te olvides de mirar más de cerca el reloj de la plaza, enmarcado por una vid tallada de hierro fundido y adornada con tres estatuillas. Al mediodía, 2 pm, 5 pm y 8 pm puedes observar cómo las estatuillas bailan al son de la canción local, la "passacalla".

La Plaza Mayor es donde se llevan a cabo todas las fiestas del pueblo y es el lugar considerado el verdadero corazón de la vida del pueblo. Naturalmente, hay una fantástica tiendecita de vino en la Plaza Mayor que tiene algunos de los mejores vinos que produce esta región. Explorar este pueblo mágico con su antiguo ayuntamiento, muralla medieval, las preciosas mansiones, impresionantes iglesias (incluida la espléndida Iglesia de Santa María de los Reyes), es como viajar al pasado.

From spicy chorizo to succulent lamb and piquillo peppers, the **cuisine** in this region is as exceptional as its wine. Fresh produce abounds in these fertile lands and luckily for all who visit, the locals of Laguardia have developed an outstanding palate for wine *and* food. Locals often say that what they like most in life is to eat and drink.

INSIDE THE MEDIEVAL WALLS

The heart of Laguardia is the **Plaza Mayor**, its central square, where King Carlos V's royal coat of arms adorns the façade of the 15th century Ayuntamiento. When you visit, don't forget to take a closer look at the clock in the square, framed by cast iron carved grapevines and adorned with three figurines. At noon, 2pm, 5pm and 8pm you can watch how these statuettes dance to the tune of the local folkloric song, the "passacalla".

The Plaza Mayor is where all the town's fiestas are held and is the spot considered to be the true heart of village life. Naturally, there is a fantastic little wine shop in Plaza Mayor that carries some of the best wines this region produces. Exploring this magical town with the old town hall, medieval wall, the gorgeous mansions, stunning churches (including the splendid Iglesia de Santa María de los Reyes) is like travelling back in time.

EL MEJOR MOMENTO PARA VISITARLO

El otoño es una estación maravillosa para visitar Laguardia, cuando los intensos colores caoba, malva y carmesí de los viñedos y colinas circundantes dan lugar a increíbles paisajes.

BEST TIME TO VISIT

Autumn is a gorgeous season to visit Laguardia, when the rich auburn, mauve and crimson colours of the surrounding vineyards and hills make for incredible scenery.

TRUJILLO

Cáceres   **Trujillo**

Guadalupe

Mérida

Badajoz

Extremadura

Trujillo

Trujillo

España posee abundantes secretos escondidos, lugares especiales que aún no han sido descubiertos por las masas. El glorioso antiguo pueblo medieval de Trujillo, en Extremadura, la región en la España oeste que bordea con Portugal, es uno de esos sitios. Irónicamente, Trujillo es casi un sinónimo de descubrimiento. Fue en Trujillo donde nació **Francisco Pizarro**, a menudo llamado el "descubridor de Perú". Y aquí, otros exploradores como Pizarro (conocidos como conquistadores) volvieron y disfrutaron de una vida lujosa, construyendo palacios opulentos para mostrar sus nuevas riquezas.

Enclavado entre espectacular campiña y hogar de algunas de las mejores sorpresas culinarias, Trujillo presume de una larga e ilustre historia. No es raro entonces que Trujillo sea tan popular entre los madrileños (los residentes de Madrid), los cuales vienen aquí los fines de semana para escapar del ajetreo de la gran ciudad. Siendo el hogar de 10000 personas, Trujillo no es pequeño, pero da la sensación de menudo y encantador.

UN PASO HACIA ATRÁS EN EL TIEMPO

Los lugareños padecieron muchas adversidades durante el primer milenio de la existencia del pueblo; el asentamiento original romano de *Turgalium* fue conquistado por los visigodos en el siglo V, y después en el siglo VIII por los musulmanes, los cuales reinaron durante más de 500 años. Entonces el pueblo era hogar de varias mezquitas, que aun así fueron demolidas cuando los cristianos reclamaron Trujillo en el siglo XIII. Sin embargo, no se pudieron borrar todos los rastros de influencia islámica.

Spain has plenty of hidden secrets - special places that haven't yet been discovered by the masses. The glorious old medieval town of Trujillo, in Extremadura, a region in western Spain bordering Portugal, is one of those places. Ironically, Trujillo is almost synonymous with discovery. It was in Trujillo that **Francisco Pizarro**, often called the "discoverer of Peru", was born. And here, other explorers like Pizarro (known as conquistadors) returned and enjoyed a luxurious life, constructing opulent palaces to display their new wealth.

Set amidst spectacular countryside and home to some of Spain's finest culinary treats, Trujillo boasts a long and illustrious history. Little wonder then that Trujillo is so popular with Madrileños (Madrid residents), who come here on weekends to escape the bustle of the big city. Home to 10,000 people, Trujillo is not tiny, but it feels small and enchanting.

A STEP BACK IN TIME

The locals endured much hardship during the first millennia of the town's existence; the original Roman settlement of *Turgalium* was conquered by the Visigoths in the 5th century, and then in the 8th century by the Muslims, who ruled for more than 500 years. Back then the town was home to several mosques, yet they were demolished when Christians reclaimed Trujillo in the 13th century. However, not all traces of Islamic influence could be erased.

Es el contraste arquitectónico el que hace que Trujillo sea un lugar tan genial para descubrir, especialmente por aficionados de la historia y de la arquitectura. El siglo XVI es a menudo llamado la "edad dorada" de Trujillo ya que fue entonces cuando los conquistadores volvieron a su patria, cargados de riquezas que habían acumulado en el "Nuevo Mundo". El consiguiente boom económico garantizó que Trujillo permaneciera como un pueblo precioso, sede de los palacios más señoriales de España.

TRUJILLO EN EL DÍA DE HOY

Explorando este laberinto medieval de calles adoquinadas, majestuosas residencias, plazas encantadoras y bonitas iglesias, uno pronto tiene la impresión de que la apariencia de Trujillo no ha cambiado mucho desde el siglo XVI. La plaza principal de la ciudad es la despampanante **Plaza Mayor**, considerada por muchos como una de las plazas más bonitas de todo el país. La plaza está rodeada de mansiones renacentistas y adornada con elegantes arcadas. Sin duda, lo primero que atraerá tu mirada será la gran **estatua de bronce de Pizarro montado a caballo**, la cual verás justo en frente de la iglesia del siglo XIV, la **Iglesia de San Martín**. Sirviendo como el lugar de encuentro de Trujillo desde tiempos medievales, hasta el día de hoy la plaza aún celebra fiestas religiosas, festivales llenos de vida y mercados semanales, preservando tradiciones que datan de hace siglos.

It is this architectural contrast which makes Trujillo such a brilliant place to discover, especially for history and architecture aficionados. The 16th century is often called the "golden era" for Trujillo because it was then that the conquistadors returned to their homeland, loaded with the riches they had accumulated in the "New World". The ensuing economic boom guaranteed that Trujillo remained a beautiful town, home to some of Spain's most stately palaces.

MODERN DAY TRUJILLO

Exploring this medieval maze of cobblestone streets, regal residences, charming plazas and beautiful churches, one soon gets the impression that Trujillo's appearance hasn't changed much since the sixteenth century. The main square of the city is the striking **Plaza Mayor**, considered by many as one of the most beautiful plazas in the whole country. The plaza is lined with Renaissance mansions and adorned by graceful arcades. Your eyes will certainly be attracted first to the large **bronze statue of a horse-mounted Pizarro**, which you'll see right in front of the 14th century **Iglesia de San Martín**. Serving as Trujillo's gathering place since medieval times, to this day the plaza still hosts religious celebrations, lively festivals and weekly markets, preserving traditions that date back centuries.

Trujillo

Pasar toda la tarde en esta plaza no sólo es relajante, sino una manera magnífica de interactuar con los lugareños, los cuales se encuentran en cafeterías y restaurantes para comer, beber y socializar. A medida que el sol empieza a ponerse, la plaza entera se vuelve de un precioso color ámbar. Disfruta de una cerveza bajo el toldo de una de las cafeterías y observa a los niños que intentan atrapar lagartijas que echan a correr de forma juguetona entre las fisuras de los adoquines. Es una escena bastante remarcable e inolvidable.

Uno tampoco puede evitar fijarse en el opulento palacio que la familia Pizarro construyó tras su retorno de América Latina. Llamado apropiadamente **Palacio de la Conquista**, fue la residencia del medio-hermano e hijo político de Francisco Pizarro, Hernando Pizarro. Hernando vivió en

Trujillo

Spending a whole afternoon in this plaza is not only relaxing, but a great way to mingle with locals, who gather in the cafés and restaurants to eat, drink and socialize. As the sun starts to set, the whole plaza turns a gorgeous amber hue. Enjoy a cerveza under the awning of one of the cafes and watch as children try to catch lizards that playfully bolt through the cobblestone cracks. It's a rather remarkable and unforgettable scene.

One also cannot help but notice the grand palace that the Pizarro family built upon their return from Latin America. Appropriately-named **Palacio de la Conquista,** it was the residence of the stepbrother and son-in-law of Francisco Pizarro, Hernando Pizarro. Hernando lived in

el palacio con su mujer Francisca Pizarro Yupanqui, la cual a la vez era su sobrina. No te preocupes…esperaremos hasta que lo hayas entendido.

Las estrechas calles adoquinadas que se alejan de la plaza te invitan a explorar el resto del tentador barrio histórico. No te pierdas una visita a la **Iglesia de Santa María la Mayor**, construida en el terreno de una mezquita. Santa María pasó por numerosas reparaciones a lo largo de los siglos, culminando en una ecléctica mezcla de estilos románico, gótico y plateresco. Dos cabezas de león de piedra vigilan la entrada y, cuando al fin entres en la iglesia, descubrirás un retablo de madera pintada de 25 piezas, que cuenta la historia de la Virgen María. El retablo, de la escuela flamenca, tiene los característicos brillantes tonos dorados y rojizos que están tan a menudo asociados con este estilo. Sube a la cima de la Torre Julia de la iglesia para ver las increíbles vistas de los planos tostados por el sol de Extremadura y las cuestas rocosas de la **Sierra de Gredos** en la distancia.

Cuando hayas acabado de explorar y de admirar las joyas centrales de Trujillo, dirígete hacia arriba al **Castillo de Trujillo**, el punto de referencia más alto de Trujillo, donde te esperan increíbles vistas panorámicas. Con sorprendente campiña y techos de tejas rojas hasta más allá de donde alcanza la vista, las vistas podrían hacer que pasaras aquí todo el día. Desde su punto de observación puedes apreciar bien la **muralla** del pueblo de 900 metros de largo, enmarcada por numerosas torres de piedra y puertas. La muralla, como el castillo, data de tiempos moriscos.

the palace with his wife Francisca Pizarro Yupanqui, who was also his niece. It's okay - we'll wait until you've figured that one out.

The narrow, cobblestone streets leading away from the plaza invite you to explore the rest of the enticing historic quarter. Don't miss visiting the **Iglesia de Santa María la Mayor,** built on the site of a mosque. Santa María has endured numerous repairs through the centuries, culminating in an eclectic mix of Romanesque, Gothic and Plateresque styles. Two stone lion heads guard the entrance and, when you eventually enter the church, you will discover a 25-piece painted wood altarpiece that retells the story of the Virgin Mary. The altarpiece, from the Flemish school, has the characteristic brilliant hues of gold and red so often associated with this style. Climb to the top of the church's Julia Tower to see incredible views of the sun-baked plains of Extremadura and the rocky slopes of the **Sierra de Gredos** in the distance**.**

When you're done exploring and admiring Trujillo's central jewels, head uphill to the **Castillo de Trujillo**, the town's highest landmark, where unbelievable panoramic views await you. With striking countryside and red-tiled roofs as far as the eye can see, the vista could keep you here all day. From this vantage point you can properly appreciate the town's 900-meter long **city wall,** marked by numerous stone towers and gates. The city wall, like the castle, dates from Moorish times.

La fortaleza era usada por los cristianos del siglo XIII, aunque sus excepcionales torres son típicas de las anteriores alcazabas musulmanas que están esparcidas por toda España y Portugal. Los visitantes pueden subir a las murallas de la fortaleza y al campanario para ver mejores vistas todavía del paisaje que rodea Trujillo. Dentro de las densas murallas del castillo hay un patio con un arco de herradura y dos cisternas de agua: más recordatorios del pasado islámico del castillo.

LAS DELICIAS CULINARIAS DE TRUJILLO

Extremadura produce una de las mejores gastronomías de España: tipos especiales de jamón, chorizo, olivas y queso, por nombrar algunos. Si te encanta la comida (¿y a quién no?), entonces te enamorarás de Trujillo, a no ser que seas vegetariano o, desafortunadamente, ¡alérgico a la lactosa!

Hablando del tema, empecemos por el queso. **El queso Ibores**, una delicia local, tiene una increíble textura cremosa, y está hecho de leche de cabra. Hay otro queso delicioso y único, llamado **La Serena**. Hecho de leche de oveja, está espesado con extracto de cardo de alcachofa, curado durante 60 días, y después se come con una cuchara. ¡"Espectacular" no empieza ni siquiera a describir esta suave y rica delicia!

Si tienes la suficiente suerte de no ser alérgico a la lactosa, entonces visita Trujillo en la primavera, durante la Feria Nacional del Queso del país. Hay queso hasta donde alcanza la vista en la Plaza Mayor, cientos de tipos de todas partes de España. Seguro que, si

The fortress was used by Christians from the 13th century, yet its exceptional towers are typical of the former Muslim alcazabas that are scattered all over Spain and Portugal. Visitors can climb the fortress walls and bell tower for even better views of Trujillo's surrounding landscape. Inside the dense castle walls is a courtyard with a horseshoe arch and two water cisterns - more reminders of the castle's Islamic past.

TRUJILLO'S CULINARY DELIGHTS

Extremadura produces some of the best food in Spain: special types of jamón, chorizo, olives, and cheese, to name a few. If you love food (and who doesn't?), then you'll fall in love with Trujillo, unless you're a vegan, a vegetarian or, regrettably, lactose intolerant!

On that note, let's start with the cheese. **Ibores cheese**, a local delicacy, has a wonderful creamy texture, and is made from goat's milk. There's another unique and delicious cheese, called **La Serena**. Made with sheep's milk, it is thickened with extract from artichoke thistle, aged for 60 days, and then eaten with a spoon. "Yum" does not even begin to describe this soft, rich delight!

If you are lucky enough to not be lactose intolerance, then visit Trujillo in spring, for the country's National Cheese Fair. There is cheese as far as the eye can see in the Plaza Mayor - hundreds of kinds from all over Spain. Sure, if

Trujillo

no eres alérgico a la lactosa cuando llegues, al final de este festival de cinco días puede que lo seas. De todas formas, ¡vale la pena arriesgarse!

Otra delicia local que no hay que perderse es el famoso jamón curado de Extremadura: **jamón ibérico de bellota**, también conocido como **pata negra**. Los españoles y los extranjeros sienten bastante pasión por este manjar, y hacen bien. Elaborado de cerdos negros ibéricos que deambulan por los bosques de Extremadura cebándose de bellotas, este jamón pasa por un proceso especial de curación que dura semanas y a veces años. El resultado es un jamón curado que prácticamente se deshace en tu boca y tiene un sutil sabor dulce, que recuerda a las bellotas.

Trujillo

you're not lactose intolerant when you arrive, by the end
of this five day festival you may be. However, it's worth
the risk!

Another local delicacy not to be missed is Extremadura's
famous cured ham: **jamón ibérico de bellota**, also known
as **pata negra**. Spaniards and foreigners are quite passionate about this food, and rightly so. Made from the black
Iberian pigs that roam the forests of Extremadura feasting
on acorns, this ham undergoes a special curing process
that lasts weeks and sometimes years. The result is a cured
ham that practically melts in your mouth and has a subtle
sweet flavour, reminiscent of acorns.

LOS ESPLÉNDIDOS ALREDEDORES DE TRUJILLO

Trujillo es la base ideal desde la que explorar tres de los otros tesoros de Extremadura: **Cáceres, Mérida** y el **Real Monasterio de Santa María de Guadalupe**, todos en la lista de Patrimonio de la Humanidad de la UNESCO, y todos a apenas una hora del pueblo. En la ciudad amurallada de Cáceres, preciosas mansiones renacentistas delinean las calles y plazas. El centro, sólo para peatones, es encantador y está preservado maravillosamente, haciendo que este pueblo de verdad parezca que está en el siglo XVI. Mérida, que una vez fue una de las ciudades más importantes del Imperio Romano, tiene la mejor colección de restos romanos de España. Transpórtate hacia el pasado, dos mil años atrás, para descubrir los sitios históricos de la antigua ciudad de *Emerita Augusta*: templos, villas, acueductos, mosaicos, un teatro, un anfiteatro, un circo romano, y un magnífico puente de 800 metros de largo. El Real Monasterio de Santa María de Guadalupe, en un encantador pueblo con el mismo nombre (Guadalupe), fue establecido en 1340 y ofrece un maravilloso complejo de claustros, una basílica, un museo y ocho torres despampanantes. Considerado una obra maestra de la arquitectura gótico-mudéjar, el monasterio rebosa de obras de arte que no tienen precio, reliquias religiosas y muchos artefactos antiguos. Uno de ellos es el famoso santuario de la **Virgen de Guadalupe**, la Madonna negra que da nombre al pueblo y al monasterio.

TRUJILLO'S SPLENDID SURROUNDINGS

Trujillo is an ideal base from which to explore three of Extremadura's other treasures: **Cáceres**, **Mérida**, and the **Real Monasterio de Santa María de Guadalupe**, all UNESCO heritage listed, and all only an hour from town. In the walled-city of Cáceres, beautiful Renaissance mansions line the streets and squares. The pedestrian-only centre is enchanting and it´s wonderfully-preserved, making this place feel like it really is the 16th century. Mérida, once one of the most important cities in the Roman Empire, has Spain's finest collection of Roman remains. Step back in time two thousand years to discover the sites of the ancient city of *Emerita Augusta*: temples, villas, aqueducts, mosaics, a theatre, an amphitheater, a Roman circus, and a magnificent 800-meter long bridge. The Real Monasterio de Santa María de Guadalupe, in a charming town with the same name (Guadalupe), was established in 1340 and offers a marvellous complex of cloisters, a basilica, a museum and eight stunning towers. Considered a masterpiece of Gothic and Mudéjar architecture, the monastery is brimming with priceless artwork, religious relics and many ancient artefacts. One of these is the famous shrine of the **Virgin of Guadalupe**, the black Madonna for whom the town and monastery are named.

Cañón del Sil

A Coruña

Lugo

Santiago de
Compostela

*Ribeira
Sacra*

Pontevedra

Cañón del Sil

Ourense

Galicia

CAÑÓN DEL SIL

Cañón del Sil

La región española vinícola de la **Ribeira Sacra**, escondida en el interior del corazón de la región noroeste de Galicia, es una de las partes del país menos exploradas, aunque más espectaculares del país. *Ribeira Sacra* en gallego significa "Ribera Sagrada", y esta área es ciertamente sagrada. Caracterizada por despeñaderos, cañones, valles y viñedos, esta área es mayoritariamente conocida por los destacados vinos que produce, aun así ofreciendo una remarcable mezcla de belleza natural e historia fascinante. Galicia puede ser hogar del delicioso vino de boutique y de la catedral de Santiago de Compostela, uno de los lugares de peregrinaje cristiano más famosos del mundo, pero la región parece haber escapado milagrosamente de la avalancha del turismo en masa. Los pueblos históricos son abundantes y preciosos y abundan los paisajes distintivos. ¿No suena perfecto?

EL CAÑÓN

Sólo a dos horas en coche desde la ciudad de Santiago de Compostela encontrarás la Ribeira Sacra y uno de los escondites naturales más impactantes de España: el Cañón del Sil. Aquí, convergen los ríos Miño y Sil, y el cañón más impresionante puede ser explorado. Empinado y rocoso, el cañón recuerda a algunas de las cordilleras más veneradas de Europa. Sin embargo, a causa de su relativo pequeño tamaño, uno puede subir caminando fácilmente, y andar de lleno por su corazón, en apenas un día. Con **crestas áridas y rocosas** separadas por **bosques verdes** y espléndidos **viñedos** a los lados de las colinas, este

Spain's **Ribeira Sacra** wine region, hidden in the heart of the northwest region of Galicia, is one of the least explored, yet most spectacular parts of the country. *Ribeira Sacra* means "sacred riverbank" in Galician, and this area is sacred indeed. Characterised by gorges, canyons, valleys and vineyards, this area is mostly known for the outstanding wines it produces, yet offers a remarkable mix of stunning natural beauty and enthralling history. Galicia may be home to delicious boutique wine and to the cathedral of Santiago de Compostela, one of the most famous Christian pilgrimage sites in the world, yet the region seems to have miraculously escaped the onslaught of mass tourism. Historic towns are plentiful and gorgeous and distinctive scenery abounds. Doesn't that sound perfect?

THE CANYON

Just a two hour drive southeast from the city of Santiago de Compostela you'll find Ribeira Sacra and one of Spain's most stunning natural hideaways: Cañón del Sil. Here the Miño and Sil Rivers converge, and the most dramatic gorge can be explored. Steep and rocky, the canyon is reminiscent of some of Europe's revered mountain ranges. However, due to its relatively small size, one can easily hike over it and walk right through its heart, in just a single day. With **arid and rocky ridges** dissected by **green forests** and splendid mountainside **vineyards**, this

Cañón del Sil

cañón ofrece una verdadera oportunidad de escapar hacia uno de los milagros de la Madre Naturaleza.

Los miradores salpicados por el Cañón del Sil brindan introducciones despampanantes a la Ribeira Sacra. Para experimentar algunas de las mejores vistas, dirígete a los **Balcones de Madrid**, uno de los puntos más altos a lo largo de la ruta escénica y un punto increíble para obtener un vistazo del área completa. Desde aquí puedes ver cuántos viñedos cubren las laderas del cañón como colchas, aferrados a las cuestas casi verticales del cañón.

Cañón del Sil

canyon offers a truly rewarding chance to escape into one of Mother Nature's miracles.

The lookout points that dot the Cañón del Sil provide stunning introductions to the Ribeira Sacra. To experience some of the best views, head to the **Balcones de Madrid**, one of the highest points along the scenic route and an incredible spot to get an overview of the entire area. From here you can see how the vineyards cover the sides of the canyon like quilts, clinging to the almost-vertical slopes of the gorge.

LA HISTORIA VINÍCOLA DEL CAÑÓN DEL SIL

No es ningún secreto que los antiguos romanos disfrutaban frecuentemente de una gota o dos (o tres) de vino. Fue justo a lo largo de las laderas de este cañón donde cultivaron uvas hace más de dos milenios. La vinicultura ha sido una forma de vida para los residentes del Cañón del Sil desde que los primeros esclavos romanos esculpieron las rocas. Los monjes de los muchos monasterios del cañón continuaron con las tradiciones vinícolas a lo largo de la Edad Media y en tiempos modernos. ¡Amén!

EL CAÑÓN DEL SIL HOY

Hasta hoy, el vino se produce con muchas de las mismas técnicas utilizadas hace siglos, y encontrarás algunos viticultores que aún cultivan sus viñas a mano. Estos viticultores han tenido que adaptarse al paisaje. A diferencia de viticultores en ubicaciones más convenientes, ¡algunos cultivadores del Cañón del Sil tienen que transportar las uvas a la cima del cañón en sus espaldas! Algunas bodegas sólo son accesibles por barco desde el río, donde las uvas se transportan a las bodegas para su fermentación y embotellamiento.

El siglo XXI puede haber llegado a la Ribeira Sacra, gracias a las crecientes alabanzas que sus deleitables vinos reciben internacionalmente. Pero si quieres desandar los pasos que hicieron las uvas de tu botella de Mencía o Albariño, entonces dirígete al Cañón del Sil y observa lo lejos que está la modernidad de aquí. El área es reconocida como hogar

CAÑÓN DEL SIL 'S WINEMAKING HISTORY

It is no secret that the ancient Romans frequently enjoyed a drop or two (or three) of wine. It was right along this canyon's slopes that they grew grapes over two millennia ago. Winemaking has been a way of life for the residents of the Cañón del Sil ever since the first Roman slaves chiselled away at the rocks. The monks of the canyon's many monasteries continued these winemaking traditions through the Middle Ages and into modern times. Amen!

MODERN DAY CAÑÓN DEL SIL

To this day, wine is produced with many of the same techniques used centuries ago, and you'll find some vintners still cultivating their vines by hand. These vintners have had to adapt to the landscape. Unlike winemakers in more convenient locales, some Cañón del Sil growers have to carry the grapes to the top of the canyon on their backs! Some wineries are only accessible by boat from the riverside, where grapes are transported to wineries for fermentation and bottling.

The 21st century may have arrived to Ribeira Sacra, thanks to the increasing praise that its delectable wines receive internationally. But if you want to retrace the steps of the grapes which made your bottle of Mencía or Albariño, then head to Cañón del Sil and see just how far modernity is from here. The area is renowned as a home

de familias vitícolas que prefieren "hacer el vino...no el dinero". Así que parece que esta **tierra antigua**, con sus uvas antiguas y sus métodos antiguos, no desaparecerá en un futuro cercano.

Puede que hayas adivinado que debe haber algo especial en esta tierra, si los lugareños se toman tantas molestias para elaborar sus vinos. El área posee una colección completa de microclimas creados por la topografía única de la región. La tierra, gracias a la abundancia de minerales, ha producido algunas de las mejores gotas de vino que se han hecho jamás en España. Aunque los entendidos en vinos de todo el mundo ya han empezado a apreciar estas geniales creaciones, los turistas extranjeros aún no han descubierto lo bonita que es esta zona, con o sin vino. (Pero sí, ¡con vino es siempre mejor!)

El área rebosa de actividades para entusiastas de la naturaleza: **caminos de montaña** y **rutas en bici** que hacen zig-zag por los bosques y los valles te llevan a sitios históricos y viñedos. Navegar en canoa a lo largo del Río Sil brinda un cambio pacífico de escena y una forma excelente de ver el cañón y los viñedos desde una perspectiva distinta.

LUGARES HISTÓRICOS

Entre los valles verdes y los densos bosques de pino y roble, uno encuentra monasterios medievales, iglesias, palacios y pequeñas aldeas increíblemente encantadoras.

to wine-making families who prefer to "make wine…
not money". So it seems that this **ancient land**, with its
ancient grapes and its ancient methods, will not disappear
any time soon.

You may have guessed that there must be something
special about this land, if locals go to this much trouble to
make their wines. The area possesses an entire collection
of microclimates created by the region's unique topography. The soil, thanks to an abundance of minerals, has
produced some of the best drops of wine ever made in
Spain. Although wine connoisseurs around the world
have already begun to appreciate these fantastic creations,
foreign tourists have not yet discovered just how beautiful
this area is, wine or no wine. (But, yes, *with* wine is always
better!)

The area abounds with activities for nature enthusiasts:
hiking trails and **cycling routes** zigzagging through
forests and valleys lead to historic sites and vineyards.
Canoeing along the Sil River makes for a peaceful change
of scenery and an excellent way see the canyon and
vineyards from a different perspective.

HISTORICAL SIGHTS

Among the green valleys and the thick forests of pine
and oak, one finds medieval monasteries, churches,
palaces, and incredibly charming small villages.

Sin duda, lo más prominente aquí son, el **Monasterio de Santo Estevo**, una maravilla del siglo X convertido en un precioso hotel, y el **Monasterio de San Pedro de Rocas**, que se cree tiene casi 1500 años. Capilla increíblemente rústica tallada en la ladera de una roca, San Pedro ciertamente se mantiene fiel a su nombre, y es a menudo descrita como el templo cristiano más antiguo de España.

Highlights here certainly are the **Monasterio de Santo Estevo**, a 10th century marvel converted into a gorgeous hotel, and the **Monasterio de San Pedro de Rocas,** thought to be almost 1,500 years old. An incredibly rustic chapel carved into a mountainside rock, San Pedro certainly stays true to its name, and is often described as the oldest Christian temple in Spain.

Playa de Rodas

Isla de Monteagudo

Playa de Rodas

Isla del Faro

Isla de San Martiño

N

A Coruña

Cangas

Vigo

Baiona

Galicia

Playa de Rodas

Playa de Rodas

O tro de los escondites secretos de Galicia es tan espectacular, tan remarcable, que viajar a Galicia y no encontrar tiempo para visitar este precioso lugar sería un pecado.

Las **Islas Cíes** puede que hayan sido nombradas por *USA Today* y *The Guardian* como hogar a una de las playas más bonitas del mundo: **Playa de Rodas** en la isla de Monteagudo. Sin embargo, la lejanía de la isla y su estado protegido significa que el turismo masivo aún no ha llegado aquí, y que nunca lo hará. El paisaje inmaculado ha sido vehemente protegido por el gobierno, que declaró las islas parque nacional, limitó el número de visitantes y prohibió los vehículos. ¡Genial!

Para llegar a las Islas Cíes, debes dirigirte a Vigo desde el Cañón del Sil (cerca de una hora y media en coche) aparca el coche, y navega en un ferry durante 45 relajantes minutos. También puedes acceder a las islas desde Cangas o Baiona. Ambos son encantadores pueblos costeros y populares entre los españoles que buscan un respiro del sofocante calor del verano, y escapan a Galicia. Los tickets de ferry diarios a las Cíes están limitados en verano, y las islas permanecen fuera de límites en invierno.

Con impresionantes acantilados y exquisitos bosques de pinos y de eucaliptos, las Cíes son famosas por la larga extensión de arena blanca, en forma de media luna de la Playa de Rodas. Las **aguas cristalinas** y el **marco tropical** crean un oasis absoluto. Pero recuerda que esto *no* es el

Another of Galicia's secret hideaways is so spectacular, so remarkable, that travelling to Galicia and not making time to visit this gorgeous place would be a sin.

The **Islas Cíes** may have been named by *USA Today* and *The Guardian* as home to one of the most beautiful beaches in the world: **Playa de Rodas** on the island of Monteagudo. However, the island's remoteness and protected status means that mass tourism has not arrived here - and it never will. The pristine landscape has been vehemently protected by the government, which declared the islands a national park, limited the number of visitors and forbade vehicles. Brilliant!

To reach the Islas Cíes, you must make your way to Vigo from the Cañón del Sil (about an hour and a half drive), park your car, and ride a ferry for a relaxing 45 minutes. You can also reach the islands from Cangas or Baiona. Both are lovely seaside towns and popular with Spaniards looking for a break from the sweltering heat of summer by escaping to Galicia. Daily ferry tickets to the Cíes are limited in summer, and the islands remain off-limits in winter.

Featuring dramatic cliffs and luscious pine and eucalyptus forests, the Cíes are famous for the long crescent-shaped expanse of white sand of Playa de Rodas. The **crystal blue waters** and the **tropical setting** create an absolute oasis. Remember though that these are *not* the

trópico, y la temperatura del agua puede ser un poco fría, aun así nadar y hacer esnórquel siguen siendo muy agradables. Este trecho divino de arena conecta las islas de Monteagudo y El Faro. Las islas están llenas de **caminos de montañas**, cada uno ofrece escenas preciosas de playas vírgenes y fantásticas vistas sobre el Océano Atlántico.

tropics, and the water temperature can feel rather chilly; yet swimming and snorkelling are still really enjoyable. This heavenly stretch of sand connects the islands of Monteagudo and El Faro. The islands are full of **hiking paths**, each offering beautiful scenes of unspoilt beaches and fantastic views over the Atlantic Ocean.

Photo Credits:

Cover: Albarracín (Cover Design by Nada Orlic; Fotolia photo)

p. 9, Albarracín vista (Juan Carlos Gil, Wikimedia Commons)

p. 14, Albarracín vista (Orval Rochefort, Flickr)

p. 15, Albarracín door with cast iron figurine (Jesus Abinzanda, Flickr)

p. 18, Albarracín streets (Juan Carlos Gil, Flickr)

p. 19, Albarracín view of Iglesia de Santiago with the Catedral de El Salvador in the distance (Orval Rochefort, Flickr)

p. 23, Castillo de Loarre (Wikimedia Commons)

p. 28, Castillo de Loarre Capital (Emilio Triboniano, Flickr)

p. 29, San Juan de la Peña (Kom Bo, Flickr)

p. 35, Oviedo - Catedral de San Salvador (Javier Losa, Flickr)

p. 42, Oviedo – Santa María Naranco (Fernando García Redondo, Flickr)

p. 43, Oviedo – San Miguel de Lillo (Zarateman, Wikimedia Commons)

p. 49, Laguardia countryside (Fotolia)

p. 52, Laguardia plaque (Daniel Cruz Valle, Flickr)

p. 53, Laguardia underground bodega (Pablo Monteagudo, Flickr)

p. 61, Trujillo - Plaza Mayor (Fotolia)

p. 66, Trujillo – Iglesia de Santa María la Mayor (Ángel M. Felicísimo, Flickr)

p. 67, Trujillo's Castle (Javier Losa, Flickr)

p. 72, Trujillo vista (Ardo Beltz, Wikimedia Commons)

p. 73, Trujillo's Castle (David Jones, Flickr)

p. 77, Cañón del Sil (José Antonio Gil Martínez, Flickr)

p. 80, Cañón del Sil (José Cernadas Iglesias, Flickr)

p. 81, Cañón del Sil (Linda Hartley, Flickr)

p. 89, Playa de Rodas (Flickr user "sesargz")

4399525R00057

Printed in Great Britain
by Amazon.co.uk, Ltd.,
Marston Gate.

Edith Wharton

The House of Mirth
The Custom of the Country
The Age of Innocence

EDITED BY STUART HUTCHINSON

Series editor: Richard Beynon

ICON BOOKS

Published in 1998 by Icon Books Ltd.,
Grange Road, Duxford, Cambridge CB2 4QF
e-mail: icon@mistral.co.uk

Distributed in the UK, Europe, Canada, South Africa and Asia by the
Penguin Group: Penguin Books Ltd., 27 Wrights Lane, London W8 5TZ

Published in Australia in 1998 by Allen & Unwin Pty. Ltd.,
PO Box 8500, 9 Atchison Street, St. Leonards, NSW 2065

Series editor: Richard Beynon
Series devised by: Christopher Cox
Cover design: Christos Kondeatis
Typesetting: Wayzgoose

ISBN 1 84046 023 7

Printed and bound in Great Britain by
Cox & Wyman Ltd., Reading

Contents

INTRODUCTION

EDITH WHARTON was born in New York on 24 January 1862, the only daughter of parents who already had two much older sons and who belonged to a wealthy social elite, described by Wharton herself as, a 'little aristocratic nucleus. . . . a society in which all dealers in retail business were excluded as a matter of course'.[1] A continuing theme of her work, and especially of the three novels discussed in this Guide, is the demise of this society. In her words:

■ the really vital change is that, in my youth, the Americans of the original States, who in moments of crisis still shaped the national point of view, were the heirs of an old tradition of European culture which the country has now totally rejected. □

(*ABG*, 1.2)

It was never 'totally rejected' by Wharton herself, even though she recognised it as a stifling and anaemic inheritance, which the First World War finally buried. It is exhumed, for example, in *The Age of Innocence* (1920), reinforcing suspicions about the unadventurousness of Wharton's imagination as a novelist. In *A Backward Glance* she tells us:

■ the small society in which I was born was 'good' in the most prosaic sense of the term, and its only interest, for the generality of readers, lies in the fact of its sudden and total extinction, and for the imaginative few in the recognition of the moral treasures that went with it. □

(*ABG*, 1.3)

What these 'moral treasures' were is a fundamental question for any student of Wharton's work. How convincingly are they realised in novels and stories that resist the incursions of the twentieth century? What are members of Wharton's 'imaginative few' subscribing to?

In recent years it has been customary to imply a Wharton unfulfilled by her upbringing, as if she might have supported the sentiment in the first line of Larkin's 'This Be the Verse'. Admittedly, *A Backward Glance* confesses to an 'agonizing shyness' when she was young (*ABG*, 6.3), but it also remembers wonderful trips to Europe in the company of 'my handsome father, my beautifully dressed mother, and the warmth and sunshine that were Doyley [my nurse]' (*ABG*, 2.2). Until her father died in her twentieth year there were frequent stays in Europe with her parents. Age ten returning to America, 'my first thought was: "*How ugly it is!*" I have never since thought otherwise, or felt otherwise than as an exile in America'.[2] Meanwhile in 1878, when she was sixteen, her mother had paid for the private printing of her first volume of poems[3] and, as far as reading was concerned, 'by denying me the opportunity of wasting my time over ephemeral rubbish . . . [had thrown] me back on the great classics, and thereby helped to give my mind a temper which my too-easy studies could not have produced' (*ABG*, 2.3). As she remembers her parents, she is especially aware that her father 'was a lonely one, haunted by something always unexpressed and unattained' (*ABG*, 2.4), but even in reflection there is no exploration of this matter, just as in the novels there is minimal probing beneath the surface vitality of a Lily Bart, an Undine Spragg or a Newland Archer. If discretion rules in her father's case, might it be superficiality in the case of her characters? Critics habitually link Wharton's *Ethan Frome* (1911) with Hawthorne's 'Ethan Brand' (1850), as if shared character names and a common New England setting left nothing more to be said. The manifest difference between the prose of the respective works is confirmed, however, when a single recollection in *A Backward Glance* reveals Wharton to have an entirely different order of consciousness and sense of self from Hawthorne's. She is remembering her father's family:

■ A little lower down the Sound (on the actual site of East Eighty-first Street) stood my grandfather Jones's pretty country house with classic pilasters and balustraded roof. A print in my possession shows a low-studded log-cabin adjoining it under the elms, described as the original Jones habitation; but it was more probably the slaves' quarters. □

(*ABG*, 1.3)

Ancestral involvements such as the last apparently leave Wharton untroubled. The equivalent burden Hawthorne with guilt.

Among her twenty-two novels and novellas, her eighty-seven short stories, her nine volumes of non-fiction, and her two volumes of poetry, *Ethan Frome*, along with *The Age of Innocence*, has remained consistently popular and in print. The story of an impoverished farmer trapped in a loveless marriage in bleak New England circumstances, it might be argued that it alone takes Wharton into territory different from her habitual realm. In *A Backward Glance*, she tells us:

■ For years I had wanted to draw life as it really was in the derelict mountain villages of New England, a life . . . utterly unlike that seen through the rose-coloured spectacles of my predecessors, Mary Wilkins and Sarah Orne Jewett. In those days the snow-bound villages of Western Massachusetts were still grim places, morally and physically: insanity, incest and slow mental and moral starvation were hidden away behind the paintless wooden house-fronts of the long village street, or the isolated farm-houses on the neighbouring hills. □
(*ABG*, 12.1)

'Rose-coloured spectacles', however, is hardly an accurate description of the perspective of either Wilkins or Jewett, and the partiality of this judgement is matched by Wharton's prejudice against the experience she depicts in *Ethan Frome*. She learns nothing she did not already know, her vision of the deformity of life outside the kind of enclave she enjoyed in the Rue de Varennes in Paris being confirmed by the fates she contrives for the novella's principal characters. Beyond such enclaves degeneracy lurks and breeds, as on the 'Mountain' in *Summer* (1917). Not for Wharton Henry James's doubts about 'the mere aesthetic instinct of mankind'.[4] She has a simplifying inclination, even a compulsion, to rest on aesthetics alone. Incipient twentieth-century America is 'ugly', and she feels 'for ugly people an abhorrence, a kind of cruel hate, that I have never been able to overcome' ('LI', p. 1072).

She had based herself in the Rue de Varennes in 1907, returning to 'The Mount', the house she had designed in western Massachusetts and lived in since 1902, for the summers. In 1885 she had married Edward Robbins Wharton ('Teddy'), a man thirteen years her senior and an intimate friend of her brothers. Initially they had houses in Newport and New York, but they also embarked on long visits to Europe. It was a troubled, probably unconsummated, marriage, and Wharton suffered a long breakdown during 1894–95. Eventually, in 1908 she had a passion-ate two-year affair with Morton Fullerton, the Paris correspondent of the London *Times* and a disciple of Henry James. She was divorced from her husband in 1913. By this time she had become a long-standing friend of Henry James (his friendship 'was the pride and honour of my life'[5]), whom she had visited at various times in Rye, Sussex, and who had accompanied her on motor-trips in England and France. James also stayed with her at 'The Mount' during his last visit to America in 1905. It was sold on her separation from Teddy in 1911, Wharton herself making her final visit to the US in 1923 to receive a Doctorate of Letters from Yale.

The French awarded Wharton the Cross of the *Légion d'Honneur* for her war work with refugees and orphans. *Fighting France* (1915) describes her trips to the French front, and in the same year she edited *The Book of the Homeless* to raise money for refugees. She also met André Gide, a fellow relief worker. After the war she divided her life between living in a converted medieval monastery, overlooking the Mediterranean at Hyères, and in Pavillon Colombe, a villa in the village of St. Brice-sous-Forêt about ten miles north of Paris. She died at Pavillon Colombe on 11 August 1937, aged seventy-five, and was buried in the Cimetière des Gonards in the town of Versailles.

As well as to her writing, her life had been mainly devoted (and why not?) to pleasure. Like her character Undine Spragg, she was a consumer of the twentieth century's goods and opportunities but, unlike Undine, she was restrained by the conscience of old New York. It expressed itself in a residual conservatism, apparent in *A Backward Glance* when she recalls:

■ that ancient curriculum of house-keeping which, at least in Anglo-Saxon countries, was so soon to be swept away by the 'monstrous regiment' of the emancipated: young women taught by their elders to despise the kitchen and the linen room, and to substitute the acquiring of University degrees for the more complex art of civilized living. The movement began when I was young, and now that I am old, and have watched it and noted its results, I mourn more than ever the extinction of the household arts. Cold storage, deplorable as it is, has done far less harm to the home than the Higher Education. □

(*ABG*, 3.2)

It is not obvious how someone with such views can be as acclaimed by feminists as Wharton has been in recent times. George Eliot, a principal but neglected influence on Wharton, was also conservative, but her positions were related to a substantial ideology to do with nemesis and the tragic nature of life. She also imagined an antithesis in passionately rebellious female characters such as Madame Laure in *Middlemarch* (1871-2) and Princess Halm-Eberstein in *Daniel Deronda* (1876). They exemplify that 'alienated, guilty, passionate, diminished outlaw, [who] becomes Satanic for [nineteenth century] women writers'.[6] Where is the equivalent in Wharton, and where too is the body of ideas bolstering the fates she imposes on her characters? The titles of her early collections of stories, *The Greater Inclination* (1899), *Crucial Instances* (1901), gesture towards ideas, as do several moments in her novels. In *The House of Mirth* (1905), for example, we meet Selden and the 'republic of the spirit', but does he or Wharton or anyone know what this phrase might mean? Elsewhere, in chapter 38 of *The Reef* (1912), we have 'a startled sense of hidden powers, of a chaos of attractions and repulsions far beneath the ordered surface of intercourse'. Admittedly, this sense is ascribed to the character Anna Leath, but, aside from her view of 'the ordered surface of intercourse', *The Reef* has no other values to rest on. Nor does it know much about 'a chaos of attractions and repulsions'. The terms of the debate, in other words, offer a simplified polarisation which may be typical of Wharton's novels.

CHAPTER ONE

The House of Mirth (1905): Edith Wharton's Comments on the Novel; Henry James's Response; The Contemporary Reviews

R.W.B. LEWIS[1] quotes Wharton's recollection that she began work on *The House of Mirth* 'about Sept 1903'. He adds that 'as early as 1900, in fact, she had been mulling over the subject – fashionable society in New York and perhaps in Newport – and had hit upon several of the characters' names', though Lily Bart 'was not truly born until the end of the summer of 1903'. Work on the novel was interrupted by the illness of Wharton's husband, and it was August 1904 before she made a sustained commitment to it in order to meet the serialisation deadline. The novel appeared in *Scribner's Magazine* January–November 1905 and was published as a book by Scribner's in October of the same year. R.W.B. Lewis and Nancy Lewis[2] record that 'the novel's enormous and instantaneous success became an element in the publishing-house lore', W.C. Brownell, the head of Scribner's book publishing department, declaring it to be 'the most rapid sale of any book published by Scribner'. Wharton's own comments begin with a letter to Brownell of 5 August 1905. She is alarmed by the illustrations appearing in *The House of Mirth* and by the epigraph from *Ecclesiastes*, 7,4: 'The heart of the wise is in the house of mourning; but the heart of fools is in the house of mirth'. Wanting her novel to speak for itself, she insists:

■ Even when I sank to the depth of letting the illustrations be put in the book – &, oh, I wish I hadn't now! – I never contemplated a text in the title-page. . . .

I think the title explains itself amply as the tale progresses, & I have taken the liberty of drawing an inexorable blue line through the text. □

(*Letters*, p. 94)

Brownell, however, had also praised the construction of the novel (Lewis, *A Biography*, p. 154), and the above letter continues with a response to this praise revealing authorial self-doubts generally ignored by later critics:

■ I am pushing off to the end any reference to what you say about my story. I am so surprised & pleased, & altogether taken aback, that I can't decently compose my countenance about it. I was pleased with bits, myself; but as I go over the proofs the whole thing strikes me as so loosely built, and with so many dangling threads, & cul-de-sacs, & long dusty stretches, that I reach the point of wondering how I had ever dared to try my hand at a long thing. So your seeing a certain amount of architecture in it rejoices me above everything – my theory of what the novel ought to be is so exorbitant, that I am always reminded of Daudet's 'Je rêve d'un aigle, j'accouche d'un colibri' ['I dream of an eagle, I give birth to a hummingbird']. □

(*Letters*, pp. 94–5)

Wharton's next significant letter, 11 November 1905, raises a topic that was to become recurrent in discussions of the novel, namely the nature of the society she presented in *The House of Mirth*. She is writing to William Roscoe Thayer, a Boston writer, biographer and historian:

■ I am particularly & quite inordinately pleased with what you say of my having to your mind been able to maintain my readers' interest in a group of persons so intrinsically uninteresting, except as a social manifestation. I knew that my great difficulty lay there, & if you think I have surmounted it, I shall go about with a high head. But before we leave the subject I must protest, & emphatically, against the suggestion that I have 'stripped' New York society. New York society is still amply clad, & the little corner of its garment that I lifted was meant to show only that little atrophied organ the group of idle & dull people that exists in any big and wealthy social body. If it seems more conspicuous in New York than in an old civilization, it is because the whole social organization with us is so much smaller & less elaborate & if, as I believe, it is more harmful in its influence, it is because fewer responsibilities attach to money with us than in other societies.

11

Forgive this long discourse but you see I had to come to the defense of my own town, which, I assure you, has many mansions outside of the little House of Mirth. □

(*Letters*, pp. 96–7)

Wharton's 'great difficulty', to maintain interest in a 'group of idle & dull people', would be a challenge for any novelist, and whether or not she overcame it remains an unavoidable critical question. As we shall see, later critics will follow Wharton and explain the society by contextualising it in various ways. So Wharton herself points to the smallness of New York social organisation and to the lack of developed relationships between money and responsibility.

Her last noteworthy letter about the novel, written to Morgan Dix, rector of Trinity Church in New York, is dated 5 December 1905. She was responding to Dix's letter which declared that *The House of Mirth*:

■ places you at the head of the living novelists of our country or of the English-writing authors of our day. It is a terrible but just arraignment of the social misconduct which begins in folly and ends in moral and spiritual death. . . . To me the reading of your book has been like walking the wards of some infirmary set apart for the treatment of pestilential disease: the same ghastly wrecks of humanity, the same mephitic odours, the same miasma of efflorescent corruption. □

(*Letters*, pp. 99–100)

To this very high praise of her achievement, and especially of her moral realism, 'just arraignment', Wharton replied:

■ You would have to write in a very different strain to keep me even twenty-four hours from answering your letter; & I must begin by telling you how touched I am that you would have found time to send it, & how proud – yes, quite inordinately so! – that you should have thought my novel worthy of such careful reading & close analysis. – Few things could have pleased me more than the special form which your commendation has taken; for, lightly as I think of my own equipment, I could not do anything if I did not think seriously of my trade; & the more I have considered it, the more has it seemed to me valuable & interesting only in so far as it is a "criticism of life." – It almost seems to me that bad & good fiction (using the words in their ethical sense) might be defined as the kind which treats of life trivially & superficially, & that which probes deep enough to get at the relation with the eternal laws; & the novelist who has this feeling is so often discouraged by the comments of readers & critics who think a book "unpleasant" because it deals with unpleasant conditions, that it is a high solace & encouragement to come upon the recognition of one's motive. *No* novel worth anything can be anything but a novel "with a purpose," & if anyone who cared for the moral issue did not see in my work that *I* care for it, I should have no one to blame but myself – or at least my inadequate means of rendering my effects.

Social conditions as they are just now in our new world, where the sudden possession of money has come without inherited obligations, or any traditional sense of solidarity between the classes, is a vast & absorbing field for the novelist, & I wish a great master could arise to deal with it – but perhaps I may have a chance to talk of these things with you, for I do not mean to be again in New York without making a very determined effort to see you & Mrs. Dix. □

(*Letters*, pp.98–100)

'Criticism of life', 'eternal laws', 'novel "with a purpose"', 'moral issue' – reading these phrases it comes as no surprise that Wharton was an admirer of George Eliot.[3] Different as her American scene is, there is a suggestion also in the letter that she shares something of Eliot's conservatism. It might be that her 'criticism of life' in *The House of Mirth* and other novels is on behalf of 'inherited obligations' and a 'traditional sense of solidarity between the classes'. If it is not on behalf of these values, which, as she recognises, were to be challenged and broken by the very nature of American energy, what others does it suggest or look for?

Nearly thirty years after the above letter, in her final reflection on *The House of Mirth*,[4] she returns yet again to the problem of its social world:

■ In what aspect could a society of irresponsible pleasure-seekers be said to have, on the 'old woe of the world,' any deeper bearing than the people composing such a society could guess? The answer was that a frivolous society can acquire dramatic significance only through what its frivolity destroys. Its tragic implication lies in its power of debasing people and ideals. The answer, in short, was my heroine Lily Bart. □

The earlier aim 'to get at the relation with the eternal laws' is modified here into a wish that her material should have a bearing on her rather fatalistic sense of the 'old woe of the world'. Nonetheless, this passage sets the terms for critical debate of *The House of Mirth*. For example, we might claim more for the society in the novel than the author herself claims, and the novel might then be all the richer. Or we might agree with Wharton's account of 'a frivolous society', but disagree that *The House of Mirth* is saved by Lily Bart, since we discover too little about the 'ideals' that are debased. The fundamental question is whether Lily is worth enough to earn 'tragic implication'.

Henry James[5] responded initially to the February episode of the novel, recording in his letter to Wharton his sense of its 'compact fullness, vivid picture and "sustained interest"' *(Letters,* p. 346). In November, half an hour after finishing the last episode, he wrote again to its author:

■ Let me tell you at once that I very much admire that fiction, and especially the last three numbers of it: finding it carried off with a high, strong hand and an admirable touch, finding it altogether a superior thing. There are things to be said, but they are – some of them – of the essence of your New York *donnée* – and moreover you will have said them, to a certainty, yourself. The book remains one that does you great honour – though it is better written than composed; it is indeed throughout extremely well written, and in places quite "consummately." I wish we could talk of it in a motor-car: I have been in motor-cars again, a little since our wonderful return from Ashfield; but with no such talk as that. There are fifty things I should like to say – but, after so long an interval there are so many I want to, in general; and I think that my best way to touch on some of the former would be by coming back to the U.S. to deliver a lecture on "The question of the *roman de moeurs* in America – it's deadly difficult." But when I do that I shall work in a tribute to the great success and the large portrayal, of your Lily B[art]. She is very big and true – and very difficult to have kept true – and big; and all your climax is very finely handled. Selden is too *absent* – but you know that better than I can make you. I hope you are having a boom. □

(Letters, pp. 373–4)

Would this praise have satisfied Wharton, or would it have left her feeling slightly damned? Probably the latter, especially as James ('better written than composed') reinforces her own initial doubts about the overall construction of *The House of Mirth*. She might also have been alarmed, even annoyed, by James's presumption (a nice way of slipping in a criticism) that she knew only too well about the problem with Selden, and that she, along with everyone else, needed to hear a lecture on the 'deadly difficulty' of the novel of manners in America. *The House of Mirth* after all was a novel of manners!

Our first reviewer,[6] who was also responding to the ongoing serialisation, seems initially to concur with Wharton's reflection on the novel in *A Backward Glance*. In believing 'the answer was my heroine Lily Bart', Wharton could not have wished for more agreement than she gets from the following passage. As this reviewer sees it, Wharton:

■ has selected a situation in that circle of society where conditions make for the destruction rather than the development of honor and virtue. The heroine, a capable, well poised woman, is inmeshed in it. And this is the tragedy – that a creature so morally sane should be subjected to a process sure to prove disintegrating. Her acting, her subterfuges, her pitiful treacheries are simply the threads of a common web which entangles with her every person in her set. She is surrounded by men and women whose aesthetic sensibilities are so highly developed that they have become emasculated. Their pleasures are self-indulgences founded upon some social form of almost every vice. Meanwhile beauty is her own spirit's art of expression, just as religion might be a nun's. The need of money, the petty intrigues and delicately veiled temptations which follow, sully conscience and damage self-respect, even if they do not betray the woman to her moral death. And the whole picture is the more distressing than if the victim were a man, because the destroying of a woman means the passing of a finer spiritual nature. The thing must be accomplished with a frightful delicacy which is not so essential in the destruction of a man's character. □

The later twentieth century may have little time for the reviewer's (and Wharton's?) belief in 'the finer spiritual nature' of women, but the above definition of Lily's 'tragedy' matches what Wharton came to believe was her central achievement in *The House of Mirth*. It is followed by the remarkably suggestive observation that Lily's 'beauty is her own spirit's art of expression, just as religion might be a nun's'. Recalling Wharton's reference to 'ideals' in the comment in *A Backward Glance*, we might wonder if beauty is Lily's only ideal, the only resource in which she seeks sublimation. Then we might ask how the novel responds to this quality in its heroine. Its sympathetic criticism of Lily may fail to offer any measure of her life other than the aestheticism she herself espouses, for example in the *tableau vivant* scene at the Wely Brys'. The reviewer points also to her moral sanity, but if this attribute is itself an ideal, it has to be recognised that it leads only to a final apathy. Where in such a conclusion is the tragedy Wharton and the reviewer claim for the novel?

These issues are related to the reviewer's perception of the novel's fatalism and environmental determinism:

■ We all have the diathesis of iniquity in us, to be sure; but the question is how far right are these authors who prove that the development of the disease depends upon environment? And since it is such an excusing doctrine, it will be easy to inculcate. Then what will be the effect when these people accept it and resign themselves to being the inane creatures of circumstances? If Mrs. Wharton could write a story dramatizing a means of escape for her victims she would do a better business.

Never since the old days in Greece, when men accepted fate with pagan cheerfulness, has fatalism been so emphasized as it is now, particularly in fiction. The difference is that we lack the pagan cheerfulness. □

Inane or not, it is true that the characters in *The House of Mirth* resign themselves to being 'the creatures of circumstances' and, taking the reviewer's point further, it is worth asking if Wharton herself is equally fatalistic. Does she indulge in her characters' resignation and thereby evade a critical analysis of the materials she presents? To answer yes to this question would provide support for the reviewer's final comment on Wharton's style, a comment which, in the light of the reviewer's initial position, may surprise us by its dismissiveness. The review as a whole exemplifies how we may be both convinced and unconvinced by Wharton:

■ Now some years ago, when Mrs. Wharton's stories first began to attract attention, it was claimed that she had that rare thing, distinction in literary style. And she still has a fine manner, but it is like the fine gowns of her heroines, a fashion of the times for interpreting decadent symptoms in human nature. What she says will not last, because it is simply the fashionable drawing of ephemeral types and still more ephemeral sentiments. □

In contrast to this judgement our second review[7] is unstinting in its praise:

■ *The House of Mirth* marks the transition in Mrs. Wharton's career from the region of cultivated tastes and skill to that of free, direct, individual creation; she has often stood on the threshold of life; now she has entered into its tragic and mysterious secrets. To say that this story is far and away the best novel of society written by an American is to give it pre-eminence in a very small class; for the society novel, in the strict sense of the term, has never laid hold of the imagination of the writers of a country engrossed in settling the more pressing problems of life. □

In commending *The House of Mirth* for its pre-eminence as a 'society novel' this writer takes a different view from Wharton's own. 'Society novel' may seem an insignificant classification, but it becomes more interesting if it is related to 'the novel of manners' form written by many English novelists – for example Richardson, Austen and George Eliot. This kind of novel hardly emerges in American literature till the end of the nineteenth century, and a traditional argument for its absence begins with what Fenimore Cooper[8] identified as 'the poverty of materials'. By this he meant the absence of history and of social diversification: 'I have never seen a nation so much alike in my life, as the people of the United States'. The diagnosis was famously elaborated by Henry James in chapter 2 of *Hawthorne* (1879), and a twentieth-century re-statement of it appears in Lionel Trilling's chapter, 'Manners, Morals and the Novel', in *The Liberal Imagination* (1949). Admittedly, Henry James himself and William Dean Howells were writing American versions of the novel of manners before Wharton, who went so far as to complain about 'the continued cry that I am an echo of Mr James (whose books of the last ten years I can't read, much as I delight in the man)' (*Letters*, p.91). It is important, however, to be aware of Wharton's particular contribution to this form and of how few her American predecessors were. In *The House of Mirth* and later novels she is maintaining new American ground in social fiction. The reviewer continues:

■ No tract for the times could have been more scathing and opportune; but no novel of the hour is farther removed from the didactic mood and manner. The kind of society which it describes with merciless veracity has existed in every generation, and is to be found in every city. The story is laid in New York, but it has been told again and again of Rome, Paris, London, and it might be told of Boston, Chicago, New Orleans, San Francisco. Wherever men and women attempt to organize life for the sole purpose of pleasure, the terrible sag of society toward vulgarity and corruption inevitably shows itself. No fortunate conditions of birth and breeding can conceal the fact that a fast society is always a vulgar society. Human relations and intercourse can be kept sweet and wholesome only by generous aims and interests; without religion, art, literature, music, society always degenerates.

It is possible that the dramatic effect of the novel might have been heightened if a few men and women of a different and finer type had been introduced; for every one in the story is vulgar, heartless, uninteresting, or immoral. □

Here *The House of Mirth* is given a universality that Wharton was ambitious to achieve, but which was denied her by the previous reviewer. It is an issue all readers must decide, demonstrating their conclusion with more particularity than the above passage provides. The apparent praise for the lack of didacticism is contradicted by the review's own moralistic tone, and it is hard to see how the comment on the narrow range of the novel's characters agrees with universality. If we also find the range of characterisation to be narrow, are we not inevitably limiting the novel's significance? The reviewer concludes:

■ Mrs. Wharton makes no concession to the optimistic mood which is supposed to dominate American readers, and no evasion of the inexorable logic of life. From the first chapter, trifling indiscretions, careless compromises, minor infidelities, begin to close round Lily Bart and bind her hand and foot until she becomes the victim of a series of circumstances none of which is really serious in itself, but which taken together forge an iron chain of fate. And to this achievement, which lies within the reach of the novelist of genius and of no other, Mrs. Wharton adds the equally great achievement of exposing the chief actor in her story to contamination at every turn, forcing compromise after compromise upon her, lowering her stage by stage in position and in her own self-respect, and yet preserving a core of integrity at the heart of her nature and sending her out of life with such compassion of comprehension that not a hand can be raised to hurl a stone. In the closing chapter Mrs. Wharton rises to a height not only far beyond the reach of her earlier work, but where only a few among her contemporaries can find place with her. A story of such integrity of insight and of workmanship is an achievement of high importance in American life. □

'Fate' again! It will be a recurrent term in discussions of *The House of Mirth*. The reviewer believes that none of the circumstances affecting Lily 'is really serious in itself', but is this the novel's position when, for example, it presents Lily as the victim of the Furies? If we agree with the review, it may be that the novel is making too grandiose a claim for what is happening to Lily at this juncture. '[A] core of integrity at the heart of her nature' reminds us of the previous reviewer's recognition of Lily's moral sanity. These are qualities that might occasion tragedy, but to do so they need more critical exploration than has so far been provided. A tragic effect in the novel would certainly contribute to what the reviewer sees as the novel's counterstatement to 'the optimistic mood which is supposed to dominate American readers'. In resisting this mood *The House of Mirth* might be associated with the later Twain, and with works by James, Dreiser and Scott Fitzgerald.

'A figure which has at least the possibilities of tragedy in it' becomes essential in our next reviewer's sense of the novel. In this piece[9] the anticipation of Wharton's own argument in *A Backward Glance* is so noticeable as to suggest the author may have echoed the reviewer:

■ The obvious criticism of novels dealing with this subject-matter is that the *dramatis personae*, as a rule, are so worthless or futile that it is impossible to feel any sympathy with them in their misfortunes. Mrs. Wharton, like a true artist, has realised that the society with which she is dealing, being highly sophisticated, can only be rendered really interesting by the introduction of a figure which has at least the possibilities of tragedy in it. This figure she has discovered in the highly complex, vivid, ill-starred heroine of her ironically named romance. □

What follows is very much what Wharton must have wished for:

■ The sacrifices of self-respect which Lily is driven to make in order to satisfy her thirst for luxury might well be supposed to alienate the reader, but in every phase of her devious career she never wholly forfeits sympathy, and in the end excites the liveliest compassion. With such antecedents and opportunities disaster was inevitable, but it is a disaster infinitely more tragic than the conventional unhappy ending of a lovely woman who stoops to folly. The relations between some of Lily's extravagant friends and their wives growing somewhat strained, the situation is saved by the sacrifice of the one honest woman of the set, – Lily herself. Perhaps Mrs. Wharton has shown too elaborate an ingenuity in contriving that every indiscretion, however venial, should ultimately recoil on her heroine with accumulated force, and the supreme humiliation of her failure to "range herself" by marrying the odious Mr. Rosedale is almost unbearably painful. Yet the story is so closely knit, so logically carried out, that one cannot but acquiesce in its inevitableness, and admire the skill with which Mrs.

Wharton has contrived to reconcile her readers to a conclusion which at first seemed mercilessly inconclusive. □

Only the reviewer's remark about 'contriving' hints at a qualification, though we may also disagree with the description of Rosedale as 'odious'. The contriving, if true, would relate to the question of 'fate', and to whether this force is an expression of impersonal, even metaphysical circumstance (what Wharton in her letter to Dix called 'the eternal laws'), or merely a matter of Wharton's own devising.

By now the main themes of the reviews are emerging. Not surprisingly, they have to do with Wharton's characterisation of Lily, with society, and with fate. Beginning with token praise of the novel, William Morton Payne[10] goes further than our previous reviews with the attack on its social world:

■ It is a story elaborated in every detail to a high degree of refinement, and evidently a product of the artistic conscience. Having paid this deserved tribute to its finer characteristics, we are bound to add that it is deficient in interest. The reason is not far to seek. There is no section of American society – or of society anywhere, for that matter – so absolutely devoid of appeal to the sympathies of normally-constituted intelligence as the vain and vulgar element that disports itself in our larger cities as the only society worth considering, this pretension being based upon wealth alone, with its natural accompaniment of self-seeking display and frivolity. A novelist of archangelical powers could not make interesting so sorry a phase of humanity as this, and because Mrs. Wharton has described for us this type and this alone, we turn her page impatiently, and look in vain for relief from their emptiness. □

Nor is Payne persuaded, as was Wharton herself, that the answer is Lily Bart. He quotes nearly all of the paragraph in Book Two, chapter 13 when Lily reflects on her parents' and her own rootlessness (paragraph beginning: 'It was no longer, however, from the vision of material poverty . . .'). Seizing especially on Lily's acknowledgement that 'there had never been a time when she had any real relation to life', he makes the following judgement, first of the passage and then of the whole novel:

■ This is so fine and true that it reconciles us in part to the complex of empty talk and petty intrigue and ignoble aim through which, as through a desert waste, we have toiled to reach it. But the question remains persistent whether it was worth while to describe at such length and with such infinite pains the career of any woman of whom it must be said in the end that she had never had any real relation to life. We are much inclined to doubt that it was worth while – for a writer of Mrs. Wharton's exceptional gifts. □

It might be argued that Payne turns the phrase, 'real relation to life', too simply against the novel and ignores the heart of the matter, which is *why* Lily has not had such a relation. He nonetheless raises a central critical question, and readers making a high claim for *The House of Mirth* must themselves give a convincing account of what Payne may be ignoring.

In our next review[11] Lily's relation to life is all too real and all too culpable:

■ Many novelists have described the social career of this ill-fated young person, generally representing her as a victim of circumstance, herself possessing intrinsic virtues which either conquer superficial and accidental attributes or at least make a good enough showing to engage the reader's sympathy. Not in this lenient fashion has Mrs. Wharton seen and judged Miss Lily Bart. The image most constantly and consistently before her, most vividly presented, is not that of a naturally good girl, of an essentially nice girl, hurt, hardened, degraded by contact with a wicked world, but that of a girl born at the wicked world's level, who, failing to get a firm footing therein, is driven by bitter and repeated disappointment to take her leave by the agency of an over-dose of chloral. Miss Bart never willingly faces life beyond the precincts of the House of Mirth, but outstays her welcome there, resorting to ignominious shifts, pocketing rather deadly insults, until she is pushed out of doors and down, step by step, to the common highway.

Occasionally Mrs. Wharton's clear, severe vision wavers. She intimates that her Lily Bart is superior to her world, that she chafes in chains, and has intermittent attacks of soft and even sanctifying emotions. Mrs. Wharton is weakest when she is merciful. Miss Bart does seem to throw up her game at a critical moment and to let coveted prizes slip through her fingers; but such misfortunes strike us as unforeseen results of her folly or of an unexpected checkmate. There is no evidence of instinctive recoil from an intention recognized as ignoble. Even her final rejection of the monstrous conditions on fulfilment of which Mr. Rosedale has expressed a willingness to marry her, fails to establish any moral worth.

Blackmail is a resort of the infamous. A decent girl, one not necessarily clever or kind or well-bred, would have sent Mrs. Dorset's compromising letters back to her as soon as they fell into her hands. It is by the temptations that Miss Bart permitted to visit her that her character finally fails to commend itself for sympathetic judgment or compassion. "Dingy" is her favorite appellation for those who do not live in splendor on their own or other people's incomes. She had a mortal horror of dinginess, external dinginess, but lived and moved delightedly among souls of dinginess incomparable, beyond furbishing. The poor girl's inward eye was a feeble organ not susceptible of cultivation. □

Here the reviewer finds exactly the opposite of the effect that Wharton, in *A Backward Glance*, claimed she wanted to produce; the author is seen at her weakest in intimating that 'Lily Bart is superior to her world'. It may be that the review is too morally simplistic. It fails to recognise that Lily's availability to temptation and her complicity provide for the novel's essential conflict. To the contrary, it finds Lily to be too much of a moral vacancy for conflict to have a hold in her:

■ She has not a particle of genuine, fundamental, good human feeling, and has very little bad. Her assumed tender emotion for the cautious, not to say canny, Mr. Selden (a cold prig), never convinces any one, not even him. She cherishes no affectionate sentiments towards the mother who did her poor best for her, the aunt who supported her, the rich women who dressed her, or the poor friend who adored her. In no society could such a being exist except in that where the dismal and (to the reader) often tedious drama of her life goes on. The denizens of her House of Mirth are revolting. They eat and drink, expensively and often, but are never merry. They never think, and their talk is as the crackling of thorns. They break the seventh commandment without the excuse of passion, apparently playing with adultery and divorce (as they seem to play bridge for high stakes and drive motor cars) in order to assert privilege, to earn the absurd epithet, "smart." They have no ideas, no intellectual interests, neither wit nor humor nor tact nor grace. □

Just as it seems this review is heaping all the blame on Lily, it turns to the society in which she exists, going further than Wharton herself in condemnation. Obviously, this writer is left with nothing at all from *The House of Mirth*.

Mary Moss[12] gets to the heart of the case Wharton is making for Lily: 'She is too fastidious for the life she is leading, but unfit for any other available one'. Moss continues:

■ As a point of probability, would not Lily have either early succumbed or managed her way to better things? But when you find yourself discussing the truth of a novel, you are really paying it a high tribute. □

In other words the very discussion *The House of Mirth* provokes is an indication of its stature. According to Moss: 'Mrs Wharton knows the truth about Lily. She was incapable of *meanness* as any other form of economy.' What follows demonstrates Moss's complete knowledge of the social world Lily inhabits. Her review is thoroughly responsive to the novel, yet it ends with a damning criticism: 'You see, you understand, but, unfortunately, you do not greatly care.'

If Moss is right about our not caring, Olivia Howard Dunbar[13] may supply a reason:

■ . . . the greatest defect of the book is undoubtedly its lack of contrast. It has no high-lights. Its figures are all of one exceedingly unpleasant tone, the interplay of different types of character, one of the chief functions of the novelist, being excluded altogether. In short, the book is a little too much like a fastidiously conducted literary "raid" – which may result in displaying a garish group of frightened transgressors, but which cannot be accepted as a sober and comprehensive interpretation of life. □

We do not greatly care because the novel is too much the demonstration of a predetermined case and is short, therefore, on contrasts, surprises and changes of direction. As Dunbar puts it:

■ As to the essential truth of the narrative, that is to say, there is not the faintest doubt in the world. Granted a Lily Bart, and a certain set of conditions, and her doom would be inevitable.

What one disturbedly wonders, however, in following the girl's unlovely history, is how much of it Mrs. Wharton has suppressed. Just as she insists upon Miss Bart's remarkable eyelashes because she feels responsibility to her as a heroine and a beauty, so we suspect there are various things about Lily which, because she is a heroine, we never learn at all. The reader is not allowed to know her with real intimacy, to get behind the scenes. One thinks of her, after all, as gloved, veiled, smiling, erectly on her guard.

Mrs. Wharton is not lacking in invention. It is the more surprising, therefore, that she should have permitted herself so old a device as that of the blackmailing charwoman who reclaimed the compromising letters most unnaturally cast by the punctilious Selden, half-torn, into the waste-basket. This entire episode is trumpery and melodramatic and weakens the plot. □

Dunbar is right about Selden. He would not have carelessly discarded those compromising letters. As for the reader not knowing Lily, this may be because there is very little to know after we have registered her beauty and integrity. For Lily, Wharton herself, and therefore the reader, the veil may conceal a blank.

Continuing this theme, Alice Meynell[14] finds that it is Wharton herself who is veiled or, in Meynell's word, 'sequestered'. Meynell begins by seeing the society of the novel as other reviewers have seen it. She then argues that:

■ To observe this horde without serious irritation is a work demanding self-control, and Mrs Wharton watches them from the sequestered bower of her fine art, taking wide views, keeping her own counsel. . . .

And in this extremity of reserve lurks the one fault of art in the book – that is the indefiniteness of the 'better part' which Selden has to offer to the self-loving and money-loving heroine. In the character of this young New York woman, about whom the whole history is written, we recognise two likenesses. She is partly Gwendolen Harleth and partly Hedda Gabler, yet with something modern in the place of Gwendolen's thirst after righteousness, and something intelligible in the place of Hedda's vice and Hedda's despair. Both resemblances therefore are slight. Now, in her slight resemblance to Gwendolen Harleth she should have a kind of external conscience in the form of a man – a man at least esteemed, at least admirable. But the man in whom the role is just suggested, in *The House of Mirth*, is very little estimable. He has borne a part in the 'cold obstruction' of the intrigues of man and woman in the world he lives in – a squalid past, we are compelled to see, because of the manner of woman who has been his random mistress. And the better art he shows the heroine, half-heartedly, as a way out of her pursuit of luxury, is vague. If it were definite we are sure it would be inadequate, and Mrs Wharton ably leaves it in a little cloud. We choose, however, to pause where she passes, and to ask a closer question. All the answer we get is a tender of liberty, and obviously liberty is what the unfortunate egoist, the woman of the New York 'world', needs urgently, and all but desperately; but in what liberty does the apostle of this vague apostolate himself abide? We see him in the beloved luxury in which all the persons of the book roll themselves with revolting joy. We cannot imagine Lawrence Selden following liberty into a hard, or a useful, or a wild, or a sacramental life. He sets open, or rather ajar, to the woman who inclines to love him, a door into a better world too dubious for faith, a better world open to nothing but a very justifiable suspicion; and where there is no definite place to go, or object in setting out, she does not go. She is less to blame than Mrs Wharton. □

The comparison with Gwendolen Harleth from Eliot's *Daniel Deronda* is well made. It may be that readers of both novels would insist that a Deronda is the last kind of male advisor Lily needs. Nonetheless, Meynell's case against Selden's function in *The House of Mirth* is arresting. She is claiming that he is useless for providing a perspective on Lily, since he himself stands for nothing that is worthwhile. In this respect he represents the 'sequestered' Wharton's inability to offer (in her own voice or in Selden's) a view of life different from Lily's own. Lily, therefore, 'is less to blame than Mrs Wharton'.

We began with a review which initially was full of acclaim, and it is fitting to end in a similar vein with the response in the English *Times Literary Supplement*.[15]

■ [Wharton] registers to the last degree of delicacy the jumble of crudity and overcivilization which she finds in New York life of to-day. She describes coolly and patiently, without a touch of journalism or sentimentality, the interminable race after pleasure which that fierce little world, like many another, engages in till it unconsciously becomes more absorbed in the race than in its object. In the middle of this turmoil move the figures she selects: Selden, an extremely subtle discovery of the writer's, sympathetic and cultivated, slipping in and out of the society round him, a detached spectator, independent of what Mrs. Wharton calls the sumptuary side of life, who cannot help loving with his taste as well as his instinct, inevitably missing his opportunity when it arrives, as spectators of life will do; Rosedale, the Jew millionaire, who knows the place in society that he wants, knows exactly what it is worth his while to pay for it, and is prepared to pay it, who with all his meanness gets somehow to the heart of life, touches reality in a way in which the Seldens of the world, who are worse egotists than the Rosedales, will never do; and then, moving between the two, like a far more sophisticated Manon Lescaut, is Lily Bart, the central figure of the book, a portrait on which Mrs. Wharton has lavished all her skill and insight. She fights passionately to hold her precarious position in the House of Mirth, and, with all her advantages and all her efforts, is slowly forced out of it. Now and then, for a moment, she half believes that it is not worth the trouble, and that Selden and the less complicated life that he represents has something curiously seductive to offer. And then at last, when she loves Selden, he fails her after all, and she has to face her catastrophe alone. It is hardly possible to praise too highly the way in which Mrs. Wharton has followed out this history, the truth she has put into it and the continuity she gives it, making this vacillating mind, among the crowd who know their own minds so well, shift and change without ever losing its identity. □

It would be difficult to better this summary for its awareness of the explicit and implicit relationships and contrasts. Its sensitivity of engagement with the novel, especially in the last lines on Lily and 'the crowd', makes all the more telling its final reservations:

■ What Mrs. Wharton appears to lack is in a word the creative gift at its fullest. She sees with certainty, and her hand is as sure as her eye. But with the richest imaginations something takes place beyond this. Detail may be rough and incorrect, but something entirely new has been conceived and embodied. That is what happens when fiction reaches its very highest point; and *The House of Mirth* may well be below this, and yet be what it is, an exceptional book. □

There is no precision about 'the creative gift at its fullest', but it seems that the writer finds *The House of Mirth* too explicable and too sure of itself. If we agree, we too might find the novel limited, and not an example of fiction reaching 'its very highest point'.

CHAPTER TWO

The Critical Response to *The House of Mirth*

A DISCIPLE OF Henry James, Percy Lubbock[1] had known Wharton since he met her in 1906 at 'Queen's Acre', the house in Windsor of James's friend Howard Sturgis. Until an eventual falling-out he was to remain her friend for a number of years. As he sees it, Wharton's previous work had presented America merely as 'an assumed background, conditioning the action without taking part in it'. In *The House of Mirth*, by contrast:

■ New York is no background; it is an urgent and voluble participator in the drama. It is an actor, indeed, so vehemently alive that Mrs. Wharton's easy and immediate control of such exuberance is a triumph of stage-management. *The House of Mirth* is thoroughly the novel of a novelist; it shows, that is to say, no sign whatever that its author had been accustomed to find her subjects in momentary glimpses that did not ask for broader development. She refocuses her sight, apparently without effort, to include one of the most remarkable spectacles in the history of manners – the sudden unfolding of a social growth fertilized by vaster streams of private wealth than the world has ever yet known. The glittering show which we associate with the name of Fifth Avenue may, for the service of art, leave something to be desired. But its very intractability is so vividly marked, in a world in which social definitions are everywhere becoming vaguer, that it clearly challenges art to the attempt to make use of it.

The evident difficulty is that the growth has been too sudden to strike us as organic. A living society, as we understand the word, can draw its being only from a stored inheritance of traditions; and the leading feature of this particular New York is its freedom from any discernible debt to the past. This, no doubt, is a superficial view of the matter, for we are presumably not prepared to regard the millionaire as a miraculous and unrelated species. The millionaire and his hierarchy have had their own origins; and evolution is not the less natural for being rapid. The structure of this singular House of Mirth is therefore no more meaningless than any other; and the novelist who could expound its meaning by showing the continuity which it must have with its mysterious past would have a brilliant subject to his hand. Unfortunately the novelist, as things are, is scarcely in a position to do this, cut off as his experience is likely to be from the conditions of life which have brought about these huge accumulations. He cannot see the new society as the inevitable outcome of ancestral forces, for the necessary links lie in a region which it is usually forbidden him to tread, the region densely veiled from him under the name of "business." Till that veil is rent he must chiefly be struck by the passion with which this society has flung itself into the attempt to buy everything that can be bought, and its amazing success in doing so. For the romance of expenditure this is all very well, but the novel of manners looks for something more coherent. No picture could be made of a promiscuity which streams beyond the limits of any frame that might be imposed upon it. A writer like Mrs. Wharton, who touches nothing but to give it finality, could treat Fifth Avenue's indiscriminate raptures in only one way. Her Trenors and Dorsets and Van Degens, scattering their millions on both sides of the Atlantic, do not and could not give her a subject for direct study; but it is a different matter when she annexes and uses them for particular issues. If it is difficult to see what they mean or how they were created, what they are devouring or supplanting is less obscure. Mrs. Wharton accordingly pictures, not the Trenors themselves, but their disturbing impact upon other and more impressionable surfaces. □

This account of the effect on New York society of 'vaster streams of private wealth than the world has ever yet known' recalls Wharton's own comments in the letters quoted in the first chapter of this Guide. It seems also that Lubbock had read James's essay 'The Question of the Opportunities'.[2] Arguing that above all others 'the typical American figure' is the 'business man', James had anticipated Lubbock in recognising how cut off the novelist is from the business world: 'those who know it are not the men to paint it; those who might attempt it are not the men who know it'. *The House of Mirth* appeared seven years after this essay, but Lubbock clearly feels Wharton has not solved the problem diagnosed by James. She cannot treat the fortunes of 'her Trenors and Dorsets and Van Degens' as 'a subject for direct study'. Instead she presents the 'disturbing impact upon other[s]'. As Wharton herself was to argue, the answer was Lily Bart. Lubbock continues:

■ In *The House of Mirth* it is Lily Bart whom they devour, or rather whom they so mold and train that when, by what might have been the fortune of her life, they cease to find a use for her, she can only drop helpless by the way. Lily's fineness of grain, her central independence of spirit, perpetually prevent her from harvesting the profit which her cultivation of the Trenors and their like brings under her hand. The fruits of her dependence have a certain grossness of texture which always makes her, when choice has to be made, neglect to appropriate them. She pays for her fastidiousness by finding herself abandoned by the vivid crowd; and she pays for her courtship of the crowd, so carefully taught her by nearly all the conditions of her life, by discovering that her independence is only strong enough to destroy and not to remake her. In the wavering drama of Lily's hesitations her independence is represented by the one friend who is both near enough to affect her and critical enough to have kept himself free on his own ground. Selden knows, and she knows, that if she is to create an existence of finer values for herself it can be only with his help. Yet between them they fail; and Lily, cast off at last by the crowd for her failure to treat with them consistently on their own terms, does not, at the moment of need, find the outstretched hand. So her drama must necessarily end; for, in the middle of a world which with all accuracy knows what it wants, there is no time for hesitation to feel its way and grow tentatively into strength. This we can easily recognize; but Mrs. Wharton appears, in arranging her effects, to have assumed a little too much for the pace and stress of the hurrying world. That Lily must drop out is clear; and doubtless her subsidence would be rapid. But that her disappearance into obscurity should seem so little remarked, that she should vanish without more splash, is difficult to reconcile with the conspicuousness of her preceding triumphs, especially as her reluctant exile is no further in space than from the palaces of one street to the boarding-houses of the next. We feel that it would take even the Trenors more time than Mrs. Wharton allows them to ignore Lily so completely, with the splendor of her beauty languishing within five minutes' walk. If this only means that we do not know the race of Trenors as Mrs. Wharton knows them – which indeed is likely – there was then all the more need to convince us securely. But except at this one juncture there seems no detail wanting to our knowledge of Lily's tyrannous world, so direct is Mrs. Wharton's use of sharp descriptive strokes. Nothing could be more unobtrusively right than the way in which the gilded crowd surges over the picture, and parts, at the due moments, to give place to the sensitive quiet of the scenes between Lily and Selden with which the book is exquisitely punctuated. □

Writing a very good account of the novel on its own terms, Lubbock gets exactly to what Wharton wants to show in Lily. We might wonder why 'her central independence of spirit' finds nothing to say 'yes' to, as opposed to everything she says 'no' to, and we might associate this issue with Lubbock's doubts about the reality of the novel when Lily disappears 'into obscurity'. Lubbock is suggesting that Wharton is rather manipulating Lily's fate, and such an authorial tactic, if it were the case, would undoubtedly require a Lily whose imputed 'independence of spirit' was impotent.

It would require a Lily who was entirely a victim. In Edmund Wilson's words:[3]

■ [Wharton's] tragic heroines and heroes are the victims of the group pressure of convention; they are passionate or imaginative spirits, hungry for emotional and intellectual experience, who find themselves locked into a small closed system, and either destroy themselves by beating their heads against their prison or suffer a living death in resigning themselves to it. Out of these themes she got a sharp pathos all her own. The language and some of the machinery of *The House of Mirth* seem old-fashioned and rather melodramatic today; but the book had some originality and power, with its chronicle of a social parasite on the fringes of the very rich, dragging out a stupefying routine of week-ends, yachting trips and dinners, and finding a window open only twice, at the beginning and at the end of the book, on a world where all the values are not money values. □

This account seems to lose confidence in *The House of Mirth* even as Wilson is writing. 'Tragic' becomes 'pathos', and the book's 'originality and power' are seen as qualities belonging only to the time in which it was written.

Alfred Kazin[4] also has a sense of Wharton's limitations, but this time they are to her class. As he sees it:

■ It is easy to see now that Edith Wharton's great subject should have been the biography of her own class, for her education and training had given her alone in her literary generation the best access to it. But the very significance of that education was her inability to transcend and use it. . . .

. . . She escaped the tedium and mediocrity to which her class had condemned her, but the very motivation of that escape was to become a great artist, to attain by the extension of her powers the liberation she needed as a woman; and a great artist, even a completely devoted artist, she never became. . . .

The greater consequence of Edith Wharton's failure to fulfil herself in art was its deepening of her innate disposition to tragedy. She was conscious of that failure even when she was most successful, and in the gap between her resolution and her achievement she had recourse to a classical myth, the pursuing Eumenides who will not let Lily Bart or Edith Wharton rest. She was among the few in her generation to attain the sense of tragedy, even the sense of the world as pure evil. □

Like Wilson, Kazin does not believe Wharton has a reach beyond her time and circumstances. He finds nothing universal in her and his position, therefore, needs to be countered by those who respond to Wharton only with acclamation. Sometimes it is not clear whether Kazin is discussing the novels or Wharton herself as a subject, his last sentence above being a case in point. Perhaps it could be applied to Wharton's own sense of life, but where, in *The House of Mirth* or any other of her works, do we find a realisation of 'the sense of the world as pure evil'? In 1942, when Kazin's claim was published, there was certainly enough real evil around to provide him with a measure.

Diana Trilling[5] might well be responding to Kazin's charge that Wharton was unable to transcend her class:

■ It is as if our failure to have waged successful class war in the Thirties now makes it mandatory that we deny any reality of class, any distinctions of social topography, or, certainly, any healthy conjunction between a writer's place in society and his moral vision. . . .

Looked at in this light, *The House of Mirth* can hardly be expected to give satisfaction, for it is nothing if not a novel about social stratification and the consequences of breaking the taboos of class. In addition, its author is in important part identified with the distinctly upper-case Society which she is putting under such rigorous inspection – and this is not merely a matter of what we know of her life, it has also to do with where Mrs. Wharton locates herself in relation to the story she tells. Writing of Lily Bart, a beautiful young woman fated to destruction because she violated the laws of her social group, Mrs. Wharton never renounces her community with Lily's harsh judges, not even when she is exposing their most vicious hypocrisies. Her attack is always within the family. *The House of Mirth* is nevertheless one of the most telling indictments of a social system based on the chance distribution of wealth, and therefore of social privilege, that has ever been put on paper. Indeed, what accounts for its extraordinary moral texture no less than its complex accuracy as a piece of social reporting is Mrs. Wharton's simultaneous acceptance of the social group into which she was born and her unflinching confrontation of the evils it perpetrates. □

Here the word 'evils' seems to mean something less than Kazin's 'sense of the world as pure evil'. Presumably the destruction of Lily is an example of the evils, though it is debatable whether this word is appropriate for what actually happens, and Trilling needed to develop its relevance. She goes on to see Wharton engaging in *The House of Mirth* with 'the inexorable process of history as it worked itself out in the America with which she was best acquainted'. It is a process in which the 'world of privilege' is attacked by 'the insurgent democratic horde'. One of the representatives of the 'new social dispensation' is:

■ . . . a very rich Jew, Simon Rosedale, who is intent upon making a marriage which will fittingly ornament his enormous wealth and ensure him a place in Society. Not only the innermost circles but even the outlying sections of the old aristocratic world are at first resistant to Rosedale's intrusion; but they are unable to withstand the power of his money, and his urgency of personal ambition. This most alien of Mrs. Wharton's characters at last penetrates the central strongholds; and if his worldly success coincides with the steady revelation of a far more feeling nature than showed in the days when he was failing so dismally in his social effort, we can take this as not the least pointed of Mrs. Wharton's comments on the connection between social realities and the life of the emotions. Obviously Mrs. Wharton is not saying that an achieved position in Society is the warrant of good feelings: her panorama of Lily's brutally shallow and callous friends argues quite the opposite. But she surely is saying that our gentler emotions have a hard time thriving when we lack a sense of our secure niche in the world, whatever it may be, or, as in Lily's case, without the nourishment of money.

The historical moment, then, of *The House of Mirth* is the moment when a Jew – and a self-made Jew at that, uncouth and charmless, whose deviations from accepted deportment are as conspicuous as his wealth and as grating on the sensitive nerve of Society – can aspire to associate on equal terms with the old Hudson Valley families. But this is still the moment when the old social monarchs, aware that a new dynasty of wealth storms the inherited realm, cling most tenaciously to their rights of blood; the struggle is the fiercer because eventually so futile. Through most of *The House of Mirth* Rosedale takes social and personal insult to a degree that would flatten any except a man of iron will – except a man, that is, whose personal will was synonymous with the will of history. His strength of endurance lies in his awareness that it is only so long as the old fortunes hold out that the old families can maintain their prestige and power, and in his sure knowledge that his own shrewd speculations on Wall Street are in the process of blasting their hereditary fortress. □

In a general sense this account is irrefutable, though there is some confusion at the end of the first paragraph when Trilling is debating the benefits of worldly success. If this confusion is also Wharton's, it would rather confirm Kazin's case that she only believes life to be possible in the very society she is attacking. One might also have expected Trilling to be more critical of the presentation of Rosedale. Might not Wharton have given him some religious and cultural baggage? All that defines him as a Jew in her eyes is his success in making money and his imperviousness to insult.

Trilling continues:

■ It is clear that what Mrs. Wharton is captured by in Lily Bart is her ambiguity of purpose, the conflict between her practical good sense and the pull of spirit. And what makes Lily a heroine for the reader – one of the greatly appealing heroines of fiction, worthy of association with Emma Bovary and Anna Karenina – is the ultimate triumph of spirit over good sense, even though the transcendence guarantees her destruction. Were Lily's spirit more in tune with her society, the novel might have ended with her practical victory over the poor souls who surround her, but the achievement would make her no better a creation than they. On the other hand, it is a mistake to think of Lily as Mrs. Wharton's model of virtuousness. She is "pure" neither in her own nor her author's eyes. The poignancy of her fate lies in her doomed struggle to subdue that part of her own nature which is no

THE HOUSE OF MIRTH

better than her culture. Where a less pliant imagination than Mrs. Wharton's would surely have conceived Lily's conflict with her world as the battle between Innocence (Lily) and Experience (Society), Mrs. Wharton has the courage to recognize the extent to which Lily has herself been tainted by her environment. □

This is uncontroversial until we reach the word 'tainted', which refers back to Trilling's use of the 'evils' in our first quotation from her. It is true that Lily shares some of the faults of her society, but how deep is either her taint or her society's? Does 'tainted' mean, or even imply, corrupt? Dare Wharton take her novel into this kind of territory which might indeed lead it to a tragic destination? Lily is actually brought down by her own negligence, especially in connection with how Trenor's money is compromising her, rather than by wrongdoing. 'Tainted', therefore, might be thought to be an overstatement.

Later Trilling returns to the point she was making in our second quotation from her:

■ For Mrs. Wharton's heroine, wealth is much more than a matter of worldly security – and this despite her luxurious tastes whose indulgence plays such a large part in her undoing. It is the means for living a life of harmony and grace, free of the dingy and sordid: Mrs. Wharton repeatedly uses these two words to describe an existence where there is insufficient money to enhance one's own potentialities or to disguise the less lovely aspects of life. That the same small segment of society which is lucky enough to have the means for making life into a thing of beauty should be as lacking in virtue and generosity, as lacking, actually, in the instinct to art, as Lily's friends are is a major irony of her story. With the considerable bitterness of her intimate experience of the spiritual desolation of Society, Mrs. Wharton assures us that the rich are morally unworthy of the beauty they can afford, that at heart they are all of them of a piece with Mrs. Peniston, whose expensive dismal furniture is so accurate a reflection of her charmlessness and such an offense to her niece. Whatever one's wealth, one cannot buy spiritual grace; nor, by extension, can art redeem a callous humanity. □

Again there is a confusion here, which may well reflect a confusion in *The House of Mirth* itself. In the passage and the novel there is a yearning for art and beauty to be separated from materiality: if only Lily could stay free of the 'dingy and sordid'; if only she could be beautiful without having to worry about providing for herself! But was not Yeats right in 'The Circus Animals' Desertion', when he identified 'the foul rag-and-bone shop of the heart' as the source of art and beauty? Their production, in other words, has everything to do with the corruptions of our mortality and materiality, and, contrary to what Trilling claims, the result may well redeem a callous humanity. Its effect may transcend its source.

Blake Nevius[6] begins his response to *The House of Mirth* by referring to Wharton's own reflection on the novel in *A Backward Glance* (quoted in chapter one of this Guide). In his words:

■ It is to Edith Wharton's credit that she recognized the perilous transparency of the human nature she had to deal with – a human nature subject to no stresses that money could not alleviate, and therefore incapable of expressing itself with the greatest intensity. The characterization of Lily Bart was central to the problem; and since Lily, in order to satisfy her function in the novel, had to take her cue from the more worldly of her associates, she remains, so far as the moral significance of her actions is concerned, until almost the end of the novel an essentially lightweight and static protagonist. Nevertheless, she has, if only in embryo, certain qualities which raise her above her associates and make her distinctly worth saving, so that her fate, if not tragic according to any satisfactory definition of the term, at least impresses us with the sense of infinite and avoidable waste. Edith Wharton's own answer to her question was "that a frivolous society can acquire dramatic significance only through what its frivolity destroys. Its tragic implication lies in its power of debasing people and ideals." Change the word "frivolous" to "materialistic," and the story of Lily Bart assumes a larger significance. Edith Wharton was one of the first American novelists to develop the possibilities of a theme which since the turn of the century has permeated our fiction: the waste of human and spiritual resources which in America went hand in hand with the exploitation of the land and forests. □

Nevius is questioning whether Lily has the stature to be, as Wharton claimed, a figure on whom 'tragic implication' could centre. His answer is to substitute 'waste' for tragedy, and though this term may be persuasive, it is surely an exaggeration to link it with 'infinite'. Nor are there grounds for replacing 'frivolous' with 'materialistic', especially when the latter is associated with 'the exploitation of the lands and forests'. Such exploitation, a familiar theme in nineteenth-century American literature, hardly registers in *The House of Mirth*.

But Nevius is working towards a consideration of the novel as a 'naturalistic tragedy':

■ There is some indication that Mrs. Wharton conceived of her action, perhaps unconsciously, in terms of naturalistic tragedy. In *A Backward Glance* she recalls her introduction to "the wonder-world of nineteenth century science" and the excitement of reading for the first time the works of Darwin, Huxley, Spencer, Haeckel, and other evolutionists. It is impossible, perhaps, to calculate their influence, but it has never been considered. She was perfectly acquainted, moreover, with the French naturalistic tradition beginning with Flaubert, and it is not impossible that Emma Bovary is the spiritual godmother of Lily Bart. But this is at best circumstantial evidence, whereas the novel itself adequately conveys the suggestion. Its theme is the victimizing effect of a particular environment on one of its more helplessly characteristic products. It was the discovery of the nineteenth century, as someone has said, that Society, rather than God or Satan, is the tyrant of the universe; and the society into whose narrow ideal Lily Bart is inducted at birth conspires with her mother's example and training to defeat from the start any chance of effective rebellion. In the naturalistic tradition, the action of *The House of Mirth* is in a sense all denouement, for Lily's conflict with her environment – no more than the feeble and intermittent beating of her wings against the bars of "the great gilt cage" – is mortgaged to defeat. . . .

Lily, in short, is as completely and typically the product of her heredity, environment, and the historical moment which found American materialism in the ascendant as the protagonist of any recognized naturalistic novel. Like any weak individual – like Clyde Griffiths or Carrie Meeber – she is at the mercy of every suggestion of her immediate environment; she responds to those influences which are most palpably present at a given moment. Although we are asked to believe that two sides of her personality are struggling for possession, there is no possibility of a genuine moral conflict until near the end of the action when as a result of suffering she experiences the self-realization which is the condition of any moral growth. Through no fault of her own, she has – can have – only the loosest theoretical grasp of the principles which enable Selden to preserve his weak idealism from the corroding atmosphere in which they are both immersed. □

What is striking here is Nevius's recognition of Lily's helplessness and feebleness – qualities that render her nearly incapable of bearing 'a

genuine moral conflict'. It is to compensate for this analysis that Nevius
has to stress the naturalism. We may wonder, however, whether the impersonal forces of social Darwinism, in which only the fittest and luckiest
survive, really make their presence felt in *The House of Mirth*. Is there not
more difference than similarity between it and the Dreiser novels that
Nevius refers to? In contrast to the worlds of Clyde Griffiths and Carrie
Meeber, Lily's world is peripheral and hermetic. Wishing it could be
heedless of where the money comes from, it is, as Wharton knows,
already obsolescent, and we may conclude that Wharton is no more
capable than Lily of an engagement with the rampant energies of capital,
enterprise and industry that are transforming the American scene. These
energies are the very stuff of a Dreiser novel. Nevius concludes:

■ It should be clear, at any rate, that we are deceiving ourselves if we
try to account for the compelling interest of *The House of Mirth* by the
nature or intensity of the moral conflict. Besides the reasons I have
suggested, the alternatives proposed to Lily Bart in the persons of
Selden and Gerty Farish are not at all attractively urged. It was beyond
Edith Wharton's powers of sympathy and imagination, and at odds
with her distrust of philanthropy, to make Gerty Farish, with her
social work, her one-room flat, and the unrelieved dinginess of her life
in general, an engaging figure. And what can we say of Selden, who
maintains his integrity at the cost of any nourishing human relationship? Like Winterbourne in *Daisy Miller*, he is betrayed by his
aloofness, his hesitations, his careful discriminations. He is the least
attractive ambassador of his "republic of the spirit," and Mrs. Wharton
knows this as well as her readers. In fact, the tragic effect of Lily Bart's
fate is jeopardized by an irony directed principally at Selden, for she
accidentally takes an overdose of sleeping pills while he is trying to
make up his mind to marry her.

The quality in the novel that seizes and holds the reader, and that
accounts more than any other for its persistent vitality, is the same
which we find in the novels of Dreiser. In the spectacle of a lonely
struggle with the hostile forces of environment, there is a particular
kind of fascination which is not at all diminished by the certainty of
defeat. □

Here Nevius is dealing with the perspectives Wharton casts on Lily in the
persons of Selden and Gerty Farish. As he makes clear, they fail as perspectives because Wharton has little faith in them. James's
Winterbourne is a good comparison with Selden, but is it not the case

that James maintains a more critical hold on Winterbourne than Wharton has on Selden? James knows Winterbourne's case thoroughly, whereas it is not clear that Wharton knows anything more than Selden about what a 'republic of the spirit' might be.

Irving Howe's balanced, intelligent appraisal[7] owes something to Lubbock:

■ We see Lily and Selden together, each a little uneasy with the other, yet decidedly attractive as a pair and civilized enough to take pleasure in knowing they are attractive – Mrs. Wharton had a fine eye for the pictorial arrangements in the social intercourse between the sexes. They amuse and test each other with small talk – Mrs. Wharton had a fine ear for the conversation that carries subtle burdens of meaning. We see Lily and Selden taking each other's measure, Lily admiring his quiet style yet aware of his handicaps and hesitations, Selden admiring her beauty yet aware that "she was so evidently the victim of the civilization which had produced her, that the links of her bracelet seemed like manacles chaining her to her fate." This striking sentence is put to several uses: it prepares us for the ordeal of a Lily Bart neither at ease with nor in rebellion against her life as a dependent of the rich; it provides a convincing example of Selden's gift for superior observation; and because, ironically, this gift is matched with his tendency to self-protection and self-justification, it suggests that Mrs. Wharton will not require nor allow Selden to serve as a voice of final judgment in the novel. Given the caustic style of these opening pages, we are entitled to suppose that Mrs. Wharton will reserve that task for herself.

There quickly follows the encounter between Lily and Rosedale. At this point Rosedale is mostly stock caricature, the "pushy little Jew" taken from the imagery of social, that is, polite, anti-Semitism; later Mrs. Wharton will do more with him. Rosedale trips Lily in a lie and is not gentleman enough to refrain from stressing his petty triumph, but the main point is that Lily, usually so nimble at handling social difficulties, has been caught off balance because she is still glowing with the pleasure of having met Selden. This too prefigures a major theme: the price, here in embarrassment and later in deprivation, that genuine emotion exacts from those who have chosen a life of steady calculation. Coming always at inconvenient moments – for it is Selden's presence which repeatedly causes her to falter – the spontaneous feelings Lily neither can nor wishes to suppress will lead to her social undoing.

Lovely as Lily Bart seems, Mrs. Wharton is careful to establish a firm dissociation between author and heroine, though never to the point of withdrawing her compassion. The similarity between Rosedale and Lily, each trying in a particular way to secure a foothold in the world of the rich, is faintly suggested by Mrs. Wharton as a cue for later elaboration. □

Here the 'price' that 'genuine emotion exacts from those who have chosen a life of steady calculation' is an especially noteworthy comment. We may question, however, Howe's claim that there is a dissociation between Wharton and both Selden and Lily. While it is true that Wharton offers ironic commentary on them, the novel as a whole endorses the direction their lives take, and in this overall sense there is no dissociation. As Howe acknowledges later:

■ In no way is the old aristocracy, or even the idea of the old aristocracy, held up as a significant model for behavior. Indeed, in *The House of Mirth* the moral positives seem almost disembodied, hovering like ghosts over the figures of Lily Bart and Lawrence Selden. When the new rich make their assault upon the world of the established rich, there occurs a brief contest between an aspiring and an entrenched snobbism, and soon enough, as one might expect, a truce is struck. The victim of that truce is Lily Bart. □

Dissociation would surely require the 'moral positives' to be embodied.
But there is no better appraisal of Lily than Howe's:

■ The social setting of *The House of Mirth* is elaborated with complete assurance: one is always persuaded of the tangibility of Mrs. Wharton's milieu, the precision with which she observes nuances of status and place. But what finally draws and involves us is the personal drama enacted within this setting. Lily Bart is a victim of taste, both good and bad: she has a natural taste for moral and aesthetic refinements which causes her to be repelled by the world of the rich, and she has an acquired taste for luxury – that can be satisfied only in that world. She is too fine in her perceptions to act ruthlessly enough to achieve her worldly aims, and too much the captive of those aims to be able to live by her perceptions. She has enough moral awareness to respect civilized structures of behavior, but not enough moral courage to abandon the environment in which they are violated. She is trapped in a heart struggle between the pleasures of this world, that is, to lure the dismal millionaire Gryce into marriage, and the refinements of personal relations, which means to drop Gryce for the privilege of walking with Lawrence Selden on a Sunday afternoon. . . .

Through a steady accumulation of incidents Mrs. Wharton makes it clear that Lily is pitifully lacking in any core of personal being. At home neither in the Trenor mansion nor Selden's book-lined rooms nor the shabby apartment of her cousin Gerty Farish, Lily is at the mercy of her restlessness, a strangely disabling kind of restlessness which marks an unfinished self. Yet all of these judgments are stated or implied by Mrs. Wharton with a profound compassion, a sense of the sadness that comes to one in observing a lovely human being dash herself against the rocks of her own bewilderment. If Lily cannot maintain those flashes of self-awareness that come to her in moments of failure, she is still a generous and warm-hearted woman, open, in Mrs. Wharton's magnificent phrase, to "one of those sudden shocks of pity that sometimes decentralize a life." □

'Trapped in a heart struggle', 'pitifully lacking in any core of personal being', 'a strangely disabling kind of restlessness' – all these phrases rise to the occasion of Lily in ways few other critics manage. They make claims for the novel that are all the more persuasive for being balanced against Howe's sense of its limitations. Having acknowledged the 'high polish, austere irony, epigrammatic conciseness' of Wharton's commentary in the novel, he concludes:

■ But even as one comes to savor the crispness of Mrs. Wharton's prose, there are passages in *The House of Mirth* that leave one uneasy. Usually these are passages in which she reveals the unfortunate tendency toward ladies' magazine rhetoric that broke out in her later years. And usually they are passages in which she must confront a theme – the satisfactions of romantic love – she finds either too embarrassing or too upsetting to handle with ease. Writing about an encounter between Selden and Lily, she composes a sentence that, at least in its second clause, seems decidedly forced: "It was one of those moments when neither seemed to speak deliberately, when an indwelling voice in each called to the other across unsounded depths of feeling." Here is Mrs. Wharton's description of the last talk between Selden and Lily, utterly right in its first sentence and a purple lapse in the second:

Something in truth lay dead between them – the love she had killed in him and could no longer call to life. But something lived between them also, and leaped up in her like an imperishable flame: it was the love his love had kindled, the passion of her soul for his.

To notice this stylistic problem is to approach a central limitation of Mrs. Wharton's writing. . . . Her work overwhelms us with its harsh truths, but finally it seems incomplete and earth-bound. Mrs. Wharton believed firmly in the moral positives she had inherited, but she could seldom project them into her work; all too often they survive only in terms of their violation. Hence the grinding, unrelenting, impatient tone of her work as if she sensed some deficiency, perhaps in the very scheme of things or only in her own vision, and did not know how to fill the need. Mrs. Wharton was a thoroughly conservative writer but there are times one is inclined to say, a bit paradoxically, that she is too hard on the rich, too glacial in her contempt for their mediocrity, too willing to slash away at them because she does not know anyone else to turn toward or against. □

Like Howe, Geoffrey Walton[8] offers one of the best accounts in praise of *The House of Mirth*, whether that means seeing it, for example, in terms of Nevius's naturalism or the aestheticism of later interpreters. Accepting the novel on its own terms, he writes:

■ . . . the first big scene opens at Bellomont, the country house of the Trenor family, with its park, its church near the gates, and all its domestic detail indistinguishable from contemporary England, but made slightly absurd, as with the Sunday church-going. The central Society group is created and exposed with devastating brilliance from Mrs. Trenor, the hostess, whose

> rosy blondness had survived some forty years of futile activity without showing much trace of ill-usage except in a diminished play of feature. It was difficult to define her beyond saying that she seemed to exist only as a hostess, not so much from any exaggerated instinct of hospitality as because she could not sustain life except in a crowd. . . .

to Mrs. Fisher, the divorcée, "her eyes and gowns as emphatic as her 'case,'" Lady Cressida Raith with her "ethnographical trinkets," and Miss Van Osburgh, "a large girl with flat surfaces and no high lights." Again Edith Wharton shows her genius for significant external details;

one is just sufficiently conscious of the idea of the "scarlet woman"
when Mrs. Trenor advises Lily not to wear red at dinner. □

Perhaps we should accept Walton and have done with it, not even wondering, for example, what Wharton might mean by 'Bellomont'. To
make a connection with the 'Belmont' of Shakespeare's *The Merchant of
Venice* which, like *The House of Mirth*, also has a challenging Jew, is only to
be led nowhere, so it may be that 'Bellomont' is no more than an authorial
flight of fancy. As an indication of the cultural superficiality and preten-
tiousness of the builders or owners of the house, it seems too easily
satirical, though Walton presumably would think not, since he praises
the author's 'devastating brilliance'. This praise is for the comment on
Mrs Trenor, but does not devastatingly brilliant satire make its targets
more interesting than Mrs Trenor is made here? Such satire is not so
detached and superior. It tends to recognise a complicity in what it satirises.
    According to Walton, Lily Bart:

■ . . . has certain ideals of a civilized and cultivated life, though they
have been corrupted by a corrupt Society into something parasitic and
materialistic. Her tragedy results from her pursuit of these falsified
ideals in the face of an increasingly hostile Society. It is a further irony
that Society, as we see it, has no right to be hostile or censorious, and a
further irony still that Lily Bart's good qualities are quite as fatal to her
as those of which we may disapprove. The poignancy of her tragedy
lies there. She is too good for Society, as Selden later feels, and consequently, though she cannot escape, she cannot play its game to the
logical conclusion. Selden, who understands and foresees so much, is
a type of young man who appears several times in Edith Wharton. He
represents old New York, which does not otherwise contribute very
much to the wealthier and newer social pattern of the novel, except
insofar as the established families pay lip-service to its social forms.
He is cultivated and full of good intentions, but, because of a certain
excessive fastidiousness, he is sometimes ineffectual to the point of
unkindness. One gathers that there were many such men in old New
York Society, where the possession of adequate means or an assured
professional position, as in Selden's case, combined with a retiring
gentlemanly ideal, made any sort of enterprise – economic, intellectual
or moral – seem unnecessary and even rather improper. Edith Wharton
shows both the merits and weaknesses of the type; the heavy-handed
condemnation of Selden by Edmund Wilson, for example, misses the
point. Lily Bart makes a mistake of another kind when she snubs the

young Jewish financier. This is an indiscretion of her fastidious good taste rather than recklessness, but the two reinforce each other and Lily is fated to be involved with Rosedale for the rest of the book. If Selden with his advice is a kind of ineffectual good angel, her association with Rosedale brings her eventually to her lowest point of degradation. At the same time there is an implied comparison between her career and his; she has a long start of him, but he succeeds where she ultimately fails – because she has scruples where he has none. Rosedale is a specially brilliant character study. □

This account undoubtedly captures Wharton's intention, and its response to Lily and 'the poignancy of her tragedy' recalls the very first review in this Guide. 'She is too good for Society' – in other words, she is not the kind of tragic figure whose hands are stained. She is not a perpetrator and, challenging Walton, we may conclude she is less tragic than characters (for example, Eliot's Gwendolen Harleth) who are. As for Selden and Rosedale, we may agree with Walton's response, but question their function in the novel as a whole. Why is it that Wharton exposes the falsity and frivolousness of her New York world, and yet remains invidious towards the characters who are outsiders? It is as if Wharton, while recognising that old New York is obsolescent, has to feel herself superior to the new. Rosedale is a case in point, and Walton sides with her in reference to it. Why should Lily's 'lowest point of degradation' be her association with a Jew, someone very much from the outside? What signal, accepted by Walton, is Wharton giving her readers?

Walton returns to Rosedale following his comment on Lily's association with the Sam Gormers:

■ In the desperate circumstances a rapprochement between Lily and Rosedale is just plausible. He has reached almost the desiderated heights by his own efforts and she now wonders wistfully whether she could persuade him to marry her for love "now that he [has] no other reason." We are about to witness another of those extraordinary displays of highmindedness and foolhardiness in rapid succession which have characterized her before, and the next two sections of the novel are built up on a complex pattern of irony. Lily refuses a chance of revenge on her enemy, Mrs. Dorset, and then almost at once does something fatally reckless in the worldly sense and shockingly cheap morally; she offers herself to Rosedale. Far from accepting for love, he laughs at the offer, but later says he will have her on condition that she completes his social ascent by straightforward blackmail of the same lady. Lily again refuses the opportunity of revenge, although it would also have brought financial salvation. From one point of view, one might call it as fatally stupid a mistake as her offer of marriage at the beginning of the scene; from another, one sees that it is one of the occasions when Lily Bart emerges from her social setting as a tragic heroine.

The final tragic movement, direct or ironical, has now been established firmly, and Lily is shown, little over a year since the glamorous beginning of the book, living in an inferior hotel in New York, completely alone except for the intense and rather uncomprehending Gerty Farish and pursued by "horrors" in her nights of insomnia. She touches her lowest level socially by taking a job as "secretary" to Mrs. Norma Hatch, resident at the Emporium Hotel. Mrs. Hatch's name is the last in the sequence, and everything is thematically appropriate: she lives in a strange under-world of luxury that has no conventions and no routine, not even mealtimes. Edith Wharton was to use this indication of social anarchy even more tellingly twenty and again thirty years later. More so than the Gormer milieu, it is an almost phantasmagoric parody of Society life. Lily's unsuccessful attempts to work in a fashionable milliner's, her lack of the skill complementary to her chief interest in life, is a touching and also profound piece of symbolism. By early spring she is walking the streets to kill time. The symbolism is again both obvious and tragically painful; Lily Bart, who was once warned not to look like a "scarlet woman" at dinner might now look to the ignorant like an ordinary prostitute; it is both pathos and poetic justice. The last scenes show the finer side of Lily uppermost, and we see her looking back over her career with a clarity of vision that indicates again her intelligence, as well as expressing her agony of mind:

> She had learned by experience that she had neither the aptitude nor the moral constancy to remake her life on new lines; to become a worker among workers, and let the world of luxury and pleasure sweep by her unregarded. She could not hold herself much to blame for this ineffectiveness, and she was perhaps less to blame than she believed. Inherited tendencies had combined with early training to make her the highly specialized product she was: an organism as helpless out of its narrow range as the sea-anemone torn from the rock. She had been fashioned to adorn and delight; to what other end does nature round the rose-leaf and paint the humming-bird's breast? And was it her fault that the purely decorative

mission is less easily and harmoniously fulfilled among social beings than in the world of nature? That it is apt to be hampered by material necessities or complicated by moral scruples?

In both content and phrasing the blending of Lily Bart's reflections and the author's interpretation of the situation is at this point especially harmonious; it would be crass to boggle at the rhetorical questions. We know that by now Lily can see nearly everything that her creator sees and it is this steadily deepening self-awareness and social perceptiveness which, along with her fundamental moral integrity and dignity, give her ultimately her tragic stature. They have been growing throughout the book, in step with the deterioration of her circumstances. This is the tragic pattern and the words in fact take us back forcibly to Selden's reflections at their opening meeting in New York eighteen months before. The "moral scruples" that have all along interfered with her single-minded pursuit of material comforts are that "fineness" which Selden then saw. □

Again this could hardly be bettered as an account of the novel on its own terms. Is it, however, only 'crass to boggle', for example at the passage Walton quotes from the novel? In her review of Leslie Stephen's *George Eliot*[9] Wharton defended Eliot from 'the principal charge against her', that she was 'too scientific' by aligning her work with 'that vast speculative movement which was just then opening countless new avenues into the mind of man and the phenomena of the universe'. From the scientific analogies in the passage Walton quotes one can see why Wharton would have an investment in this defence. Yet only superficially might the passage be likened to Eliot. Rather than offering analogies for consideration, in the Eliot manner, it offers them as complete explanation, as if Lily were no more than 'an organism as helpless out of its narrow range as the sea-anemone torn from the rock'. Authorial voice, moreover, coincides with the character's, so that all possibility of critical distance is lost, and Wharton excuses Lily more than Lily excuses herself. Experience, which Walton so often describes as tragic, is to be judged as free of troublesome culpability. Lily, it seems, is superior by definition, even though her superiority, having no positive desires, is expressed negatively in what she rejects. Similarly, the superiority we are asked to have over Mrs Norma Hatch is also a superiority by negation on Wharton's part. What Walton calls 'this indication of social anarchy' is only to be so judged with reference to old New York, about which Wharton says little that is positive.

Informative as he is, R.W.B. Lewis[10] hardly takes matters further:

■ The nature and status of women in that society are suggested by the other two titles Edith Wharton originally contemplated. The first was "A Moment's Ornament": women were regarded as ornamental, beautiful objects to be collected and displayed; they were expected to strike elegant attitudes and poses; and their career was a fleeting one. But women were also required to appear flower-like, gentle, fragile, innocent, lovely; the second title was "The Year of the Rose." Lily Bart was an exceptional flower, but only to a degree. At the end, refusing a gambit which would have restored her social and financial fortunes, she takes an overdose of a sleeping potion and dies.

"Lily" was the name given Edith Jones by the Rutherford children in the Newport days, and Lily Bart undoubtedly incorporates some of Edith Wharton's features. She is endearing, proud, sensitive, and exasperating by turns. Through Lily Bart, moreover, Edith Wharton conveyed her sense of herself as essentially unfitted for the only American society she knew, and as gravely misunderstood by that society. By the same token, if she pointed to no means of escape for Lily, it was because she was aware of none – or any viable alternative life to the one she depicted.

Lawrence Selden, the attractive and seemingly astute lawyer who is drawn to Lily in the opening phases of the narrative, is the one human being who might have supplied such an alternative. He has a vision, about which he is given to holding forth, of what he calls "the republic of the spirit," where the keynote is freedom and where only two or three are encouraged to gather together. But although this betimes was also one of Edith Wharton's ideal images, Selden himself, as she told Sara Norton, was "a negative hero," a sterile and subtly fraudulent figure whose ideas were not much to be trusted.

Selden was also an emblem of masculinity in Edith's world. Fond as she was of her Walter Berrys, her Egerton Winthrops, her Eliot Gregorys – and Selden has a little of each – she knew they had insufficient blood in their veins and could provide little of what an intelligent and ardent woman might crave.

There were, of course, enormous differences in the outward and material circumstances of Edith Wharton and Lily Bart; a reviewer might well be skeptical about the mistress of The Mount coming truly to grips with the downward spiral of Lily's life. Yet behind the trappings of Lenox and Park Avenue was a soul that was familiar with pain, with the feeling of entrapment, with psychological and physical deprivation. The crucial difference between the author and her heroine was Edith Wharton's unshakable belief in the possibilities of life. □

Where, in *The House of Mirth*, are we aware of this 'unshakeable belief'?

Cynthia Griffin Wolff,[11] the first of the feminist readings we are to encounter, develops Lewis's charges against Selden. Selden exemplifies a world that destroys women by turning them into aesthetic objects. As the novel opens:

■ The narrator begins in Selden's mind, presents Lily only as *he* sees her, and shows him to have the lingering, appraising, inventorial mind of the experienced collector: he is fascinated with her surface appearance, misses no detail of her exquisite finish. He remarks the chiaroscuro effect of "[h]er vivid head, relieved against the dull tints of the crowd," takes in the details of her clothing and "the purity of tint, that she was beginning to lose after eleven years of late hours and indefatigable dancing". As they walk up Madison Avenue, the inspection continues, with Selden "taking a luxurious pleasure in her nearness: in the modelling of her little ear, the crisp upward wave of her hair . . . and the thick planting of her straight black lashes".

Selden's reactions to this surfeit of decorative art reveal, even here, his inbred moral-aesthetic ambiguities. There is first the self-indulgence of his appreciation of her, then the startled, guilty awareness of the monetary implications of even such indulgence as this, then disapproval – but not of his own indulgence, rather disapproval projected onto Lily – and finally the longing to see such beauty allied in some indefinable way with the lofty virtue that his nature craves:

> Everything about her was at once vigorous and exquisite, at once strong and fine. He had a confused sense that she must have cost a great deal to make, that a great many dull and ugly people must, in some mysterious way, have been sacrificed to produce her. He was aware that the qualities distinguishing her from the herd of her sex were chiefly external: as though a fine glaze of beauty and fastidiousness had been applied to vulgar clay. Yet the analogy left him unsatisfied, for a coarse texture will not take a high finish; and was it not possible that the material was fine, but that circumstance had fashioned it into a futile shape?

Selden's musings might almost pass for social criticism were it not for the fact that the "futile shape" he seems to deplore is a shape he obviously and extensively admires and that his admiration is part of the continuing "circumstance" that fashions it. There is satire, of course; but it inheres in the narrator's use of irony – an irony which places Selden as part of the *uninformed* audience.

His assessment of Lily is gradually revealed to deal almost entirely with externals: he is willing at every point to accept the appearance for reality. Thus, while people have indeed "been sacrificed" to "produce" Lily, the reader learns (though Selden never fully does) that the principal sacrifice has been Lily herself. ☐

Wolff gets Selden exactly, but, as we have already seen, the separation between his and Wharton's view of Lily may not be as clear as she claims it to be. Selden's last question in the passage quoted by Wolff may also be Wharton's, since the novel's significance depends on there being fine material beneath Lily's futile shape. If Wharton is as uncertain as Selden about this fineness, it is not easy to see the function of any satire or irony directed at him. Apart from the determination of 'circumstances', what other explanation for Lily's fate is Wharton herself to offer?

Wolff's own difficulty in identifying Lily's fine material is revealed in the following passage:

■ Lily never does learn her mother's capacity for management, and in the transactional portions of her life she suffers a failure of will, a revulsion, perhaps, from the final human compromise. The everyday habit of self-adornment indicates that Lily has internalized the New Art's notion of woman; but the merely decorative is in the end not entirely sufficient for her. Even when she was very young, "there was in Lily a vein of sentiment . . . which gave an idealizing touch to her most prosaic purposes. She liked to think of her beauty as a power for good, as giving her the opportunity to attain a position where she should make her influence felt in the vague diffusion of refinement and good taste". But this pining after moral significance brings with it no capacity to make choices, draw difficult distinctions, or bear hardship; it is, like much else in her nature, diffuse and indolent and undeveloped . . . She is genuinely puzzled by the difficulties (when they come to her attention, as they rarely do) of the moral life conscientiously lived . . . "She could not breathe long on the heights; there had been nothing in her training to develop any continuity of moral strength: what she craved, and really felt herself entitled to, was a situation in which the noblest attitude should also be the easiest".

She would be like the Wood Nymph of the Art Nouveau, her

evocative purity casually, "naturally . . ." placed in a bower of flowers – or like the unwaveringly chaste women of the neoclassical school, poised to preside majestically over significant public events . . . In other words, virtue and nobility should be effortless companions to her artistically rendered self . . .

Most often, Lily handles her moral queasiness by choosing not to know the full implications of her plight . . . She permits the pleasing aesthetic *appearance* that she can give to a situation to substitute for its reality . . . "She was always scrupulous about keeping up appearances to herself . . . Her personal fastidiousness had a moral equivalent, and when she made a tour of inspection in her own mind there were certain closed doors she did not open". When an acceptable interpretation cannot be found, Lily characteristically removes herself to a different, more spiritually consoling atmosphere . . . After all, "moral complications existed for her only in the environment that had produced them; she did not mean to slight or ignore them, but they lost their reality when they changed their background". This need to avoid serious moral reflection is, of course, a principal cause of her social downfall . . . She must accept Gus Trenor's stock market "tip" as a fraternal gesture; she is not prepared to sort out the moral and financial problems that would be revealed by a frank appraisal . . . She must perceive Bertha Dorset's invitation to join in her vacation as springing first from mere friendship and then from deep wells of human need; the option of recognizing Bertha's malicious and immoral use of her raises problems that she has not the stamina to resolve . . . She must linger lazily in her secretary/companion role to Mrs. Hatch until all the world believes in her actual duplicity and moral compromise; she has not the discipline to refuse (nor, ironically, the sustained habit of calculation to partake in that lady's social rise) . . . In the end when Lily tries to review her relationship to Bertha and Selden dispassionately, she cannot overcome the deficiencies of a life devoted to evasion: "What debt did she owe to a social order which had condemned and banished her without trial? She had never been heard in her own defense; she was innocent of the charge on which she had been found guilty: and the irregularity of her conviction might seem to justify the use of methods as irregular in recovering her lost rights". But she cannot think her way through these complexities (the possibility of going directly to Selden does not occur as an option, for reasons that we shall discuss later); she has not been bred to offer anything more than the appearance of moral righteousness . . . "Was it her fault that the purely decorative mission is less easily and harmoniously fulfilled among social beings than in the world of nature? That it is apt to be hampered by materialistic necessities or complicated by moral scruples?".

When Lily's habits of moral evasion fail her as she meets one reversal after another, she does not put her aesthetic-moral talents to a real examination of the problem: instead she reverts to a more energetic summoning of the Grand Manner, an infusion of her being with the appearance of spiritual command which in no way corresponds to the fact of increasing inner desolation . . . □

'Diffuse and indolent and undeveloped', 'a life devoted to evasion'; Wolff gets Lily as well as she gets Selden, and her own words for Lily might have caused her to expect that Lily herself would be the subject of satire. Indeed she very nearly is in 'the vague diffusion of refinement and good taste'. What restrains Wharton is the need to maintain Lily's implied value, even though this value may remain elusive. All Wolff can finally resort to on Lily's behalf in the above passage is the prescriptive determinism with which the novel itself is replete ('she has not been bred . . .'). This determinism is complemented by a question about nature and society which leads nowhere. In response to it, we might ask how much nature there is in Lily. Her 'decorative mission', with all its connotations of artifice, suggests the quantity is very little.

The methodology of Elizabeth Ammons[12] is very similar to Wolff's. Both seek to demonstrate the value of *The House of Mirth* by supplying a context. For Wolff the novel 'is built upon a series of explicit allusions to the art of the day [which] would have been immediately clear to a reader in 1905'. Failing to acknowledge that contemporary reviews of *The House of Mirth* do not mention this art, she insists it victimised women by shaping them as aesthetic objects. In Ammons's case it is Charlotte Perkins Gilman's *Women and Economics: A Study of the Economic Relation between Men and Women as a Factor in Social Evolution* (1898) and Thorstein Veblen's *The Theory of the Leisure Class: An Economic Study of Institutions* (1899) that supply the context. For both Wolff and Ammons it seems that the act of supplying a context necessarily validates the novel. Whether the context is itself more or less complex than the novel is not questioned. Lily, as Ammons sees it, 'beautifully illustrates Veblen's observation that "the servant or wife should not only perform certain offices and show a servile disposition, but it is quite as imperative that they show an acquired facility in the tactics of subservience"'.[13] Ammons continues:

■ But only on the surface. In fact Lily has merely learned to suppress and camouflage her own impulses and ambitions. Even though she acquits herself of the social arts in which she has been so carefully bred, she transgresses other moral and social regulations with which society expects compliance. She visits Selden alone in his apartment; she gets deeply into debt; she borrows money from a married man, Gus Trenor, and is seen leaving his town house late at night; she spends time alone with another married man, Dorset, and becomes the object of rumors; she takes a job as a private secretary to the flashy, nouveau-riche Mrs. Hatch. Her behavior is nonconformist, as are her real ambitions. She has "fits of angry rebellion against fate, when she longed to drop out of the race and make an independent life for herself".

The seal on her stationery, with its flying ship and the motto "*Beyond!*," images her true aspiration: she wants to escape – she wants to govern her own course in life. Her problem is that she is equipped for no life except the one she leads.

The job she has been trained for is highly specialized and her skills, if she does not choose to use them as some rich man's wife, are not transferable (or at least not in any way compatible with her pride: she has the opportunity to make money as a human mannequin modeling hats in a millinery shop, but refuses the job; it is simply a vulgar variant on what she is trying to escape). All her training and hard work wasted, Lily realizes late in the novel that she is "no more than some superfine human merchandise," and admits: "I can hardly be said to have an independent existence. I was just a screw or a cog in the great machine I called life, and when I dropped out of it I found I was of no use anywhere else". Lily is absolutely correct. She has utility only so long as she remains in good standing within the class that produced her.

Her utility within that class is clearly spelled out by Wharton. Men go out into the commercial world to accumulate goods and money, but unless the rich man also accumulates a woman, all his money and property and power do not extend beyond the narrow mercantile world into the social realm, into the society at large. Therefore for a rich man, ownership of a woman is not a luxury, but a necessity. She is his means of disseminating Wall Street power beyond the limited masculine world of Wall Street. Hence the economics of being a woman in Lily's world amount to working as a wife, and working hard, to translate financial power into social power by displaying a particular man's wealth for him. Put simply, the man makes money on Wall Street which he then brings to Fifth Avenue for a woman to turn into social power to aggrandize him (and by association herself). □

This is a seductive account of Lily as a victim, and we may feel sorry for victims as such. In literature at least, however, their significance depends on the value of what has been sacrificed. Again we return to the question of the value embodied in Lily. What are her 'impulses and ambitions' which, according to Ammons, distinguish her? The actions listed in the first paragraph above demonstrate further victimisation rather than independence. Not even by implication, it seems, has Wharton given any meaning to '*Beyond*'. As Lily herself recognises, she could have been nothing other than 'a screw or a cog in the great machine I called life'.

Nevius is right; Lily is not characterised by Wharton so as to embody a significant conflict in herself. Her interest, therefore, has to derive from her representativeness within an irresistible social order. According to Ammons, this order is governed by men. *The House of Mirth* exemplifies her reading of Gilman and Veblen, and implicitly she invites us to believe the novel to be as an all-embracing account of the way life was in turn-of-the-century New York. Suppose, however, we doubt Lily's representativeness, arguing that not all women (Wharton herself and Bertha Dorset, for example) were as incapacitated as she? Such an argument would undoubtedly weaken Ammons' case, and it might cause us also to wonder what it is that Wharton is saying about Lily and women of her kind. What is she also saying about the men? Ammons' phrase, 'ownership of women', hardly applies to Gus Trenor's, George Dorset's and Lily's father's relationship with their respective wives. All of these men seem as victimised as the women.

Ammons, however, insists that behind Lily's refusal to marry Gryce, Dorset and Rosedale lies:

■ . . . a repugnance toward a relationship in which a woman is powerless. The same reason explains Lily's nervous rejection of Selden. She gives as her reason his relative poverty: life with him would be an extension of the parasitical existence she hopes to escape. He could not afford to provide the things she requires, so it would be foolish to marry him. More significant, however, are Selden's Pygmalion impulses – his desire, like George Darrow and Ralph Marvell after him, characters in *The Reef* and *The Custom of the Country*, to rescue (which means change) the woman he loves. Selden finds his beloved too beautiful for the coarse world; he wants to save her, he wants to "lift Lily to a freer vision of life". As in the Pygmalion story, the key scene is one in which the female appears as a human statue. In Wharton's version, Selden gazes on Lily's frozen beauty as Reynolds's

Mrs. Lloyd in a tableau vivant and, yielding to the "vision-making influences as completely as a child to the spell of a fairy-tale" . . . decides to renew his proposal of marriage. Wharton's choice of the painting by Reynolds comments on Selden's romantic impulse, for Mrs. Lloyd, wearing a diaphanous gown, is a graceful yet voluptuous woman captured in the act of inscribing the surname Lloyd on a tree. Obviously this portrait/tableau appeals to Selden's aesthetic sense and at the same time to his sensuality, but also and perhaps more importantly to his vanity – the real motive of Pygmalion, a storybook hero who also fell in love with a statue he envisioned bringing to a higher order of existence. No doubt Selden, the product of his upbringing and environment just as Lily is, would like to remodel his beloved in the image of his mother. □

In response to Ammons' claim for women's powerlessness it is worth pointing out how confident Lily is with Gryce as she prepares for their encounter at the beginning of the book. Had she really wanted this man, she could have had him and ruled him: '. . . one spring that she had only to touch to set his simple machinery in motion'. Selden, it is true, is more complicated, but the complication derives mainly, as has already been suggested, from Wharton's own uncertainty about him. Contrary to Ammons' argument, Selden's desire to 'lift Lily to a freer vision of life' is the best alternative, vague as it is, that Wharton herself can conceive for her heroine. Similarly, Lily's appearance as Reynolds' 'Mrs. Lloyd' appeals as much to Wharton's 'aesthetic sense' as to Selden's. Why otherwise do hers and Selden's points of view merge during this episode? So implicated indeed is she in both Lily and Selden, she can hardly manage a critical stance on either of them. Her excuse for both is deterministic and fatalistic: they are victims of their culture. Ammons' predisposition, by contrast, is to apply the determinism only to the women.

Wai-Chee Dimock[14] is responding to Ammons and others when she argues that:

■ Power in *The House of Mirth*, many critics have suggested, is patri-archical. They are right, no doubt, about the basis for power, insofar as power is economic and insofar as money making is a male prerogative, but the actual wielders of power in the book are often not men but women. On the whole, Wharton is interested less in the etiology of power than in the way power comports itself, in the mode and manner of its workings. She is most interested, that is to say, in the mediated and socialized forms of power, power that women do enjoy and that they use skilfully and sometimes brutally. □

This argument is a development of the thesis suggested by her title. Her essay begins with a quotation from Gus Trenor's confrontation with Lily in Book 1, Chapter 13:

■ ". . . you got reckless – thought you could turn me inside out, and chuck me in the gutter like an empty purse. But, by gad, that ain't playing fair: that's dodging the rules of the game. Of course I know now what you wanted – it wasn't my beautiful eyes you were after – but I tell you what, Miss Lily, you've got to pay up for making me think so –"

"Pay up?" she faltered. "Do you mean that I owe you money?"

He laughed again. "Oh, I'm not asking for payment in kind. But there's such a thing as fair play – and interest on one's money – and hang me if I've had as much as a look from you . . ."

The most brutal moment in *The House of Mirth* dramatizes not so much the centrality of sex as the centrality of exchange. Sexual favors are what Gus Trenor wants, but his demands are steeped in – and legitimated by – the language of the marketplace, the language of traded benefits and reciprocal obligations. Odious as it may seem, Trenor's speech merely asserts what everyone assumes. "Investments" and "returns," "interests" and "payments": these words animate and possess Wharton's characters, even in their world of conspicuous leisure. The power of the marketplace, then, resides not in its presence, which is only marginal in *The House of Mirth*, but in its ability to reproduce itself, in its ability to assimilate everything else into its domain. As a controlling logic, a mode of human conduct and human association, the marketplace is everywhere and nowhere, ubiquitous and invisible. Under its shadow even the most private affairs take on the essence of business transactions, for the realm of human relations is fully contained within an all-encompassing business ethic. Some characters – Trenor and Rosedale, for instance – obviously speak the voice of the marketplace, but even those who hold themselves aloof (as Lawrence Selden does) turn out to be more susceptible than they think.

Of all the characters, Lily Bart has the most puzzling and contradictory relation to the marketplace. A self-acknowledged "human merchandise," she is busy marketing herself throughout most of the book, worried only about the price she would fetch. She tries to induce Percy Gryce to purchase her, and if she had succeeded she would have been "to him what his Americana had hitherto been, the one possession in which he took sufficient pride to spend money on it." Much later, as she forces herself to accept Rosedale's attentions, she consoles herself by calculating "the price he would have to pay." Lily is clearly caught up in the ethos of exchange. And yet her repeated and sometimes intentional failure to find a buyer, her ultimate refusal to realize her "asset" – as her mother designates her beauty – makes her something of a rebel. She is not much of a rebel, of course, and that is precisely the point. For Lily's "rebellion," in its very feebleness and limitation, attests to the frightening power of the marketplace. It attests as well to Wharton's own politics, to her bleakness of vision in the face of a totalizing system she finds at once detestable and inevitable.

The persistent talk of "cost" and "payment" in *The House of Mirth* raises the question of *currency*. How does one compute the "cost" of an action, what constitutes a "debt," and in what form must "payments" be made? Money, the standard medium of exchange, is not the only currency in circulation. Trenor clearly does not wish to be paid back with a check. In fact, "payment in kind" is never expected in transactions in the social marketplace, and this unspoken rule makes for a plethora of business opportunities. A "society" dinner, for instance, is worth its weight in gold. Since the likes of Rosedale habitually "giv[e] away a half-a-million tip for a dinner," Jack Stepney regularly "pay[s] his debts in dinner invitations." Others – even those who protest – eventually follow Stepney's example, for the simple reason that Rosedale is "placing Wall Street under obligations which only Fifth Avenue could repay." There are other expenses, other debts, and other means of payment as well. Lily's visit to Selden's bachelor apartment is a "luxury" that is "going to cost her rather more than she could afford." Still she might have "purchased [Rosedale's] silence" if she had only allowed him to take her to the train station, since "to be seen walking down the platform at the crowded afternoon hour in the company of Miss Lily Bart would have been money in his pocket." Business, in the social world, operates by what we might call the commodification of social intercourse. Everything has a price, must be paid for, just as – on the opposite end – everything can be made to "count as" money, to be dealt out and accepted in lieu of cash. Dispensed in this manner, social gestures lose their initial character and figure only as exchange values: the dinner invitations, for Stepney and Rosedale, presumably have no meaning except as surrogate cash payments. A social world predicated on business ethics is an essentially reductive world, and the power of money lies not so much in its pristine form as in its claim as a model, in its ability to define other things in its own image. The fluidity of currencies in *The House of Mirth*, the apparently endless business possibilities, attests to the reduction of human experiences to abstract equivalents for exchange. □

This quotation exemplifies Dimock's very persuasive thesis. What is not clear is how generally applicable she is claiming the thesis to be. Does she believe it to be true of capitalist societies as such, or is it only true of the society recorded in *The House of Mirth* during a peculiar phase of its development? In relation to Dimock's reading, the significance of the novel would turn on the answer to this question. It presses its attention when Dimock writes:

■ Lily's paradoxical conformity and deviance come across most clearly in her dealings with Trenor. Having taken almost nine thousand dollars from him and finding her obligation "not the sort . . . one could remain under," she proceeds to settle her debt as soon as she receives her aunt's legacy – a decision that "cleans [her] out altogether," as Rosedale rather indelicately puts it. In repaying Trenor, Lily is indeed complying with the rules of exchange, but she is also challenging the very basis of exchange. Trenor never expects to be paid back in quite this way. "Payment in kind," the most primitive form of barter economy, has no place in a highly developed social marketplace, which trades on the putative equivalence between disparate entities. By paying back the exact monetary amount, by equating nine thousand dollars with nine thousand dollars, Lily at once obeys the principle of exchange and reduces it to tautology. Her nine-thousand-dollar debt is now just that; a nine-thousand-dollar debt, not some ill-defined and possibly limitless obligation. In other words, by making money its own equivalent, Lily reduces it to its own terms and defies its purchasing power. She has understood what it means to live under the "intolerable obligation" of an all-consuming system of exchange, and she now tries to exorcise its influence by facing up to what she owes – in all the crudeness and brutality of its cash amount – just to rescue from its dominion the other strands of her life. What appears as a gesture of submission turns out to be a gesture of defiance, for by adhering literally to the terms of exchange Lily turns the system on its head. And yet, as every reader must recognize, defiance of this sort is ultimately unavailing. The exchange system can easily accommodate rebellion like Lily's: Trenor, no doubt, will take the money and even circulate it anew. Lily's action hurts no one but herself. It remains a challenge to the exchange system in spirit but not in fact. □

It is not generally true that 'payment in kind' 'has no place in a highly developed social marketplace'. Lenders, as most of us know to our cost, are only too happy to accept money at the interest charged. This qualification aside, however, Dimock is critically alive, especially to the ending of the novel. As she sees it:

■ [Wharton's] difficulty arises only when she is confronted with the need to imagine an alternative to the exchange system, a positive ideal to complement her ringing critique. To do so Wharton can only invoke an absent ideal – something that it has never been Lily's privilege to experience:

> And as [Lily] looked back she saw that there had never been a time when she had had any relation to life. Her parents too had been rootless, blown hither and thither on every wind of fashion, without any personal existence to shelter them from its shifting gusts. She herself had grown up without any spot of earth being dearer to her than another: there was no centre of early pieties, of grave endearing traditions, to which her heart could revert and from which it could draw strength for itself and tenderness for others. In whatever form a slowly-accumulated past lives in the blood – whether in the concrete image of the old house stored with visual memories, or in the conception of the house not built with hands, but made up of inherited passions and loyalties – it had the same power of broadening and deepening the individual existence, of attaching it by mysterious links of kinship to all the mighty sum of human striving.

Wharton's image of the sanctified ancestral home, like the house of custom and ceremony Yeats prays for, is a quintessentially aristocratic ideal. As metaphor and as fact, the ancestral house stands aloof, in all its feudal strength, from the contemporary world of commodities, the world of "the wares/Peddled in the thoroughfares" [W.B. Yeats, 'A Prayer for My Daughter']. It is Wharton's fantasy of a transcendent order, for an organic life based on "blood" and "root[s]" is indeed antithetical to the mechanical exchange of capitalism. Wharton's critique of the marketplace is essentially an aristocratic critique, a critique

THE HOUSE OF MIRTH

from the standpoint of "early pieties," "grave endearing traditions," and "inherited passions and loyalties." And yet, even as she articulates her ideal, she sees that it does not exist, will not exist, and indeed has never existed, either in her own experience or in Lily's. The ideal is declared impossible even as it is invoked. The ancestral home is no alternative to the commodified "house of mirth," irrevocably present and here to stay.

Still, Wharton is not quite willing to give up the idea of transcendence. She finally compromises, ingeniously if not altogether convincingly, by grafting her ideal on a lower social order, the working class. The fantasized ancestral house does appear in the book after all, if only in the modernized and modified form of a working-class tenement. And to the occupant of this humble habitation, Nettie Struther, Wharton entrusts her vision of a life antithetical to the one she condemns. It is in Nettie's kitchen that Lily catches her "first glimpse of the continuity of life." She sees in Nettie someone who seems "to have reached the central truth of existence." It is not clear how Nettie accomplishes that feat (aside from her good fortune in having found a trusting husband); nor is it clear how her haphazard life as a wage laborer can withstand the ravages of the marketplace. As an ideal, Nettie remains curiously unsubstantiated, curiously unexamined: Wharton seems to have suspended her ironic incisiveness, her withering sense of all that entraps and compromises the human spirit. She does not look more closely at Nettie, one suspects, because she cannot afford to. Wharton is not completely persuaded by the virtues of the working class nor is she altogether sympathetic to their causes. Even though she looks instinctively to the "poor little working girl" in her search for a redemptive figure, she sees Nettie less as the representative of the working class than as the embodiment of a private ideal – Wharton's ideal. Nettie, then, is to be from the working class but not too militantly, not too clamorously of it. To be all that Wharton wants her to be, Nettie must be abstracted from the all-contaminating exchange system. She must be romanticized and, to some extent, insulated – transported, in short, from the social realm into another realm, what we might call the realm of nature, a realm Wharton metaphorically invokes. Nettie's makeshift tenement, Wharton would have us believe, has "the frail, audacious permanence of a bird's nest built on the edge of a cliff." As an organic force, a principle of tenacity and continuity, Nettie takes her place within the "permanence" of natural history, at once more primitive and (Wharton hopes) more enduring than the exchange system.

A "naturalized" working class represents Wharton's best hope for an organic life beyond the marketplace. It is the only romanticism she permits herself in the book, but even this ideal is not always easy to sustain. On a number of occasions – most particularly when Nettie expresses her innocent hope that her daughter ("Marry Anto'nette") will grow up to be just like Lily – we see the corrosive vision of the ironist subverting the "alternative" she has so painstakingly set up. The book is fueled, then, by an almost exclusively critical energy directed at the marketplace Wharton disdains. She can only confusedly gesture toward a redeeming alternative: for her, the house of mirth has no exit. □

The likely source for Wharton's account of Lily's rootlessness is the first two paragraphs of chapter 3 of Eliot's *Daniel Deronda*. In other words the passage need not be referring to 'a quintessentially aristocratic ideal' that has 'never existed'. Eliot herself certainly knew what it was to have a 'centre of early pieties', and it may be peculiar to Wharton's endlessly unsettled American scene that such a centre is always something of a fantasy. This said, Dimock's reading of Nettie Struther is invaluable.

Elaine Showalter[15] seems initially to belong more to Ammons' camp than to Dimock's. She sees Lily as a victim. In her words:

■ Wharton refuses to sentimentalize Lily's position but rather, through associating it with her own limitations as the Perfect Lady Novelist, makes us aware of the cramped possibilities of the lady whose creative roles are defined and controlled by men. Lily's plight has a parallel in Wharton's career as the elegant scribe of upper-class New York society, the novelist of manners and decor. . . . In deciding that Lily cannot survive, that the lady must die to make way for the modern woman who will work, love and give birth, Wharton was also signalling her own rebirth as the artist who would describe the sensual worlds of *The Reef, Summer*, and *The Age of Innocence* and who would create the language of feminine growth and mastery in her own work. □

If this case were tenable, it might indeed be possible to see *The House of Mirth* as the turning point in Wharton's career that Showalter is claiming it to be. But in which works was Wharton 'the Perfect Lady Novelist', whatever this title means, and where, in the writing that follows *The House of Mirth*, do we find 'the language of feminine growth and mastery'?

Later in the essay Showalter moves away from her sense of Lily as victim:

■ . . . it is often overlooked that Wharton develops a full cast of male characters in *The House of Mirth*, whose dilemmas parallel those of the women. As historians now recognize, the period 1880–1920 redefined gender identity for American men as well as for American women. Among the characteristics of progressivism and of the masculinity crisis was the increased specialization of men as workers marginal to the family and culture. According to the capitalistic ethos, men were expected to promote industry and commerce, which they did in abundance, often spending long hours at the office, the plant, or in the fields and forests. With their energies spent, they came home too weary and worn to devote much time and interest to family or friends.

Wharton's critique of the marriage system is not limited to the economic dependency of women but also extends to consider the loneliness, dehumanization, and anxiety of men. Lily's father, a shadowy figure in the prehistory of the novel, establishes the theme of the marginal man. This "neutral-tinted father, who filled an intermediate space between the butler and the man who came to wind the clocks," is a dim and pathetic fixture of Lily's scant childhood memories. "Effaced and silent," patient and stooping, he is an exhausted witness to the stresses his society places on men. Even on vacation at Newport or Southampton, "it seemed to tire him to rest, and he would sit for hours staring at the sea-line from a quiet corner of the verandah, while the clatter of his wife's existence went on unheeded a few feet off." Mr. Bart does not so much die as get discarded; to his wife, once he had lost his fortune "he had become extinct," and she sits at his deathbed "with the provisional air of a traveller who waits for a belated train to start." Unable to love her father, to feel more for him than a frightened pity, or to mourn him, Lily nonetheless comes to identify with him in her own trial, recalling his sleepless nights in the midst of her own and feeling suddenly "how he must have suffered, lying alone with his thoughts."

The story of Mr. Bart, who in his enigmatic solitude and marginality here strongly resembles Mr. Bartleby, lingers in our consciousness as we read *The House of Mirth*, coloring our impression of even the crudest male characters. If Gus Trenor is beefy and stupid, he is nonetheless repeatedly used by the women in the book, and there is some justice in the words, if not the tone, of his complaint to Lily: "I didn't begin this business – kept out of the way, and left the track clear for the other chaps, till you rummaged me out and set to work to make an ass of me – and an easy job you had of it, too." To Lily, we have seen earlier,

Trenor is merely "a coarse dull man . . . a mere supernumerary in the costly show for which his money paid; surely, to a clever girl it would be easy to hold him by his vanity, and so keep the obligation on his side." Lily repays her financial debt to Trenor, but never her human one.

If women in this system harm each other, they also do an extraordinary amount of harm to men. It's hard not to feel a sympathy for shy Percy Gryce when Lily sets out to appeal to his vanity and thus to make an ass of him: "She resolved so to identify herself with her husband's vanity that to gratify her wishes would be to him the most exquisite form of self-indulgence." Despite the loss to Lily, we must feel that Gryce is better off with even the "youngest, dumpiest, dullest" of the Van Osburgh daughters. □

Men and women are mutual victims of the 'system', and Showalter is now closer to Dimock than to Ammons. In itself her diagnosis is persuasive, though it is not clear from Showalter that it is given sufficient recognition by Wharton's own commentary in the novel. Nor does Showalter herself relate the exploitative Lily to the Lily at the beginning of her essay. To exploit is to have the kind of power that may become culpable, and in the case of a woman as beautiful as Lily would inevitably have a sexual force. Where in the novel does Wharton face these issues?

Showalter turns next to the novel's capacity to engage with the possibility of change:

■ Real change, Wharton shows us in the novel, must come from outside the dominant class-structure. Thus the figure of Simon Rosedale, the Jewish financier making it big on Wall Street, takes on increasing importance as the novel develops. . . . Rosedale, the only man in the novel who likes children (we see him through Lily's eyes 'kneeling domestically on the drawing room hearth' with Carrie Fisher's little girl) offers the hope of continuity, rootedness, and relatedness that Lily finally comes to see as the central meaning of life. □

How convincing is this view of Rosedale's function? It is true that his gesture towards the child belatedly humanises and complicates him, but 'continuity, rootedness, and relatedness' seem strange qualities to fasten on a character whom Wharton has separated utterly from his ancestral heritage. Showalter, however, is determined to bring something positive from the novel. Her reading of Lily's involvement with Nettie Struther contrasts markedly with Dimock's and that of several other critics. It is offered in relation to Edna Pontellier in Chopin's *The Awakening*:

■ Some feminist critics, however, have tended to see the images of the mother and child in this scene, and in Lily's deathbed hallucination of holding the infant, as sentimental and regressive. Patricia Meyer Spacks, for example, criticizes Lily's "escapist fantasy of motherhood." Cynthia Griffin Wolff maintains that the scene with Nettie "gives poignant evidence of Lily's inability to conceive of herself in any other way than as the object of aesthetic attention," that she is once again self-consciously arranging herself in a *tableau vivant* for Nettie's admiration. Wolff also argues that in her death Lily is relinquishing her "difficult pretenses to adulthood." Thus in Wolff's view the extraordinary passage in which Lily, as she is succumbing to the drug, feels "Nettie Struther's child . . . lying on her arm . . . felt the pressure of its little head against her shoulder" is a sign of Lily's own retreat into the safety of infantilization.

It seems to me, however, that this hallucination speaks rather for Lily's awakened sense of loving solidarity and community, for the vision she has had of Nettie's life as representing "the central truth of existence." That Nettie should be the last person to see Lily alive and that Gerty should be the first to discover her death suggests that Lily's death is an acknowledgment of their greater strength. Doing justice to Lily Bart requires that we see how far she has come even in her death. Unlike the infantilized Edna Pontellier, who never awakens to the dimensions of her social world, who never sees how the labor of the mulatto and black women around her makes her narcissistic existence possible, Lily is a genuinely awakened woman, who fully recognizes her own position in the community of women workers. Whereas Edna's awakening is early, easy, incomplete, and brings a warm liquid sense of satisfaction, Lily's enlightenment is gradual and agonizing: "It was as though a great blaze of electric light had been turned on in her head. . . . She had not imagined that such a multiplication of wakefulness was possible; her whole past was re-enacting itself at a hundred different points of consciousness." Although her awakening proves unendurable, she really tries to overcome rejection, failure, and the knowledge of her own shortcomings. *The House of Mirth* ends not only with a death, but with the vision of a new world of female solidarity, a world in which women like Gerty Farish and Nettie Struther will struggle hopefully and courageously. Lily dies – the lady dies – so that these women may live and grow. □

In his reading of Nettie Struther's function in the novel, Donald Pizer[16] is closer to Showalter than to Dimock. Acknowledging Nevius, Pizer draws attention to the novel's naturalism and the 'deterministic theme of victimization'. For him Nettie is one of the 'alternative forms of belief and value'. In his words:

■ Whether Lily's fate is shaped by the capitalistic exchange values of her society or by its patriarchal power structure or by some variation of these two central readings in contemporary criticism of the novel, it is now common – whether or not the critic employs the terms of naturalistic criticism – to view the work as in the naturalistic camp.

Absent from almost all of this recent re-examination of *The House of Mirth*, however, is an effort to reconcile a view of Lily Bart as naturalistic victim of her world and Wharton's bold and concerted attempt, at the close of the work, to modify or counter an interpretation of this kind. We seem to have returned, in this respect, to the critical climate of the 1930s, when the need to view fiction in specific cultural terms because of the social work which this reading could provide led to a simplification of the novels of such figures as Norris and Dreiser. The rediscovery of Wharton as a naturalist, in other words, has also led to the redeployment in her case of the critical assumption that American naturalism in its various forms is an unqualified representation of social determinism in action. It is this assumption about *The House of Mirth* which I wish to test. . . .

Toward the end of *The House of Mirth*, however, Wharton juxtaposes this conscious deterministic theme of victimization by one's familial and social environment – of being forced into roles and attributes which both imprison and destroy – with two striking alternative forms of belief and value. The first involves Nettie Struther, the second the final "union" of Lily and Selden. These are alternative forms of belief, I will suggest, because they are non-materialistic in their conception of the human will and emotion – that is, they posit either a transcendent strength, one which can defeat the forces making for victimization in life, or a transcendent faith, one which holds that some values exist despite their seeming defeat in life. □

Nettie is one of Pizer's tests:

■ Nettie, we learn, has returned to life through marriage with a good man who has accepted and loves her despite her relationship with a previous suitor. Nettie explains, "[I]f George cared for me enough to have me as I was, I didn't see why I shouldn't begin over again – and I did". The infant which she now dotes on is thus the symbol of the triumphant rebirth of her will to live and indeed to live happily. "The strength of the victory shone forth from her as she lifted her irradiated face from the child on her knees." Nettie's progress from "victim" to "victory" within her own category of social determinism is thus a clear gloss on a potential of a similar kind within the category represented by Lily. If Nettie can triumph in the face of the physical and social handicaps which are hers from birth, this victory is also possible for Lily within her own seeming manacles of environmental conditioning. What differs in the two instances, in other words, is not an absolute distinction but a relative one. Nettie, unlike Lily, has both a sufficiently powerful will and the providential actuality of a man willing to take a chance on her. As Lily herself tersely sums up the differences between Nettie's fate and her own: "It had taken two to build the nest; the man's faith as well as the woman's courage". □

Dimock has already offered a large qualification of claims made for Nettie, and one wonders too if Pizer goes far enough with his comments on Lily. What does it say for Lily as a heroine if, in contrast to Nettie, she has not a 'sufficiently powerful will'? Is she, in this respect, strong enough to be a heroine? Pizer's avoidance of critical questions is confirmed when he turns to the second way in which Wharton modifies the conception 'that she is participating in a conventionally conceived naturalism'. This modification is apparent in her depiction of Lily's death:

■ ... an event which would indeed seem to confirm the theme of pessimistic determinism in the novel. Lily and Selden have parted with his love for her "dead" at that point. But, we are told, "something lived between them also, and leaped up in her like an imperishable flame: it was the love his love had [earlier] kindled, the passion of her soul for his". Lily goes to bed that night therefore both with the overdose of chloral which represents her inability to overcome her socially determined fate and with thoughts or feelings of love which constitute the transcendent in human affairs – the capacity to believe that certain values and conditions have significance because of the human capacity to believe in them despite their being unachievable by some or even all of humankind. The first such belief is that encapsulated in Nettie's story, as rendered now by Lily's dream or hallucination that Nettie's child – the child that Lily had in fact held rapturously in her arms earlier that evening – is there in bed beside her. What she had not achieved in life, in short, is here achieved in the imagination and is thus affirmed and even celebrated as a human value even in the face of its actual denial in life.

As Lily lies in bed imagining the sleeping child beside her, "she said to herself that there was something she must tell Selden, some word she had found that should make life clear between them". She tries to articulate this word, "which lingered vague and luminous on the far edge of thought" but falls asleep before she can do so. The next morning, Selden, once he has determined the truth of Lily's relationship with Gus Trenor, approaches her deathbed.

> He saw that all the conditions of life had conspired to keep them apart; since his very detachment from the external influences which swayed her had increased his spiritual fastidiousness, and made it more difficult for him to live and love uncritically. But at least he *had* loved her – had been willing to stake his future on his faith in her – and if the moment had been fated to pass from them before they could seize it, he saw now that, for both, it had been saved whole out of the ruin of their lives.

> It was this moment of love, this fleeting victory over themselves, which had kept them from atrophy and extinction; which, in turn, had reached out to him in every struggle against the influence of her surroundings, and in him, had kept alive the faith that now drew him penitent and reconciled to her side.

> He knelt by the bed and bent over her, draining their last moment to its lees; and in the silence there passed between them the word which made all clear.

The language of this extraordinary conclusion is essentially religious in character. The "conditions of life" conspire to defeat the spiritual fulfillment which is human love. But love did exist and continues to exist despite this defeat. Lily and Selden's "brief moment of love" had earlier provided them with a "fleeting victory over themselves," keeping them from "atrophy and extinction," and now, in his realization of her love, has supplied him with a "faith" that has made him "penitent." Thus, in the "silence" of physical actuality there can nevertheless be transmitted the "word" – the clear expression of their love for each other – which was never spoken in life. Life seemingly defeats the human effort to believe in a spiritual force in life, but in fact that belief transcends defeat both in its functional force in human affairs during life and in its permanence despite the transience of life. □

Do we not have to be as much engaged with the quality of what a novelist writes as with a possible literal meaning? 'The passion of her soul for his' is an arresting phrase, but where in *The House of Mirth* has it been apparent that Wharton is dealing with the passion of anyone's soul? Where, with any conviction, has the novel reached to 'the transcendent in human affairs'? Ignoring the doubts of many other critics, Pizer finally sees Selden as a spokesman for Wharton. Whether he is or not (and he may well be), there is certainly a problem with the claim about a triumph over 'atrophy and extinction'. No one could be more atrophied and extinct than Lily at this stage in the novel. Nor is it clear what spiritual, intellectual or physical energies remain available to Selden.

Pizer is disappointingly superficial, and there are signs that those attempting in the 1990s to impose a thesis on Wharton are becoming more and more desperate. Candace Waid[17] exemplifies this tendency. Her thesis about *The House of Mirth* develops from her reading of Wolff who, in Waid's words, 'rightly concludes that the heroine must be sacrificed because she cannot be a productive artist'. Her approach depends on establishing a relationship as authors between Lily and Bertha Dorset: 'Although Bertha is often on the margins of the narrative, she is crucial to any understanding of Lily and the place of writing in the novel'. As Waid sees it:

■ Bertha's centrality to both the plot and the allegory of the novel originates in her identity as the author of the love letters to Lawrence Selden – the letters that set so much of the plot in motion. When the charwoman Mrs. Haffen finds the letters that Selden has carelessly discarded, she sells them to Lily Bart in the mistaken belief that Lily is the author. Although Lily ultimately refuses to make the letters public or to use them to blackmail or even influence Bertha, Lily's possession of the letters gives her a power which *may* be the source of the fear that causes Bertha to conduct her campaign to drive Lily from the social stage. Bertha's relentless campaign seems to lead in the end to Lily's suicide. The importance of these letters to the plot is finally overdetermined, however. In addition to motivating the plot, they point to Bertha's role as an author and the potential power of letters in the world of *The House of Mirth*. . . .

Bertha Dorset is not just the author of well-placed stories that frame Lily as a disreputable woman, she is also the powerful scripter of scenes in which Lily Bart is cast as a character. What will be a carefully staged production is set in motion in the final lines of Book 1 when Bertha sends a telegram to Lily inviting her to "join us on a cruise in Mediterranean". This brief written text authored by Bertha is a prelude to the more elaborate scenario that Bertha authors in Monte Carlo. Here Lily is manipulated into distracting Bertha's husband and screening Bertha's infidelities, only to be set up as a 'sacrifice' – banished in an invented scandal to protect Bertha's marriage and reputation. □

Waid's linking of Lily and Bertha Dorset is useful, but how persuasive are tendentious phrases such as 'the powerful scripter of scenes' and '[t]his brief written text authored by Bertha'? Which of us, in Waid's elastic terms, is not an author? How is such an author to be distinguished from a novelist? Her subsequent claim that, 'to understand *The House of Mirth* we must understand Lily Bart as a writer' turns on her interpretation of the *tableau vivant* scene, when Lily re-enacts the portrait of Mrs Lloyd by Sir Joshua Reynolds, a painting in which Mrs Lloyd is apparently writing her husband's name on a tree. Even though Waid acknowledges that Wharton's narrative, 'despite its descriptive detail, . . . does not note that the portrait of Mrs Lloyd is the figure of a woman engaged in writing', she asserts that 'Lily as Mrs Lloyd holds an implement of writing in her hand'. We might ask how it is possible to be sure about this matter, and whether there is even a tree, or the representation of a tree, in Lily's re-enactment of Mrs Lloyd's pose? We might also ask whether Waid engages sufficiently with Wharton's moral endorsement of Lily in the novel. This latter question arises as we consider Waid's conclusion about a Lily who refuses to become a writer. In her words:

■ Although she has become the victim of Bertha's vengeful stories, Lily refuses to tell the story that would make her Bertha's equal rather than her sacrificial double. She refuses to admit that she has a story to tell, that she secretly possesses the power of letters. . . .

. . . her death seems both an escape from and a punishment for the dangerous eroticism of the underworld that Bertha seems to embody. . . .

Despite Wharton's success in writing *The House of Mirth*, the novel imagines two untenable places for the woman writer: the defiled underworld of experience and writing represented by Bertha Dorset, and the literal death that results from Lily Bart's refusal to use the power in her hands. □

The power in Lily's hands is Bertha's letters to Selden. Is it not the case, however, that Lily's refusal to blackmail Bertha with these letters is offered by Wharton as the clinching evidence of Lily's moral superiority? In recognising this authorial intention our very first reviewer (in chapter one) was surely right: 'this is the tragedy that a creature so morally sane should be subjected to a process sure to prove disintegrating'. Where is there any suggestion that Lily's refusal represents her inadequacy? Where in Wharton herself is it apparent that her own success as the author of *The House of Mirth* derives from that experience of 'the dangerous eroticism of the underworld' regarded by Waid as a necessary dwelling place for a woman writer?

Not that sexuality in Wharton's work is a negligible subject. It is discussed in the biographies by Lewis and Wolff, and both reprint Wharton's 'Beatrice Palmato', a four-page document unpublished in Wharton's lifetime and dated 1935 by Lewis, 1919–20 by Wolff. Regarded by Lewis as 'the most startling piece of fiction Edith Wharton ever wrote' (p. 524), it should be read by anyone interested in sex in Wharton. It has two parts, the first a plot summary of an intended fiction, the second a graphically dramatised sexual encounter between an older man and a younger woman. The plot summary hints strongly at an incestuous relationship between Mr Palmato, 'a rich half-Levantine, half-Portuguese banker living in London', and his two daughters, one of whom (Wharton apparently having Beatrice Cenci in mind) is named Beatrice. In the dramatised scene the sex is usually assumed to be between Mr Palmato and Beatrice, though the young woman in the scene is not named and Mr Palmato is not certainly identified as her father. Wolff goes further than Lewis in using 'Beatrice Palmato' as evidence of Wharton's own incestuous desires for her own father, and several critics follow Wolff in reading *Summer* (1917), which ends with a young woman marrying the man who has been her guardian, as further evidence in Wharton of a fascination with father–daughter incest. Both 'Beatrice Palmato' and *Summer* feature in Gloria C. Erlich's study,[18] which also reprints 'Beatrice Palmato'. Erlich's starting-point is what she sees as the 'flaws in the mother–daughter relationship that derailed [Wharton's] emotional development and caused a massive sexual repression'. Whether or not we accept this thesis, Erlich, with the Jewishness of Mr Palmato in mind, is especially suggestive, when it comes to *The House of Mirth*, in relating Lily Bart's sexual repression to her thoughts about Simon Rosedale:

■ Lily approaches the marital project in ignorance of its personal and sexual dimension. With flirtation and wedlock split off from sexuality, she understands marriage only in terms of property, never of desire. She dismisses too easily the promptings of desire that she feels for Selden because they fail to connect to property and hence to security. When she decides that she must accept Rosedale,

> she did not indeed let her imagination range beyond the day of plighting; after that everything faded into a haze of material well-being, in which the personality of her benefactor remained mercifully vague. She had learned . . . that there were certain things not good to think of, certain midnight images that must at any cost be exorcised – and one of these was the image of herself as Rosedale's wife.

Lily's expressed misgivings about Rosedale's "race" may obscure the implication of these exorcised midnight images, surely visions of the marriage bed, which seem to be carried over from Wharton's own nightmares. □

Erlich's book becomes a psychological case-study of Wharton herself. Literary critics, however, may feel their function is to assess the terms on which Wharton's fiction represents life. In this respect it is striking that she is unable to sexualise her own race, and especially her own class, in a way which might be defined as normal. Lily Bart is sublimated beyond sexuality, and generally in Wharton's fiction sexuality exists only fancifully as a state of bliss or degradation. As in Rosedale's case, it is often associated with a race or social class Wharton would regard as inferior to her own. The high value of Lily's beauty for Wharton, therefore, is integral with its sublimation. Hence the hysteria of both Wharton and Lily when this sublimation is challenged by Gus Trenor's drunken proposition. As Erlich puts it,

■ Lily misreads social cues such as Gus Trenor's sincere belief that he has earned her sexual favors. The exhibition of her body at the *tableau* leads Gus to think that if she is thus accessible to every man, he, who has lent her money, should be the first to collect. When he tries to trap her into paying up, Lily is forced to confront raw sexual reality. She tries to deny this by disingenuously interpreting Gus's demand as a request for repayment of money, and when she realizes that Gus considers her favors already bought and paid for, she is horrified. . . .

She is devastated not by anger at her close encounter with rape, but by shame and guilt. She feels defiled by a catastrophic revelation, hunted by the Furies, "alone in a place of darkness and pollution". Turning up distraught at the home of Gerty Farish, Lily declares that she is "bad – a bad girl – all my thoughts are bad. . . . There are bad girls in your slums. Tell me – do they ever pick themselves up? Ever forget, and feel as they did before?". She now feels less honorable than these whores: "I've sunk lower than the lowest, for I've taken what they take and not paid as they pay".

Why does she feel shame instead of anger, and why such extreme self-degradation? Why should Gus Trenor's readily foiled sexual approaches make this inviolable woman feel defiled? Why does she transfer to herself, the victim of a crude attempt at seduction, so much shame that her final act in life is to send her desperately needed inheritance check to Gus, who never sought return of the money? The nature of Lily's response and its extremity break through the social envelope of the novel, taking us back to the arena of the author's sexual confusion, straight to young Edith's tendency to feel polluted by even her unuttered thoughts, her need to atone for any thoughts that were "not nice," that is, sexual. □

Whatever Wharton's own sexual problems, what she presents as Lily's response to Trenor's proposition cannot be accepted at the value Wharton herself places on it. Is it not absurd to bring on the 'Furies' after such an encounter as Lily has experienced? Would they bother to turn out over such a matter? Wharton's recourse to them may be seen as a desperate attempt to transform hysteria into tragedy. What eventually results may be no more than sentimentality: a transcendent Lily, having resisted compromise with materiality (sex and money), will die unblemished.

Finally, Erlich is another critic who makes a positive claim for Nettie Struther's contribution:

■ Nettie's experience with sex had been genuinely distressing; it resulted in an out-of-wedlock pregnancy. But instead of writing herself off as a polluted woman, she made pragmatic choices and reconstructed her life. She has married a man who can accept her child, and she is building a home for herself and her baby. This home is humble but sufficient to shelter life and sustain continuity: "It had the frail, audacious permanence of a bird's nest built on the edge of a cliff – a mere wisp of leaves and straw, yet so put together that the lives entrusted to it may hang safely over the abyss". For Nettie, home and heart unite to form a structure that, however fragile, can be trusted.

THE CRITICAL RESPONSE

Although sophisticated critics may view the poor but courageous Nettie Struther and her baby as refugees from a sentimental novel, the pair are tied into the deeper themes of *The House of Mirth*. Nettie's frail shelter is built from womanly courage, adaptability, and the capacity for love. Her self-image allows for accommodation and regeneration, capacities that the beautiful Lily Bart lacks. □

Surely Erlich regards herself as a 'sophisticated' critic and has not immersed herself in Freud to come up simple. She omits, however, the blatant ironies with which Lily's encounter with Nettie is replete and which presumably confirm for Wharton the blind needs of Nettie's kind. The working girl idolises Lily and has named her daughter 'Marry Anto'nette . . . after the French queen in that play at the Garden – I told George the actress reminded me of you'. Dimock is surely right. All we can learn from Nettie's experience is that she has been very lucky.

Carol J. Singley[19] returns us to the notion of Lily's moral superiority. In this reading, however, the problem is the likening of Lily to Christ, a desperate move if ever there was one! According to Singley,

■ In the final chapters of the novel, Wharton contextualizes Lily's out-cast position in society by evoking the Christian story of betrayal, sacrifice, and resurrection. Whereas earlier she contrasted Lily with the Old Testament "beloved," here she evokes her as a New Testament savior. Lily becomes a Christ figure destined to die for principles that her self-absorbed, ignorant "well-wishers" fail to recognize or honor. Lily is explicitly connected with Christ in Selden's mind, repeatedly declines offers for wealth and power, and refuses to seek retribution against those who malign her. However, unlike Christ's crucifixion, Lily's death redeems no one. With this allusion, then, Wharton demonstrates the unbridgeable gap between the Christian message of salvific sacrifice and modern-day materialism.

Lily's Christlike qualities are evident first in her self-restraint and silent endurance of others' injustices. She does not protest when her aunt unfairly cuts her from her will, or when her wealthy cousin Grace Stepney affects moral indignation before refusing her a simple loan. Instead, she turns the other cheek and – much to some readers' vexation – repeatedly fails to save herself when she has the means. She exemplifies the spirit of Christ's Sermon on the Mount, which not coincidentally occurs to Selden when he thinks of her: *"Blessed are the pure in heart, for they shall see God"*. (Original emphasis.)

Imitating Christ's refusal of Satan's power and riches, Lily also several times rejects "the terrible force of the temptation" that would allow her to vanquish those who shun her. After Selden has abandoned her, she thanks him for having loved her once. Although her "tired mind was fascinated" by the possibility of evening the score she refuses to use his and Bertha's love letters for personal gain. She similarly rejects "the great golden vistas of peace and safety" implied by George Dorset's suggestion that she testify against Bertha in a divorce suit. When a scheme to marry Freddy Van Osburgh to Norma Hatch presents itself, Lily withdraws from the transaction "in time to save her self-respect but too late for public vindication." The scandal is once again wrongly "ascribed to Miss Bart's connivance"; Lily herself is blameless. She rejects Rosedale's suggestion that she marry in exchange for status and money and tells him only the barest facts about Trenor's attempt to extort sex for loans, circumspectly calling it "business".

Just as Christ was deserted by most of his supporters at the time of his death, so Lily is betrayed by apparent friends, including Selden, who takes "the conventional view" of her, finding "it was much simpler for him to judge Miss Bart by her habitual conduct than by the rare deviations from it". □

As the subtitle to her book indicates, Singley wants to associate Wharton with fundamental religious, philosophical and aesthetic themes. As exemplified above, however, the association may seem glib and presumptuous. When Singley asserts that 'Wharton demonstrates the unbridgeable gap between the Christian message of salvific sacrifice and modern-day materialism', is it not relevant to ask if 'salvific sacrifice' is the Christian message? Moreover what is meant by 'demonstrates the unbridgeable gap'? Have all Christians enjoying 'modern-day materialism' been in a state of delusion since the publication of *The House of Mirth*, their faith a waste of spirit? Singley is no less immune from self-questioning, when she turns to the relationship between the aesthetic and the moral:

■ Although Lily falls short of tragic heroism, she aspires toward higher values than those in the world around her. Wharton suggests as much by describing her beauty, grace, good taste, and aversion to dinginess. Elsewhere in her writing, Wharton associates an aesthetic sensibility with a superior moral capacity. In *A Backward Glance*, for example, she contrasts "the intolerable ugliness" of New York with the "immortal beauty and immemorial significance" of Europe. Her autobiographical fragment, "Life and I," similarly equates moral and aesthetic ugliness, describing the "moral tortures" and "suffering" experienced from "certain images – impressions of scenery and more sharply-drawn visions of rooms" – that she encountered during a childhood stay in Europe. In *The House of Mirth*, then, words like "dingy" and "dreary" refer not only to superficial material conditions but to an entire quality of life. Dinginess, "a quality which assumes all manner of disguises," is "as latent in the expensive routine of her aunt's life as in the makeshift existence of a continental pension". In contrast, Lily possesses finer aesthetic and moral sensibilities – however embryonic. □

Here Singley is facing a question recurrent among the writers featured in this Guide, namely what it is that Lily stands for that makes it worth our while to take an interest in her. In attempting to provide an answer, Singley has to range outside the novel and, by the end of her paragraph, has hardly convinced herself. More worrying because more dangerous is her complacent concurrence in Wharton's association of 'aesthetic sensibility with a superior moral capacity'. Henry James, like others before and since, spent a lifetime probing this association. He might as well never have bothered.

Stuart Hutchinson[20] compares Wharton's novel, to its disadvantage, with Eliot's. His response to Wharton's aesthetic sense is the opposite of Singley's. Finding a 'diluted Keatsianism'[21] in both Wharton and Selden, he offers for evidence their response to Lily in the *tableau vivant* scene:

■ . . . in both their eyes Lily is sublimated by this enactment of her beauty into an equivalent of the eternal figures on the Grecian Urn. Whereas Keats, however, is debating the genuinely tragic interrelatedness of sublimity and material contingency, Wharton sentimentalizes the mere fact that Lily's potentially sublime beauty will be wasted by 'all that cheapened and vulgarised it'. Lily may even unconsciously echo Keats's 'No hungry generations tread thee down' ('Ode to a Nightingale'), when she insists to herself: 'No; she was not made for mean and shabby surroundings, for the squalid compromises of poverty'. Again the eventual effect of the conceptualization is sentimental. Instead of using such a moment of self-inflation for the purposes of critical engagement with Lily, Wharton exploits it only for a too simple irony of circumstance, when 'the squalid compromises of poverty' finally become Lily's fate. Eliot's analogous presentation of Gwendolen is altogether superior. Gwendolen's 'sense that so exceptional a person as herself could hardly remain in ordinary circumstances or in a social position less than advantageous' is to result in the more profound irony of her hating the very achievement of this presumption. □

Hutchinson then turns to Reynolds' painting itself:[22]

■ Though Wharton claims that Lily 'had shown her artistic intelligence in selecting a type so like her own', the Mrs Lloyd of the painting is in fact very different. When Reynolds painted her, she had either just married Lloyd or was about to do so. In the painting she is writing Lloyd's name on a tree, and for her pose Reynolds has used a reversal of Raphael's drawing of 'Adam Tempted'. The painting is full of sexuality – in the thin clinging dress, in the low neckline emphasizing the breasts as Mrs Lloyd bends forward, in the parted legs and crossed ankles drawing attention to the loins, in the bare feet shod in thin blue sandals, which themselves have a suggestion of the *seraglio*. Whether or not Mrs Lloyd may be regarded as a damsel, a damsel-fly has attached itself to her neckline. In all its blending of art and nature, the painting lives with a worldly and humane humour, shared, one suspects, between subject and painter. Both know this dressing up is playing mock heroic games. Only superficially, therefore, is Reynolds's portrait of Mrs Lloyd the 'idealized and exalted rendering of reality' that Wolff, in her search for images that violate Lily and all women, claims it to be.

Wharton also makes Lily dress up, but for both author and character it is to escape reality and not, as with Reynolds and Mrs Lloyd, to be reminded of the areas where reality and ideality, nature and art, interrelate and challenge each other. After being Reynolds's subject, Mrs Lloyd will change her clothes and get on with her life and her marriage (eventually, she was to be married again). Lily, by contrast, hardly has a life away from the *tableau*. Plagiaristic and artificial as the *tableau* is, this 'exalted rendering of reality', to borrow from Wolff's phrase, is an ultimate act of self-affirmation, regarded neither by Wharton nor by Lily as a distraction from a true self. It is the ultimate expression of a beauty which Wharton is unable to endow with natural energy and passion. Wharton writes of 'the flesh and blood loveliness of Lily Bart', but this loveliness as embodied by Lily seems entirely passive, neither capable of, nor responsive to, desire or appetite. Though Wharton knows that realistically Lily would be the object of sexual desire, she hardly wants to engage with this aspect of Lily's case, and again she shelters behind Selden. When some men respond sexually to Lily's performance in her *tableau*, Wharton immediately escapes into Selden's point of view. As he sees it, these men are as Caliban responding to Miranda. □

After nearly a hundred years of criticism of *The House of Mirth*, Hutchinson is at least attempting to return to first order questions about it.

CHAPTER THREE

The Custom of the Country (1913): Wharton's Account of its Composition; The Contemporary Reviews; Henry James's Comments

'I HAVE . . . TAKEN up again my sadly neglected great American Novel'[1] – this was Wharton's first reference from her home in Lenox, in May 1908, to *The Custom of the Country*. In May 1911, writing from Salsomaggiore, where she was taking a cure, she proclaimed the novel to be 'a real magnum opus' (*Letters*, p. 240). Three months later, back in Lenox, it was 'the Big Novel' (*Letters*, p. 252), and in November of the same year she wrote to Charles Scribner from her Paris home to discuss serialisation and a problem as to whether or not the proposed title already belonged to another book. In passing she noted it was already the title of a play – by Beaumont and Fletcher, she thought, though it is actually by Fletcher and Massinger (*Letters*, p. 263). Serialisation began in *Scribner's* in January 1913, while in August of that year she still had to face in her Paris home 'the hard grind at my last chapters' (*Letters*, p. 303). No other novel had engaged Wharton for so long, or had been so interrupted by other projects – short stories, *Ethan Frome* (1911) and *The Reef* (1912).

Our first review[2] responds to the ongoing serialisation only to write a thesis about the development of America since pioneering times:

■ In her latest novel Mrs. Wharton is concerned with a type of American womanhood which might be described as one of the stock figures of the newer fiction, if it were not for the consideration that Mrs. Wharton's Undine Spragg is not a stock figure at all, but is very much alive. The fact that the spending American woman is always turning up in our literature must be taken as a sign that she is to be found in life.

The fierce determination to "get on" in society; the passion for enjoyment which is more correctly to be described as excitement; the utter lack of concern for the father or husband who finances the process of getting on; and the lack of interest in the sources from which the supporting male procures the sinews of war – these are familiar traits which do not grow stale through repetition. That men shall earn and women shall spend, without intruding upon each other's territory, is the custom of the country as Mrs. Wharton defines it. For the husband to confide his business troubles to his wife would be almost as odd as for the wife to make her husband a repository of her troubles with the dressmaker. It is a division of functions which we have apparently developed to an unrivalled state of perfection. □

According to the writer it was different when 'the rigors of pioneer life fell more painfully upon the women than upon the men'. Now 'economic pressure' has relaxed, and 'it is natural that the women of the family should be the first to feel the relief'. 'The aspirations for the softer, finer things of life are stronger in the female of the species. The advent of leisure gives more immediate freedom to feelings long repressed.' The review is an example of supplying a context which may enlarge our sense of the novel, but which hardly refers to it. What the novel contributes to the context is not considered.

The writer of 'Critical Reviews of the Season's Latest Books'[3] is more engaged with the novel itself. The review declares that 'the American society woman of today, with her puerile ambitions, and her tenacity of purpose, is the subject of Edith Wharton's displeasure in *The Custom of the Country*':

■ She has been held up to scorn by a good many writers of fiction of late, both those who wish to preach and those who wish to depict or satirise the life of the society of wealth whose doings are chronicled in the newspapers. She provokes Mrs. Wharton into forgetting her art in the effort to be emphatic, and employing crude methods that are evidently as strange to her as to the readers of her books. These may well feel uncertain about the meaning of the title, whether it refers to the social conventions that stand in the way of her heroine or whether

THE CUSTOM OF THE COUNTRY

Mrs. Wharton applies it cynically to the American habit of letting
women have their own way, and to the abuses of the divorce laws.

  She has constructed an ideal monster, perfect in that at no time
does she betray any human feeling, a model for other women who are
pushing their way and a standard by which the people who are
watching them may measure them. She has two valuable assets, her
confidence in the power of her own beauty and the inflexible determination to have whatever she wants at once and at any cost,
characteristics which to the male observer may seem general to the
sex, but which in this case are developed to an acute degree. She is
ignorant; she is lacking in intelligence; she does not know enough to
try to find out what the society she forces herself into is like or to
acquire a superficial varnish of its manners; she is sexless, with no
feeling for men, nor for her child, nor for her parents; she is recklessly
extravagant with money, though she is not mercenary, but merely
needs it to carry out her will, and to obtain it regards neither her own
honor nor that of others[;] she is absolutely unmoral and has no sense
of decency whether as regards the truth or the marriage relation, not to
speak of the more delicate points in character or in the manners of
respectable society. She manages to obtain her desire over and over
again, only to discover, as many others have done, that what she really
wants is something she has not got yet. In Mrs. Wharton's picture she
never falters; the one hint of weakening is when she meets her male
counterpart, who understands her, but she quickly and bravely gets
over that. She is absolutely selfish, logical and repulsive. □

We may feel that the meaning of the novel's title is cleared up in the thesis
expounded by the character Charles Bowen in chapter 15. This review is
mainly interesting, however, for its response to Undine: 'an ideal
monster', 'sexless', 'absolutely unmoral', 'absolutely selfish, logical and
repulsive'. Despite the apparent prejudice against women, if this is a true
reading of Undine we need to pose a question it does not pose, namely
how Wharton sustains interest in the character. What the reviewer means
by Wharton 'forgetting her art' becomes clear in the final paragraph:

■ The contrast between the husband's and the wife's impressions in
the Italian honeymoon is a bit too tragic for humor or preciosity, and
in the careful description of French family life the reader for the first
time may feel some sympathy for the heroine and wonder why her
husband married her at all. No detail of the vulgarity of the last
alliance she enters into is passed over.

With a character such as Mrs. Wharton has drawn it is evident that we have to do with abstract types and not with live men and women; the reprehensible actions are so gross as hardly to need denunciation. For the other people are merely lay figures. It is interesting to see Mrs. Wharton emerge from her own sphere, but in this case there is a distinct loss of art, whatever effect her warning may have. □

The review has assumed throughout that its moral response to the material of the novel is also Wharton's. As for 'loss of art', it is clear that the reviewer associates this with Wharton's emergence 'from her own sphere', presumably the world of *The House of Mirth*. We may not agree with this judgement, but it indicates an interesting critical question to do with the breadth of experience Wharton's writing can engage.

L.M.F.[4] begins with quotations from Bowen's exposition in chapter 15. After declaring Undine to be 'the most repellent heroine we have encountered in many a long day – so "monstrous" that at times she seems scarcely human, yet so cleverly portrayed that she is always real', it continues:

■ The book resembles *The House of Mirth* in tone and atmosphere, but Undine Spragg is without any of Lily Bart's redeeming characteristics; she is merely greed personified – without conscience, heart, sense of honor, or sense of humor. She wants the best that can possibly be had in the way of luxury and position; scruples as to ways and means never enter her head. She is "respectable," and rather boasts of the fact, but when respectability seems to bar her from the fortune she desires she sacrifices it without an instant's hesitation or qualm. Her principal weakness lies in the lack of imagination, which makes it impossible for her to understand the aspect certain of her acts wear to other people, and this same deficiency renders her unable to calculate any save immediate consequences. Absence of imagination it is which brings her to the verge of social shipwreck, and her escape is due simply to a piece of good luck. Natural affection she has none; her parents' devotion she accepts as a matter of course, her child's birth she resents, and she is perfectly willing to resign the boy to his father's care until she discovers that she can use him as a means of extortion. Many men fall in love with her, for she is wonderfully beautiful, with a smile "like refracted sunlight," and sweet tempered so long as everything is going her way. They usually tire of her, however, because she has no intelligence; only an imitative faculty so strongly developed that soon she, who, when first invited to dine with Mrs. Fairford, came

perilously near to writing her reply on the pigeon-blood note paper
which "Boudoir Chat" had pronounced the latest thing, attained a
social competence which obliged even Bowen to admire her skill in
disposing of the companion she did not want. □

This response to Undine is more considered than in the previous review,
and it raises questions that are more critically significant. If Undine does
lack 'imagination', 'natural affection' and 'intelligence', Wharton might
be thought to have made things rather easy for herself in that she has
presented a character whose reality can only be superficial. Undine can
be made to live instantaneously for Wharton's purposes, because she will
never be capable of complicating commitments. This issue bears too on
any representative status that might be claimed for Undine. Is Wharton
offering her as a representative mid-Western product? If so, and if the
reviewer's view of Undine is accurate, are we not left with a sense of the
author's disdain for such a product, amused as the disdain occasionally is?
　　The reviewer turns next to the other characters in the novel:

■ If Undine is repellent, it cannot be said that human nature as
reflected in the pages of this novel is ever particularly attractive. The
Marvells and Dagonets of Washington Square are mere ghosts of a
narrow past, futile, bloodless, out of touch alike with the "Invaders"
who have swarmed into and captured New York society, and with the
people who are doing the real, worth-while work of the world. The
possessors of certain aesthetic tastes and a fine sense of probity, but
expert in "the vocabulary of evasion," shirkers to the very backbone,
every one of them. The Van Degens and their kind, affiliated with
those others by such bargain marriages as that of Clare, are material-
ists whose creed is eat, drink and be merry, whose religion is a frank
worship of the Golden Calf. The French aristocrats are stronger
through their sense of union, their ideal of "The Family." Raymond de
Chelles, for all his limitations, wins a respect one cannot but deny
Ralph Marvell. De Chelles had some power of the will; yet he, like
Ralph, succumbs at last before the brute force of money. Undine's
father, Abner L. Spragg, is about the only really likable person in the
book; his humorous tolerance of "a son-in-law who expected to be
pensioned like a Grand Army veteran," his resistance to Elmer
Moffatt, and his devotion to his wife and child make him an agreeable
contrast to such men as Van Degen.
　　It is Elmer Moffatt, however, who next to Undine herself is the
most impressive figure in this novel. Typical in many ways, he shows

the human quality she lacks by his kindliness and his genuine love of beautiful things. There is something symbolic in his capture of the famous de Chelles tapestries. One feels the force of the man, even during his time of defeat. He has a bigness the other characters are nearly all without; his materialism, like his success, is on a huge scale. He sweeps much before him as he moves through the hothouse in which all the scenes of the story are laid. □

'Mere ghosts of a narrow past, futile, bloodless . . . ' – if this is an accurate response, Wharton has set up very little in opposition to Undine, and we may wonder why her commitment to the representatives of her own past is so weak. It is interesting too that Elmer Moffatt has 'the human quality' and the aesthetic taste Undine lacks. Why are these things given by Wharton to a man and not to a woman? Was an Undine deprived of these qualities easier for Wharton to objectify and manipulate? Wharton might have sensed that Undine could have become too much a version of herself. Her sheer consumerism is surely Wharton's own.

H.W.B.[5] begins as a general and stimulating survey of Wharton's work. Of the early work he concludes:

■ But beneath the suavity and self-possession of her manner there has always been a restless spirit, and the time passed soon when the exercise of wit and adroitness could soothe it. She had, besides, the resource of the study, and the richest of art. Turning from the short story to the novel, she called them to her aid. She ranged herself in that school of sophistication, of finesse, half-lights, and rich, dim accessories, which was then ascendant. She knew her Meredith, her James, her Howells, and the greater masters of France – Bourget, Stendhal, and the rest. She wished to address herself to no vulgar audience. The very titles of those earlier books, *The Greater Inclination, Crucial Instances, The Valley of Decision*, were a snub to the populace and a challenge to the fastidious. The populace does not deal in comparatives, *nuances*, reservations, compunctions. □

From this provocative reflection H.W.B. arrives at disappointment with *The Custom of the Country*. Undine is a 'caricature' instead of a 'refinement' of character-type that novelists such as Dreiser were also doing. Ralph, following his suicide, 'is well out of it, and that is all we feel; with his elegance and sensitiveness, he shows the futility that besets most of Mrs Wharton's finer-grained male Americana'. In conclusion:

■ With all its amenity of manner, *The Custom of the Country* has a sharply satirical tone. The heroine is a mere monster of vulgarity; and Mrs. Wharton seems to feel a ruthless satisfaction in exposing her in all her enormity. The result is a defeat of what should have been the main purpose, to interest us in the Spragg. A caricature does not remain interesting to the length of six hundred pages. And there is no use trying to convey on paper the charm of a physical beauty which has no backing in mind or character. The mood of satire seems to be growing upon Mrs. Wharton, a dubious sign in a writer who has passed a certain age. It is hard to feel that, clever and effective and varied as her work has been, and is, she has ever yet veritably "found herself" – the self of assured power which seemed to exist potentially in her first books. Ten years ago, a stranger asking an American who was the most distinguished of our novelists would very likely have heard the name of Mrs. Wharton. It is not altogether due to the fact that other (potential) giants have arisen among us, that the answer would now hardly be the same. □

These are challenging judgements to which any modern supporter of Wharton must be able to respond. Especially arresting are the charge of ruthlessness and the uneasiness with the satire. Do these ingredients betoken a mere impatience on Wharton's part? A determination not to explore would indeed be crippling to a novelist.

This possibility of superficiality in *The Custom of the Country* arises unintentionally from points made by F. M. Colby.[6] After summarising the plot, he tells us:

■ By a stroke of fortune Undine Spragg was swept to the very summit of New York gentility through her marriage to Ralph Marvell, the flower of Washington Square aristocracy. There is an admirable description of the Marvells and their connections, who represent New York's waning *noblesse*:

> Ralph sometimes called his mother and grandfather the Aborigines, and likened them to those vanishing denizens of the American continent doomed to rapid extinction with the advance of the invading race. He was fond of describing Washington Square as the "Reservation", and of prophesying that before long its inhabitants would be exhibited at ethnological shows, pathetically engaged in the exercise of their primitive industries.

> Small, cautious, middle-class, had been the ideals of aboriginal

> New York; but it suddenly struck the young man that they were
> singularly coherent and respectable as contrasted with the chaos of
> indiscriminate appetites which made up its modern tendencies. □

The passage Colby quotes is nowadays well-known and, in contrast to
the reviewer, we may find it objectionable. There surely can be no
appropriate likeness to be made between the decline of a New York
social group and the extinction of a race. To make the analogy, as Ralph
and Wharton do, is surely to be superficial. Moreover, how convinced
are we that the ideals of Ralph's class would be 'small' and 'cautious'?
Might it be that Wharton deprives them of larger energies so that she
may manipulate them into her scheme of things? Colby further asserts:

■ It is wonderful how in a word or two she can call to the mind a type
or extinguish a pretension or present a complete picture to the eye.
Disagreeable persons are never condemned or brought obviously to
ridicule by Mrs. Wharton. They are in a delicate phrase or two artistically snubbed. For example, the "lovely, aimless" Mrs. Beringer, who
kept "a home for stray opinions and could never quite tell them apart";
Mr. Popple, the painter, whose portraits were "not pictures of Mrs. or
Miss So-and-so, but simply of the impression Popple thinks he's
made on them"; and "the Harvey Shallums, fresh from Paris, and
dragging in their wake a bewildered nobleman vaguely designated as
'the Count,' who offered cautious conversational openings, like an
explorer trying beads on savages." □

'Artistically snubbed' is the key phrase here. If it is accurate, it describes
a dubious, self-defeating habit for a novelist.

Before we get to Henry James, extracts from three other reviews
published in England are worth noting. The first[7] claims that:

■ [Wharton,] by avoiding the least hint of sentiment, and laying stress
upon the sequence of environment, upbringing, character, has made
her heroine a natural and pathetic figure. She succeeds in winning for
a cold and selfish character the kindly sympathy which comes of
understanding – an achievement of which any novelist might well
be proud. □

What Wharton's 'understanding' of Undine amounts to, especially in its
relation to her understanding of Ralph Marvell and old New York, is the
central critical question the novel poses. Our second review published in

England[8] finds quite the opposite to 'kindly sympathy':

■ Mrs. Wharton has assembled as many detestable people as it is possible to pack between the covers of a six-hundred-page novel. It is a sordid society into which we are introduced – a set of vulgar Americans, blatant and pushing, whose only standard of values is the dollar.

Undine, the daughter of Mr. and Mrs. Spragg, named after a patent hair-curler which had founded the fortune of the family, is the pivot on which the novel turns. She may be regarded as symbolic of a certain type of American woman whom Mrs. Wharton desires to hold up to scorn and reprobation. She has not a single redeeming moral feature. Cold, greedy, heartless, and wayward, without a soul and with no realisation of anything but the outward glitter and tinsel of life, she has only one passion, and that is for endless amusement. □

The disdain directed at 'Americans' and 'America' adds a piquancy to this review, especially as it assumes (wrongly?) that the disdain is also Wharton's. The review concludes:

■ Mrs Wharton's book gives us [a] general view of American marriages. It is a scathing exposure of the scandals of divorce and of the mean standards of a certain section of American society. Brilliantly written, it should be read as a parable. □

The last review of *The Custom of the Country*[9] draws attention to a part of the novel that is still rarely noticed:

■ [Wharton] draws with admirable skill the parents of Undine, people who have made money rapidly, and come to New York in order to let their daughter get into society; the description of Mrs. Spragg's loneliness in the New York hotel, of her pathetic isolation and helplessness, is one of the best things in the story. But it is written without over-colouring. Mrs. Wharton uses these scenes and situations in order to bring out the character of her heroine, and the characterisation is subtle, clever, and convincing. It is an unlovely plot. Mrs. Wharton does not conceal the inner misery of a woman who is inferior to all the men she marries, thanks to her greedy love of pleasure. But no moral is drawn. The story is left to tell its own warning. It is this which makes it effective. There is less bitterness than in *The House of Mirth*, though the situation is practically the same. □

Mrs Spragg certainly is not snubbed by Wharton, but is it true that we have a sense of Undine's 'inner misery'? Is Undine internalised at all by Wharton?

Henry James[10] is reflecting on several other novelists as well as Wharton. In contrast, for example, to his sense of the looseness of Wells and Bennett, he sees her as one of the 'votaries of selection and intention'. Turning particularly to *The Custom of the Country*, he declares it to be:

■ consistently, almost scientifically satiric, as indeed the satiric light was doubtless the only one in which the elements engaged could at all be focused together. But this happens directly to the profit of something that, as we read, becomes more and more one with the principle of authority at work; the light that gathers is a dry light, of great intensity, and the effect, if not rather the very essence, of its dryness is a particularly fine asperity. The usual 'creative' conditions and associations, as we have elsewhere languished among them, are thanks to this ever so sensibly altered; the general authoritative relation attested becomes clear – we move in an air purged at a stroke of the old sentimental and romantic values, the perversions with the maximum of waste of perversions, and we shall not here attempt to state what this makes for in the way of aesthetic refreshment and relief; the waste having kept us so dangling on the dark aesthetic abyss. A shade of asperity may be in such fashion a security against waste, and in the dearth of displayed securities we should welcome it on that ground alone. It helps at any rate to constitute for the talent manifest in *The Custom* a rare identity, so far should we have to go to seek another instance of the dry, or call it perhaps even the hard, intellectual touch in the soft, or call it perhaps even the humid, temperamental air; in other words of the masculine conclusion tending so to crown the feminine observation. □

This takes us back to H. W. B.'s detection of Wharton's 'mood of satire', though 'scientifically satiric' suggests a reflexive satire working on behalf of nothing but itself. What it might have pointed to is now seen by James as 'the old sentimental and romantic values' which he is relieved to find absent from Wharton. Whether her 'particular fine asperity', even though it constitutes a 'rare identity', is enough of a fund he is not sure, though he is certainly more sure about 'masculine' and 'feminine' than critics in our own time are ever able to be.

CHAPTER FOUR

The Custom of the Country: The Critical Response

COMMENTING ON Undine, Percy Lubbock[1] remarks that:

■ The Middle West is rich enough to float [her] to New York, but it is her unaided beauty that carries her on from that point and that scars a great disturbing track across lives as firmly rooted, as broadly civilized, as her own is unattached and unconditioned. Undine has nothing and is nothing but her beauty, with just the wit to enable her to perceive that there are worlds where noise and expense are not taken as the measure of all values. □

He continues:

■ *The Custom of the Country*, in short, is a fine book, but unluckily it is all too good for Undine. It is difficult to see, given the lines on which Mrs. Wharton has treated the action, how it could have been otherwise. Undine, as a mere bubble of rainbow tints, may possibly have substance enough to wound and destroy, though it is perhaps doubtful whether we can quite accord all that Mrs. Wharton claims for beauty so unsupported by any gifts of character whatever. At any rate, if this empty shining fairness is to be endowed with such importance, it is clear that we must be made to see it at every turn and be conscious of it at every moment. It must fill the air for us with the very same revelation of glowing light that bewitched its victims. But Mrs. Wharton for the most part chooses to look in the opposite direction; that is to say, she makes us chiefly see with Undine's eyes and watch her beauty as it is reflected in the intent gaze of her adorers. So and in no better way could we be convinced of many a vision of enchantment, but the workings of Undine's mind are altogether too rudimentary to help us out in her case. Undine, being nothing but an exquisite object, should surely have been treated exclusively as an object. This is no doubt a somewhat subversive reflection to throw out in passing, for it of course implies a point of departure and a way of approach to the story entirely different from those which Mrs. Wharton has chosen. Where in this case she could have found a controlling and unifying center is a question it might be inconvenient to tackle. But it seems as though Undine's triviality could not otherwise be made strong enough to carry the piled-up irony of her career through such a series of glittering scenes. □

'[B]eauty so unsupported by any gifts of character whatever' – is this an accurate view of Wharton's presentation of Undine? If so, we may well agree with Lubbock that Wharton is claiming too much for its likely effect on others. We may agree too that 'the workings of Undine's mind are altogether too rudimentary' for the amount of time devoted to them. Very much influenced by his reading of Henry James, Lubbock wants 'a controlling and unifying center' for *The Custom of the Country* other than Undine herself.

Q.D. Leavis[2] begins by comparing Wharton, to her advantage, with George Eliot:

■ Undeniably Mrs. Wharton had a more flexible mind, she was both socially and morally more experienced than George Eliot and therefore better able to enter into uncongenial states of feeling and to depict as an artist instead of a preacher distasteful kinds of behavior. Her Undine Spragg is better sustained and handled than the other's Rosamond Vincy. Undine's sphere of action is dazzling and she always has a fresh surprise for us up her sleeve in the way of moral obtuseness; it was cleverer to make Undine end up at the top of the tree with her only disappointment that her last husband couldn't get made Ambassador (on account of having a divorced wife) than to involve herself in disasters like Rosamond: the manifold irony of worldly success is more profitable than any simple moral lesson and artistically how much richer! □

This being said, Leavis recognises that it is Eliot 'who is the great novelist':

■ I think it eventually becomes a question of what the novelist has to offer us, either directly or by implication, in the way of positives. In

The Bunner Sisters, Summer, and some other places, Mrs. Wharton rests upon the simple goodness of the decent poor, as indeed George Eliot and Wordsworth both do in part – that is, the most widespread common factor of moral worth. But beyond that Mrs. Wharton has only negatives, her values emerging I suppose as something other than what she exposes as worthless. This is not very nourishing, and it is on similar grounds that Flaubert, so long admired as the ideal artist of the novel, has begun to lose esteem. It seems to be the fault of the disintegrating and spiritually impoverished society she analyzes. Her value is that she does analyze and is not content to reflect. We may contrast Jane Austen, who does not even analyze, but, having the good fortune to have been born into a flourishing culture, can take for granted its foundations and accept its standards, working within them on a basis of internal relations entirely. The common code of her society is a valuable one and she benefits from it as an artist. Mr. Knightley's speech to Emma, reproving her for snubbing Miss Bates, is a useful instance: manners there are seen to be based on moral values. Mrs. Wharton's worthy people are all primitives or archaic survivals. This inability to find any significance in the society that she spent her prime in, or to find "significance only through what its frivolity destroys," explains the absence of poetry in her disposition and of many kinds of valuable experience in her books. She has none of that natural piety, that richness of feeling and sense of a moral order, of experience as a process of growth, in which George Eliot's local criticisms are embedded and which give the latter her large stature. Between her conviction that the new society she grew up into was vicious and insecurely based on an ill-used working class and her conviction that her inherited mode of living represented a dead end, she could find no foundation to build on. □

Is it because 'Mrs. Wharton has only negatives' that James found the writing in *The Custom of the Country* to be 'consistently, almost scientifically satiric'? The satire in other words was entirely reflexive because it had nothing to recommend, even by implication. If in the last sentence above Leavis is right about Wharton's dilemma, a way out of it might have led to an exploration of the strategies of writing itself. Wharton, however, even as an heiress of James, showed little interest in exploring the art of fiction.

Quoting from passages describing the Spraggs' situation at the Hotel Stentorian in chapter 1, and Undine's and Moffatt's Paris residence in chapter 46, Edmund Wilson[3] observes:

■ It is a vein which Sinclair Lewis has worked since – as in the opening pages of *Babbitt*, where Babbitt is shown entangled with his gadgets; and in other respects *The Custom of the Country* opens up the way for Lewis, who dedicated *Main Street* to Edith Wharton. Mrs. Wharton has already arrived at a method of doing crude and harsh people with a draftsmanship crude and harsh. Undine Spragg, the social-climbing divorcee, though a good deal less humanly credible than Lily Bart of *The House of Mirth*, is quite a successful caricature of a type who was to go even farther. She is the prototype in fiction of the "gold-digger," of the international cocktail bitch. Here the pathos has been largely subordinated to an implacable animosity toward the heroine. □

Wilson, it seems, was the first to register Wharton's anticipation of Lewis, though he might have taken the point further with a reference to the account in chapter 43 of Moffatt's rise and fall in Apex. Here, Wharton has more of Lewis's kind of fun than in the passages Wilson cites. We may disagree too with Wilson's assertions about 'crude and harsh', and later critics will disagree that Wharton's response to Undine is one of 'implacable animosity'.

As with *The House of Mirth*, Geoffrey Walton[4] responds intelligently to *The Custom of the Country* on its own terms:

■ The dry but imaginative humor of her observation in cases such as these forms a basis for the greater asperity or indignation that inspires the creation of more important personages. A very elaborate structure of social ideals is built up and subjected to detached and impartial scrutiny, and the manners and customs of each group are displayed and their moral quality exposed as Undine Spragg sweeps forward from one to another. The central theme is her pursuit of wealth and power, cutting across the conflicts of groups and classes, old and new. The positive values are diffused. It is not merely a matter of old New York against the newly rich or European tradition against trans-Atlantic innovation. There are humane and civilized qualities and simple truth and generosity in many places, often the most unexpected. They emerge from the social struggle as it progresses and form an implicit judgment on the final ironic victory. . . .

The Spraggs carry on an absolutely rootless and utterly boring existence amid the comfortless, tasteless, and depersonalized luxury of a "Looey suite" in the Hotel Stentorian, a name happily chosen to indicate the tone of its more prominent inhabitants. Mrs. Spragg wears "as complete an air of detachment as if she had been a wax figure in a shop-window." Her one interest is the daughter's social advancement. Mr. Spragg, on the other hand, despite his drooping and dyspeptic appearance, has not altogether lost his "pioneering" energy. There is a certain Dickensian quality about their presentation in terms of typical and slightly absurd details of dress and behavior. The artificiality of the two women's existence is epitomized in the decidedly Dickensian character of Mrs. Heeny, the masseuse and manicurist, who provides them and others like them with a vicarious social life as well as physical invigoration. Her advice, "Go steady, Undine, and you'll get anywheres," is recalled at intervals during the heroine's progress. As has been indicated, Undine Spragg begins her career of conquest from the outside. She has to be shown not only the territory and the membership of Society but also its scale of values, the difference between Washington Square and Fifth Avenue, the difference between the Dagonets and Marvells, on the one hand, and the Driscolls and Van Degens, on the other, and which is the more "'swell" – plain white or pigeon-blood note paper. She is at once a formidable and an absurd figure. She is beautiful in a rather blatant way, with reddish-gold hair and dark eyebrows, and from childhood she has had a narcissistic strain that has become an ingredient in a naive but predatory egotism . . .

She tyrannizes over her parents by sheer petulance and she soon adapts her posturings to the task of subduing other worthwhile victims. She is described as "fiercely independent and yet passionately imitative" so that, while always seeking to dominate, she picks up the manners of whatever group she is placed in. Her most terrifying and far-reaching quality is her coldness. She has tremendous energy but no human sympathy, let alone passion. With one exception, her relationships with men are motivated by social ambition, sometimes of a ridiculously childish kind, and she casts them off if she is not socially satisfied. Where Lily Bart is shown as frivolous, but ultimately pathetic, Undine Spragg is ruthlessly calculating. One cannot call her contemptible, however; she rises – it is the appropriate word – to wickedness on a majestic scale in her indifference to moral principles and her freedom from the ties of affection; relative chastity is a mere by-product of her frigidity. She has none of the charm and warmheartedness of Becky Sharp, to whom she has been compared; no one would ever try to sentimentalize Undine Spragg. One thinks rather of a more respectable and more successful, but less human, Roxana; Edith Wharton's ironical detachment is indeed comparable to the coarser quality in Defoe. With all her meretricious glamor and her dominant position, Undine is a perfectly adjusted component in the satiro-comic scheme. If it can be called Undine *contra mundum*, both sides and all parts stand or fall together as art as certainly as one side stands or falls as life. □

The only critical question prompted by this reading of Undine is Wharton's motive in creating such a character. In this respect Walton's contrast with Lily Bart is telling. She disintegrates on the inside of Wharton's own social class and is 'ultimately pathetic'. Undine attacks this class from the outside and is 'ruthlessly calculating'. Is not this too simple and too self-serving a view on Wharton's part? If Undine is to have significance, she needs to be representative. Is it therefore Wharton's case that young women from the mid-West are generally of her kind? If not, what is Undine's status? '[W]ickedness on a majestic scale in her indifference to moral principles' surely needs more response than Wharton provides. '[I]ronical detachment' may conceal authorial evasiveness.

When he turns to Ralph, Walton exhibits difficulties recurrent in several critics:

■ The gist of it would seem to be that the values of old New York are morally and culturally superior to those of the newly rich, though capable of equivocation, but they are not only incapable of survival in any struggle for existence – we know Edith Wharton had read Darwin – but also mediocre and cramping for finer spirits such as Marvell, let alone the more energetic. Ralph Marvell has more energy than Lawrence Selden, but less detachment and psychological penetration. He is ready to act, but also easily deceived, so that with all his intellectual flexibility and vitality, which raise him above his own group, he is still, partly because of his cloistered upbringing and partly because of his retired and introvert temperament, predestined to be a victim of Undine. □

Walton's awkward first sentence betrays his problem in identifying what it is of value that old New York represents. Where too is the evidence of Ralph's 'intellectual flexibility and vitality', and how do these qualities relate to 'his retired and introvert temperament'? Yes, Wharton had read her Darwin, but allusion to this fact cannot account for Ralph's 'predestined' defeat. Should there not have been more of a struggle for survival?

After an eloquent summary of de Chelles' position, Walton concludes his account by turning to the novel's final concentration on the young Paul Marvell:

■ . . . he carries his significance as tragic victim and residuary legatee of both old New York and traditional France with no traces of sentimentality or awkwardness. His fruitless search for his own possessions, his desire to get at the locked-up books, and his unsatisfied curiosity about the pictures are perfectly in the character of a serious small boy and at the same time symbolize the natural civilized human being isolated amid completely artificial conditions. He not unnaturally, and from the point of view of the themes very appropriately, blurs the memory of Ralph Marvell with that of his French "father," whom he has loved, and he is outraged by Moffatt's crassness and his mother's lies about the latter. He is made to enact the fundamental criticism of Undine and Moffatt that underlies the whole story of their careers in all its significance, the cold cruelty of Undine's egotism and Moffatt's coarse-grained obtuseness. Paul Marvell's tears are deeply poignant. The last note is satiric comedy. Undine has not lost her social ambitions and she has acquired considerable social expertise, but her own past and Moffatt's vulgarity will always queer her pitch, and Moffatt has got her for his wife. They now belong to no class, and they have no traditions and no principles, inherited or acquired; they have only each other and unlimited wealth. The comic prospect is endless and unrelieved. □

Walton is very good on Paul Marvell, but his response to Moffatt fails to recognise the character's developing interest in rare and beautiful artefacts. So much does this quality distinguish him from Undine, one wonders what his remaining interest in her is, other than a sentimental tribute to a past involvement. This aesthetic passion is Wharton's affirmation of what America will inevitably need to do with its money. As in the case of Adam Verver in James's *The Golden Bowl*, it will need to acquire things having a value other than the financial. Only then will the money be validated.

According to R.W.B. Lewis:[5]

■ On deeper levels, each of the four main characters bespeaks a portion of Edith Wharton herself and tells us a little more about that complex nature. Ralph Marvell in his musings suggests Edith's growing tenderness toward the vanishing New York she had known, and which now seemed to her to display virtues she was inclined to honor. Marvell also, as it were, embodies Edith's feminine side; Moffatt her masculine side, her immense energy, her decisiveness in action, the vigor of her ironic humor. This aspect had long been recognized by Morton

Fullerton, who addressed her at times as *"Cher ami"*, and Henry James in a commentary would point to a certain masculinity, a toughness of mind, in the very texture of the novel. Edith Wharton's commitment to the traditional French way of life, meanwhile, and her gathering disgust at some of her rootless compatriots as they blundered about in the Old World are voiced in an outburst of articulate rage by Raymond de Chelles.

But the most of Edith Wharton is revealed, quite startlingly, in the characterization of Undine Spragg. No one (except possibly Ethan Frome) would at first glance seem more remote from Edith Wharton than Undine: a crude, unlettered, humorless, artificial, but exceedingly beautiful creature, with the most minimal moral intuitions and virtually no talent whatever for normal human affection. Undine did, undoubtedly, stand for everything in the new American female that Edith despised and recoiled from. But the matter, as it turns out, is much more interesting than that.

There are smaller and larger telltale similarities. As a child Undine, like Edith, enjoyed dressing up in her mother's best finery and "playing lady" before a mirror. Moffatt addresses her by Edith's youthful nickname, "Puss." Edith's long yearning for psychological freedom is queerly reflected in Undine's discovery that each of her marriages is no more than another mode of imprisonment; and Undine's creator allows more than a hint that the young woman is as much a victim as an aggressor amid the assorted snobberies, tedium, and fossilized rules of conduct of American and, even more, French high society. Above all, Undine suggests what Edith Wharton might have been like if, by some dreadful miracle, all her best and most lovable and redeeming features had been suddenly cut away.

So imagined, we see in Undine Spragg how Edith sometimes appeared to the view of the harried and aging Henry James: demanding, imperious, devastating, resolutely indifferent to the needs of others; something like an irresistible force of nature. James's image of Edith as a cyclone is borrowed (Minnie Cadwalader Jones probably showed her the letter) to describe the uproar Undine caused on one occasion, when "everything had gone down before her, as towns and villages went down before one of the tornadoes of her native state." Marvell thinks of his young bride as an eagle, and one has the decided impression of a number of men carried off seriatim, "struggling in her talons." No character Edith Wharton ever invented more closely resembles that bird of prey by which James, Sturgis, and others so often, and only half-jokingly, portrayed Edith herself. Undine Spragg is, so to say, a dark Angel of Devastation: Edith Wharton's anti-self; and like all anti-selves, a figure that explains much about its opposite. □

It is disappointing that this enlightening passage does not face up to the language it finds itself using in the second sentence. New York 'now seemed to display virtues she was inclined to honor' conveys a lack of conviction on Lewis's part, which is surely the echo of Wharton's equal lack. Does it not indicate an absence of central conflict in the novel between what Ralph and Undine respectively represent? Ralph surely needed to have more going for him than Wharton is able to create. Unfortunately, in Louis Auchincloss's words,[6] 'he goes down to speedy ruin before Undine, and his suicide is almost a matter of course. The victim . . . is too naive; one's sympathy is confounded with impatience'. Perhaps Lewis does not go far enough in identifying Undine with Wharton. The Undine who relishes 'all the surface-sparkle and variety of the inexhaustible streets of Paris' in the opening paragraphs of chapter 20, is surely the insatiably consumerist Wharton, of whom James could say: 'She uses up everything and every one either by the extremity of strain or the extremity of neglect'.[7] It is as if the custom of the country is unceasing self-gratification, and Wharton is more than resigned to it, though she asserts her dissociation from Undine, for example in the final pages. The dissociation, however, to return to Leavis's point, can find nothing to attach itself to.

Cynthia Griffin Wolff[8] responds to what she sees as the 'energy' of the novel:

■ The secret of Wharton's most ambitious masterpiece is its perversity, its constant change. It is a difficult and disorienting novel. Reading it, we are challenged always to be mindful of what it is not (not epic, not pure satire, not caricature), constrained always to wonder whether our response has been correct. The relentless forward movement of the work is countered by a tidal undertow. Nothing is fixed. The relationships among the characters shift continuously as fortunes are won and lost, married and divorced. (How often we are tempted to suppose that the cosmopolitan society that fills this fiction is all merely a shadow world and that the substance of the novel is, somehow, really the stock exchange – its "place" really the pit!) Nothing is less certain than the moral relationships among the parti-colored crew, for there is no moral center within the world of this novel, no fixed set of principles according to which we may systematically evaluate its characters. We may sympathize now with one, now with another; but the final judgment of any individual must be ambiguous. The most reliable voice within the novel is that of the Marvells' family friend, Mr. Bowen. Yet even Bowen adopts the tone, almost, of a sociologist. He can tell us certain "facts" about this world, observe the ways in which social arrangements are faulty. But he cannot formulate a code by which to judge the jumble that he observes. Nor does the narrator offer much help in this matter. Following the general pattern, the narrator's vantage shifts – to Undine, momentarily to her parents, to Ralph, occasionally to Moffatt, very often to the position of solemn, impartial spectator. There are no clarifying summations: the language of praise is inconclusively balanced against the language of condemnation.

One thing and only one is genuinely fixed; and that is a preoccupation with energy. Psychic energy – power, assertion, drive, ambition. This, more even than Undine herself, is the subject of the fiction.

The novel is postulated in an era of titanic transition. It is, perhaps, a Götterdämmerung; perhaps it is the triumph of a progressive, pioneering spirit, the dawning of a new age of strength and wisdom. The final verdict has not been rendered when the novel ends, and we cannot tell whether the world is dying or being reborn. We know only the fact of change – the nervous, restless movement that pervades the entire work – and at the heart of this change there is energy. Old orders must pass away. Some have grown enervated, their resources exhausted, the beautiful harmony of their proprieties resounding with a fainter and yet fainter echo. Others have become perverted, their energy misplaced, channeled into the preservation of empty forms whose content has been eroding for decades. By contrast the newcomers radiate energy. Their vitality is manifest in nothing so much as an apparently unending capacity to rebound from defeat, and their vigor thrusts them forward, ever forward; they are the wave of the future, these high-riding buccaneers. They swarm over the globe – never hindered by boundaries of country or continent – and, roaming at will, they plunder the castles of the rich, now become glorious tombs. Often they destroy, unmindful of the value of their spoils; just as often they preserve with a voracious need for beauty that suggests a capacity to become the preservers of the future: we cannot judge what final course these modern barbarians will ultimately follow. The novel is poised precariously upon the moment of change; the values that were revered have been sundered from the force needed to sustain them. This instant in the transition is characterized by an ominous, free-floating residue of power, and the Undine – a creature without a soul – is a perfect and monstrous emblem of the time. *The Custom of the*

Country is a money novel, a business novel, that is true. However, above all, it is a novel of energy, of initiative. □

Wolff's judgement that 'there is no moral center within the world of this novel' takes us back to James's finding the writing 'consistently, almost scientifically satiric'. Much of the rest, however, seems to belong to Wolff's fantasy version of *The Custom of the Country*. Where, for example, does it engage with 'an era of titanic transition' or offer experience which might be identified as a 'Götterdämmerung'? Like Wolff, the first reviewers identified Undine as 'monstrous'. Unlike them, however, we and Wolff need to develop this judgement beyond superficial character study. If Undine is monstrous, should not Wharton be more responsive than she is to this quality? To leave a monstrous character entirely on readers' hands might be thought to be an evasion of authorial responsibility. Wharton might be judged to be not attending sufficiently to possibilities she has created.

Despite Wolff's exclamations about the novel's energy, she colludes with its fatalism:

■ Ralph takes a rather fatalistic view of his accumulated failures. . . . There is a large measure of truth in his conclusion, for the options offered by old New York are limiting indeed. Yet it is equally true that for whatever reason, Ralph has built his life around the most pernicious of these options. He has spent all his emotion in passive fantasy . . . Free and at the same time inevitably shaped by conditions that particularize his life, Ralph is a haunting specter of the terrible possibilities that are latent in his venerable world. □

Why does Wolff need to say 'for whatever reason'? Is it not because Wharton has failed to provide any cause for Ralph's demise other than his fatalism? In this respect the novel might be seen to be endorsing this quality in Ralph rather than objectifying and exploring it. Could Wharton deal with a Ralph who was anything other than fatalistic?

Wolff's case about Undine is that 'possessing the energy needed to conquer life (possessing it even as her counterpart Elmer Moffatt does) she has been debarred from victory by reasons of her sex'. Later Wolff writes:

■ Almost all the men seem more appealing to us than the women: as *psychological* entities, they are more coherently developed and less grotesque. The goal of "everything I can" renders them human and keeps them within the bounds of reality, not spun into impossible, infantile expectations of "everything." However, precisely *because* society has offered them humanizing options and a greater degree of control over their own destiny, it adds a moral dimension to their natures that cannot reasonably be brought to bear upon their consorts. Thus as *moral* entities, the men must be judged to be even more repugnant than the women.

Yes, Moffatt can find the leisure to pity Undine and her multi-fathered son. We must not be misled by such instances of "kindness." When the moment comes to do business, he is as uncomplicatedly ruthless with her as she has ever been with others. And since Moffatt (unlike Undine) *chooses* ruthlessness – having kindness as a possibility within his repertoire – he reveals himself ultimately to be more dangerous and more satanically possessed even than she. □

It seems strange to claim that society offers the men 'humanizing options' when the different options that men have in *The Custom of the Country* are found mainly in the world of business. Wharton does not present this world as humanising, a fact that Wolff's second paragraph, with its reference to Moffatt's business ruthlessness, recognises. Moreover, how can it be said that Undine does not herself choose ruthlessness, for example when she reacts to the telegram about Ralph's illness? It seems that Wolff is too determined to excuse Undine 'by reasons of her sex'. Janet Malcolm,[9] by contrast, finding in Wharton 'a deep pessimism and equally profound misogyny', concludes that with Undine 'Wharton takes her cold dislike of women to a height of venomousness previously unknown in American letters'. 'Reasons of her sex' cannot, at any rate, apply to Undine's failure to achieve an aesthetic sensibility equal to Moffatt's.

Elizabeth Ammons[10] contextualises *The Custom of the Country* as she had contextualised *The House of Mirth*, and again Thorstein Veblen is a key reference point. As Ammons sees it, the novel 'throws a brilliant, satiric light on the institution of marriage, stripping it of all sentiment and sentimentality'. This comment invites the response that since no marriage can exist without some sentiment, the 'light' Ammons describes, if it is Wharton's, must be annihilating rather than satiric. Ammons, however, is concerned to defend Undine:

■ Not Undine Spragg, self-centered and insensitive as she is, but the institution of marriage in the leisure class is the main target of Wharton's satire in *The Custom of the Country*. The point about Undine is that, as something of an outsider and therefore a "naïf," she does not bother with the hypocritical rhetoric that rationalizes marriage – she sees what marriage is rather than what people say it is and she acts on what she sees. Consequently, her behavior and her assimilated values reflect Wharton's criticism less of the parvenu than of the established American upper class, which in her view, as in Veblen's, is looked to as the ideal by all of American culture and thus epitomizes pervasive American attitudes (even if not practices) toward women. That is, Edith Wharton *uses* Undine to reveal her criticism of the attitudes implicit in leisure-class marriage, an institution that has long, and unfortunately, been the envy of women dreaming of freedom but that in fact encourages the husband to assert his autonomy as an international playboy like Peter Van Degen or as a manager in the business world (a financier on Wall Street or a lawyer in a prestigious legal firm) while the wife, expected to be supportive and dependent, must channel her desires for self-assertion into the role of conspicuous consumer for him. Her life, in contrast to her husband's, is by definition parasitic and vicarious. □

To justify the title of her book Ammons has to make large claims. Consequently she needs to find that 'leisure-class marriage' (a rather narrow basis on which to have an 'argument with America') is 'looked to as the ideal by all American culture'. If it is not so regarded (and how could anyone know?), marriage as presented in *The Custom of the Country* has little representative status and certainly cannot be seen as a portrayal of marriage as such. In any case we may wonder if Undine, even implicitly, makes any of the criticisms of marriage summarised by Ammons. Is it not the case that she is perfectly happy in the 'role of conspicuous consumer', provided her various husbands can supply the means? Other than consumption, she has no dream of freedom. Nor is Ralph the kind of husband Ammons describes. Eventually Ammons concedes that:

■ Undine is not admirable, of course. But neither is any other character in *The Custom of the Country*, Raymond de Chelles and Ralph Marvell included. To attribute Ralph's suicide to Undine's Circe-like destructiveness is to ignore the self-pity and fatuous self-sacrifice that motivate it. "He said to himself: 'My wife . . . this will make it all right for her . . .' and a last flash of irony twitched through him" as he pulled the trigger (Wharton's ellipsis). Both Ralph and Undine have been playing the same game of trying to change the other person; put crudely, Ralph is an exceptionally poor loser. Similarly, to deplore Undine's abuse of her son as either an irrelevance or an "acquisition" –

the book plainly encourages sympathy for the boy – should not obscure the fact that she treats him as his beloved stepfather, Raymond, treated her. That by no means excuses her behavior, but it does place it in context. And within the commercial context of this novel Undine's failure as a mother emphasizes Wharton's contention that the social system, much like Wall Street, is designed to promote the success of precisely the most callous, rapacious people. Concern for others and tenderness are weaknesses in the "jungle" of social, no less than economic, competition. (Given Wharton's fondness for mythology, it is likely that she plays with the idea here that the undine, according to myth, can acquire a soul only by marrying a mortal and bearing a child. Wharton's Undine remains soulless even in maternity, suggesting perhaps that the mortal world that insemi- nates her has no soul to bestow. If so, her lack of maternal concern, figuratively as well as sociologically, accentuates the culture's as much as her own inhumanity.) Moreover, even as we recognize that Undine is a terrible mother, we should ask: in this book who, in her own way at the over-solicitous other end of the spectrum, is not? Mrs. Spragg, Mrs. Marvell, and the Marquise de Chelles dote on their children (and look at them: Undine, Ralph, Raymond) with a vested devotion only somewhat less selfish than Undine's neglect of her child. No mother in *The Custom of the Country* would win any awards. □

How significant a 'context' is provided by the claim that Undine is no worse than all the rest? Is it the case that people cannot be better than the society in which they find themselves? Ammons' reading of the novel implies a rather glib determinism. She fails to register the possibility that Wharton herself, in her sympathy for Ralph, might not characterise his suicide as 'fatuous self-sacrifice'. If it is the case that Ammons feels the authorial sympathy for the character is unwarranted, she needs to offer a critical debate about this matter. It hardly needs saying that such a debate would need to go further than suggesting, as Ammons does with reference to Undine's name, that Wharton 'plays' with an 'idea'. Where does the suggestion that Wharton is playing leave her readers?

The notionality of Ralph is an unacknowledged reason for Candace Waid's desperate thesis.[11] Incredibly, given the manifest wealth and vari- ety of American art, it tries to argue that *The Custom of the Country* 'presents a powerful vision of the impossibility of art in America'. Taking her cue from the name Marvell, Waid argues at length for a relationship between Wharton's characterisation of Ralph and the poet Andrew Marvell. Wharton makes no explicit connection between these two figures, but Waid suggests that 'in describing Ralph Marvell, Wharton often seems to experience a "releasing power of language" that is directly informed by Andrew Marvell's poems'. The particular poems Waid cites are 'The Garden', 'The Unfortunate Lover', and 'The Gallery'. Her argument is too detailed to summarise, but unconvincing for all its detail. If Andrew Marvell is to make any kind of contribution to the characterisation of Ralph, we surely need some sense in the novel of how Wharton sees the poet for himself and with respect to the character she is creating. It cannot be left to readers to happen upon 'The Gallery' and claim, as Waid does, that its fourth stanza 'could be read as an account of Ralph Marvell's spiritual death'. What validity could such an authorial expectation of readers have, especially as any association of Ralph with Andrew Marvell diminishes Ralph as a characterisation? A single line from 'The Garden' ('When we have run our Passions heat') reveals only one dimension of a generality and complexity of experience commanded by the English poet, but quite beyond Ralph's and Wharton's range.

Deborah Ann MacComb[12] places the novel in the context of Wharton's own divorce from her husband of nearly twenty-eight years, in the year the novel was published. She develops this context to provide so much information about the 'divorce industry', that we may wonder why the novel matters to her, except as another collection of data. Wharton, she insists, is arguing that:

■ . . . the logic of consumption and disposal being urged in contemporary advertising schemes extends most insidiously into the home, where familial relations that transmit identity, continuity, and tradition are similarly at risk of being "unmade." To her already potent critique of the marriage market, Wharton adds the role that the booming divorce industry plays by creating a product – marketed in terms of the increased freedom, mobility, and status it can provide – that keeps the marriage economy expanding because spouses and even families become disposable items in the rotary system of consumption. Yet, like so many advertising promises, the benefits to be secured by a quick trip to a western divorce mill proved illusory, for this legal remedy neither liberated women from the marriage economy nor advanced their fortunes within it. Rather, the divorce industry functioned as an extension of that economy by recycling women back onto the marriage market after exacting from them both their time and money. □

No matter what the validity of these arguments in themselves, they seem to be at a considerable remove from the novel. Why, moreover, is it only women who are recycled 'back onto the marriage market'? MacComb concludes:

■ One could well read *The Custom of the Country* – especially in the light of Wharton's fear that scandal might attach itself to her divorce – as an attempt to proclaim through Undine's despicable career her own alienation from 'the system' that produced and even profited by such monsters. Yet as a public document that in some way replicates the appeal contained in the private bundle of papers left to her biographer, *The Custom of the Country* participates in the process Wharton rejected, becoming an advertisement – renewed in her subsequent divorce novels *The Age of Innocence*, *The Mother's Recompense*, and *The Children* – that announced her fundamental difference from 'the invaders' and asserted her place in the old order from which she had seemed divorced. Although she proclaims an alliance with the 'real' of the old guard, the 'real' is presented in the commercial form of a book and with a character whose self-bartering figures what Wharton and her publishers will attempt to do with that book. Affirming the old pieties, Wharton cannot avoid suggesting her implication in the new – cannot dent her ties to self-advertisement even as she eschews publication of her private acts. □

Like Ammons, MacComb says things about the novel we may infer its author would not agree with. Whatever Wharton's reservations about Undine, her manifest amusement in the character is surely not registered by the phrase 'Undine's despicable career'. Nor is it the case that Wharton is caught in the contradiction MacComb outlines. To barter the self, as Undine does, is not the same as Wharton and her publishers bartering a novel.

As we near the end of the twentieth century it seems that critics of *The Custom of the Country*, in their compulsion to interpret and contextualise, are hardly bothering with the essential function of criticism, which is to explore the quality of the writing. All of Wharton's treatment of Ralph Marvell still needs considering, so that readers might have a clear understanding of what the author's investment in him and his world is. Similarly, we need to ask what depth and coherence there is to the characterisation of Undine. Several striking things are said about her: she is 'always doubling and twisting on herself' (chapter 1) and is at once 'fiercely independent and yet passionately imitative' (chapter 2); she 'might have been some fabled creature whose home was in a beam of light' (chapter 2); she is 'Venus-like' (chapter 7), 'some warrior Queen' (chapter 8), 'Ariel-like' (chapter 11), 'a startled Diana' (chapter 29); always Ralph is aware of 'the overwhelming fact of her beauty' (chapter 32). How do these pronouncements relate to the suggestions of her name and aid an understanding of her actions? Does not her hysteria over her pregnancy momentarily suggest a degree of inner disturbance which Wharton needed to develop? Whether even a beautiful young woman, so incapable of affection, let alone love, would get the consideration from others Undine receives may strike us as doubtful.

CHAPTER FIVE

The Age of Innocence (1920): The Writing of the Novel and the Contemporary Reviews

A CCORDING TO R.W.B. Lewis[1] the immediate motivation for *The Age of Innocence* began in April 1919, when Wharton received an offer of $18,000 from the editor of *Pictorial Review* for the serial rights to her next novel. It was an offer inaugurating her reign as one of the leading money-makers among contemporary authors, though it arrived when her writing of *The Glimpses of the Moon*, published in 1922, had ground to a halt. In response she proposed *A Son at the Front*, eventually published in 1923, but its war material was not what *Pictorial Review* wanted. Abandoning these two novels, Wharton proposed another. In Lewis's words:

■ . . . it bore the title 'Old New York' and the scene was laid in 1875. The two main characters, Langdon Archer and Clementine Olenska, are both unhappily married. Falling in love, they 'go off secretly', Edith explained, 'and meet in Florida where they spend a few mad weeks' before Langdon returns to his pretty, conventional wife in New York, and Clementine to an existence separated from her brutish husband in Paris. □

Lewis tells us that serialisation of the novel began in the monthly *Pictorial Review*, 'flanked by advertisements for soap flakes and "Sani-flush" for cleaning toilet bowls, in July 1920'. In book form it was more respectfully treated, and there was lavish advertising announcing Wharton as the greatest woman novelist in America. Sales were very good, and Wharton's high reputation seemed to be confirmed when *The*

Age of Innocence was awarded the Pulitzer Prize in May 1921. Actually the jury had chosen Sinclair Lewis's *Main Street* (1920), but this novel had caused some offence, so the trustees of Columbia University, the sponsors of the prize, took it upon themselves to overrule the jury and substitute Wharton's novel.

In a letter of 12 December 1920 to her close friend, the art critic Bernard Berenson, Wharton emphasised how she wanted *The Age of Innocence* 'not to be taken as a "costume piece" but as a "simple & grave" story of two people trying to live up to something that was still "felt in the blood" at that time'.[2] Any tendency to treat the novel as a 'costume piece' might, however, derive justification from her mood and feelings towards her native land after the First World War. Lewis tells us that she had remarked that:

■ '. . . the face of the world is changing so rapidly that the poor novelist is left breathless and mute, unless like Mr. Wells, he can treat things "topically", which I never could'. With *The Age of Innocence* under way, and with a clearer sense of her own creative situation, she held forth to Berenson on the relation between the Great War and the writing of fiction, saying (in Berenson's paraphrase):

> Before the war you could write fiction without indicating the period, the present being assumed. The war put an end to that for a long time, and everything will soon have to be timed with reference to it. In other words, the historical novel with all its vices will be the only possible form of fiction.

She was in addition revolted by what she could see of postwar America, and the impression grew in her that something crucially valuable had been lost. The spurt of patriotic emotion aroused by American troops marching down the Champs Elysées had quite subsided, and if she turned against Paris, it was in good part, as we have noticed, because of the hordes of Americans darkening the scene by their noisy persistent presence. She was becoming acquainted, she told Elsina Tyler, with 'the new American cad', and discoursed scathingly about two visiting members of a New York refuge committee, each in her view a worse bounder than the other. Her country's retreat into isolationism was a further cause of disgust.

> I say nothing about what you say of public affairs [she wrote the equally horrified Sally Norton] except that I agree with you on

every point, and am humiliated to the soul at being what is known
as an 'American'. All that I thought American in a true sense is
gone, and I see nothing but vain-glory, crassness, and total ignorance – which of course is the core of the whole evil.

Impelled by such angry and despairing sentiments, Edith Wharton
went in search, imaginatively, of the America that was gone. Looking
across the vast abyss of the war, she located the lost America in the
New York of her girlhood: the New York she had come back to in
1872, after six years in Europe; the world in which she had passed her
adolescence and the first years of her womanhood – a safe, narrow,
unintellectual, and hidebound world, but from the tremendous distance of time and history, an endearing and an honourable one. It was
there that she set the main action of *The Age of Innocence*. □

What were the 'vices' of the historical novel for Wharton? The form has
many virtues especially if, as in the case of Hawthorne, George Eliot and
Hardy, the account of the past is also an engagement with the present
and, thereby, the very opposite of an evasive retreat from one's time.
Lewis's account of Wharton suggests such a retreat by her, and *The Age of
Innocence* may confirm it. Admittedly, the war was, as Lewis puts it, a
'vast abyss', and securities needed to be re-found. New York of 1872,
however, far from re-appearing across 'the tremendous distance of time
and history' (it was only fifty years away!) might be a security too seduc-
tively available to Wharton. Her reflection on *The Age of Innocence* in *A
Backward Glance* (1934) suggests as much. In chapter 14, part 4, of the
later book she recalls her spirit 'heavy' with 'losses' after the war. She
wanted to express her feelings in *A Son at the Front*, 'but before I could
deal objectively with the stored-up emotions of those years, I had to get
away from the present altogether'. She continues:

■ I found a momentary escape in going back to my childish memories
of a long-vanished America, and wrote 'The Age of Innocence'. I
showed it chapter by chapter to Walter Berry; and when he had
finished reading it he said: 'Yes, it's good. But of course you and I are
the only people who will ever read it. We are the last people left who
can remember New York and Newport as they were then, and nobody
else will be interested.'
    I secretly agreed with him as to the chances of the book's success;
but it 'had its fate', and that was to be one of my rare best-sellers! □

Few critics quote this passage, and one wonders if this omission is because of the phrase 'childish memories'. Wharton is nothing if not verbally exact, and it must be significant that she does not write 'childhood memories'. As Wharton looks back on *The Age of Innocence* in the 1930s, does not 'childish' suggest a relegation, in her eyes, of its significance?

When it was published she must, however, have been pleased by the first of the reviews we shall refer to:[3]

■ A new novel by Edith Wharton is by way of being an event in the literary calendar, and in this absorbing tale the almost metallic brilliance, which in *The House of Mirth* dazzled the reading public, hypnotizes the eager eye which would not lose one significant word. New York society in the '70s – the cynically christened "Age of Innocence" – is painted with Meissonier-like clarity of detail, beginning with vast Catherine Mingott, ruler of a great family of fashionables, down to her slim, pale grand-daughter, Countess Olenska, wife of a Polish roué, seeking sanctuary with her New York kin, who prove not always kind. From the opening opera night at the old red-hung Academy of Music, with Nilsson singing Marguerite in *Faust*, the scenes of luxury, black walnut, smug hypocrisy, formal festivities, and rampant family virtue continue in perfect sequence. Little help in such a *milieu* for young Newland Archer, who, having married a handsome white and gold débutante of regulation inexperience, finds himself appallingly and passionately in love with her cousin, the dark, seductive Countess. Again and again, the apparent artlessness of the young wife scores as if by accident; thru her, backed by the solid phalanx of family, respectability triumphs and the smooth surface of convention is never punctured, tho all New York relishingly infers that which never really came to pass.

The plot is unobvious, delicately developed, with a fine finale that exquisitely satisfies one's sense of fitness, and as always with Mrs. Wharton, the drama of character is greater than that of event. One revels recognizingly in her clean-cut distinction of style, the inerrant aptness of adjectives, the vivisective phrase. No wonder that in the letters of Henry James his admiration for his dazzling disciple finds expression; she has a more human touch, a more vivacious humor. And in the closing scene her pen dwells lingeringly on the Paris she loves, rich in that warm atmosphere of beauty and art which New York of the '70s so crudely and coldly lacked. □

Here the novel is accepted entirely on its own terms. 'Metallic brilliance' and 'cynically', however, are worth a pause for thought. They take us back to Henry James's comment that in *The Custom of the Country* Wharton was 'consistently, almost scientifically satiric'. They might suggest authorial disengagement, allowing Wharton, from 'the Paris she loves', to condescend and simplify. Throughout the novel, for example, one of her too easy presumptions is that opera and theatre were mere social occasions in 1870s New York, nothing that was performed in that city at that time having a significant effect on anyone.

William Lyon Phelps[4] also greeted the novel with praise. In his view:

■ Mrs. Wharton's admirable career is a progression from the external to the internal; she began as a decorator and is now an analyst. She has always been an expert in gardens and in furniture. Her first book was called *Decoration of Houses*, written in 1897 with O. Codman, and in 1904 she produced a work on Italian villas and their gardens. These studies of interior decorating and landscape gardening are much in evidence in her novels; I do not remember when I have read a work of fiction that gives the reader so vivid an idea of the furnishing and illuminating of rooms in fashionable houses as one will find in *The Age of Innocence*. □

Remembering when *The Age of Innocence* was written, it is worth responding to Phelps with words from Virginia Woolf's landmark, 'Mr Bennett and Mrs Brown' (1924).[5] Wanting to write novels which engaged the twentieth century, Woolf remarked:

■ how serious a matter it is when tools of one generation are useless for the next. . . .

That is what I mean by saying that the Edwardian tools are the wrong ones for us to use. They have laid an enormous stress upon the fabric of things. They have given us a house in the hope that we may be able to deduce the human beings who live there. □

May we apply Woolf's criticism to what Phelps praises in *The Age of Innocence*?

Over one matter Phelps is in disagreement with Wharton:

■ Like her idol and master, Henry James, she is forever comparing America with Europe, to the latter's advantage. I have no quarrel with her on this score, for, after all, it is simply a matter of taste, so far as questions of art are concerned; but it is only occasionally in this latest book that the direct comparison is made. Describing a hot day in Boston:

Archer found a cab and drove to the Somerset Club for breakfast. Even the fashionable quarters had the air of untidy domesticity to which no excess of heat ever degrades the European cities.

It is a matter of no importance, but I do not believe that statement to be true. I should not like to compare my knowledge of Europe with hers; Mrs. Wharton has either missed city scenes in Europe in the dog days, or has shut her eyes. □

Phelps's quotation is from the second paragraph of chapter 23. He is right to expose Wharton's prejudice on behalf of Europe, but he might have broadened the charge by referring to the chapter's first paragraph. There we read:

■ The streets near the station were full of the smell of beer and coffee and decaying fruit, and a shirt-sleeved populace moved through them with the intimate abandon of boarders going down the passage to the bath-room. □

The merely snobbish exception this takes to 'a shirt-sleeved populace' on a hot day in Boston might be considered a severe handicap for a twentieth-century novelist. It makes all the more debatable Phelps's conclusion at the end of this next paragraph:

■ New York society and customs in the seventies are described with an accuracy that is almost uncanny; to read these pages is to live again. The absolute imprisonment in which her characters stagnate, their artificial and false standards, the desperate monotony of trivial routine, the slow petrifaction of generous ardours, the paralysis of emotion, the accumulation of ice around the heart, the total loss of life in uphol-stered existence – are depicted with a high excellence that never falters. And in the last few pages the younger generation comes in like fresh air. Mrs. Wharton is all for the new and against the old; here, at all events, here sympathies are warm. She would never, like Solness, fear youth knocking at the door. The two young women of the story are contrasted in a manner that is of the essence of drama without being in the least artificial. The radiantly beautiful young wife might have had her way without a shadow on it, were it not for the appear-ance of the Countess Olenska, who is, what the other women are not, a personality. Newland Archer, between these two women, and loved by both, is not at all to be envied. The love scenes between him and

Ellen are wonderful in their terrible, inarticulate passion; it is curious how much more real they are than the unrestrained detailed descriptions thought by so many writers to be "realism." Here is where Mrs. Wharton resembles Joseph Conrad and Henry James, for the love scenes in this book are fully worthy of those two men of genius. So little is said, so little is done, yet one feels the infinite passion in the finite hearts that burn. □

This summary of Wharton's presentation of New York society is unchallengeable, but given his point in the previous quotation how can Phelps conclude that 'Wharton is all for the new and against the old'? Later he finds 'the love scenes' between Archer and Ellen Olenska 'wonderful in their terrible, inarticulate passions. . . . Here is where Mrs. Wharton resembles Joseph Conrad and Henry James'. He concludes by suggesting it is an anachronism for Wharton to have Archer reading Maupassant. Phelps believes the French writer's work only appeared in New York in the early Eighties.

The review, 'An Elder America',[6] tells us:

■ Mrs. Wharton has never ranged herself with the prophets, contented, apparently, with being the most intellectual of our novelists and surveying with level, satirical eyes the very visible world. By the "Age of Innocence" she means the seventies in New York during the past century, and the innocence she finds there is "the innocence that seals the mind against imagination and the heart against experience." To the hotter attacks which angrier critics have recently been making upon that age she does not lend herself. Her language is cool and suave. And yet the effect of her picture is an unsparing accusation of that genteel decade when the van der Luydens of Skuytercliff were the ultimate arbiters of "form" in Manhattan, and "form" was occupation and religion for the little aristocracy which still held its tight fortress in the shaggy city so soon about to overwhelm it. The imminence of the rising tide is never quite indicted. How could it be, when the characters of the action themselves do not see it, bound up as they are with walking their wintry paths and hugging their iron taboos? Newland Archer suspects a change, but that is because he is a victim of the tribal order which sentences him to a life without passion, without expression, without satisfaction. The Countess Olenska suspects it, but she too is a victim, too fine for the rougher give-and-take of her husband's careless European society and yet not conventional enough for the dull routine which in her native New York covers the fineness to which also she is native. The peculiar tragedy of their sacrifice is that it is for the sake of a person, Archer's wife, who is virtuous because she is incapable of temptation, competent because she is incapable of any deep perturbation, and willing to suit herself to the least decorum of their world because she is incapable of understanding that there is anywhere anything larger or freer. The unimaginative not only miss the flower of life themselves but they shut others from it as well.

Mrs. Wharton's structure and methods show no influence of the impressionism now broadening the channel of fiction; she does not avoid one or two touches of the florid in her impassioned scenes; she rounds out her story with a reminiscent chapter which forces in the note of elegy where it only partially belongs. But *The Age of Innocence* is a masterly achievement.

Mrs. Wharton's triumph is that she had described these rites and surfaces and burdens as familiarly as if she loved them and as lucidly as if she hated them. □

'Mrs Wharton has never ranged herself with the prophets . . .'. If true, and it would seem to be, this observation might indicate a limitation in Wharton, which is related to the novel's lack of engagement with the 'rising tide' of later nineteenth-century and early-twentieth century forces. The limitation cannot be attributed entirely to the characters, for Wharton herself could have maintained a perspective different from theirs. Her failure to do so might indicate her own narrowness of view. It determines that Archer and Ellen each be a 'victim' of their time, because Wharton herself cannot face the complication of energising them with any other status. Whether authorial victimisation amounts to 'tragedy' is the question we also ask in relation to Lily Bart and Ralph Marvell. Why does Wharton so recurrently invoke victimisation, if it is not to simplify? The reviewer's last point about love and hate is very perceptive, but this authorial dilemma is also shared by Newland Archer. By 1920 we might have expected Wharton herself to have moved out of its imprisonment.

Henry Seidel Canby[7] anticipates some of the above critical moves:

■ The only objection I have ever heard urged against Mrs. Wharton's fine art of narrative is that it is narrow – an art of dress suit and sophistication. And this book is the answer. For, of course, her art is narrow – like Jane Austen's, like Sheridan's, like Pope's, like Maupassant's, like that of all writers who prefer to study human nature in its most articulate instead of its best or its broadest manifestations. It is narrow because it is focussed, but this does not mean that it is small. The story of *The Age of Innocence* could be set in a far broader background. It is the circumstances of the New York society which Mrs. Wharton knows so well that give it a piquancy, a reality that "epics" lack. They are like the accidents of voice, eye, gesture which determine individuality. But her subject is America.

This treating of large themes by highly personal symbols makes possible Mrs. Wharton's admirable perfection of technique. Hers is the technique of sculpture rather than the technique of architecture. It permits the fine play of a humor that has an eye of irony in it, but is more human than irony. It makes possible an approach to perfection. . . . □

Canby is using a broad brush, and readers must make up their own minds as to whether the other writers mentioned in this paragraph are narrow. His conclusion that Wharton's 'subject is America' is based entirely on his review's opening insistence that 'America is a land of cherished illusions'. Which land isn't?

Our first English review[8] considers the novel in relation to the end of the recent war:

■ Mrs. Wharton's new book, her first "full-length" novel for some years, is perhaps a sign of the times. When the war broke in upon the settled, accepted "present day" of the novelists, it was easy to foresee the predicament in which they would find themselves before long. Since 1914 there has been no present day, in the old sense. Now we must know from the start whether we are dealing with the world before or during or since the war, and the action must be precisely timed; any and every novel, in other words, is bound to be now "historic." And since it is a hazardous venture to set about treating very recent times historically – it needs a great deal of information or a great deal of assurance to move upon that *cineri doloso* – it was probable that a writer like Mrs. Wharton, critical of the impressions of life, should hesitate to use the crude new material of 1920, while it is still daily shifting and cracking before our eyes. And so she goes back – back to the old world, and far enough into it to make the action of her story openly historic; she goes as far back as the early seventies, in fact, and to that New York of the early seventies which is now so much more remote, as it happens, than even our own past of that day, over here. Changes of the same general kind we too have seen, no doubt, but nothing to compare in extent with the change that has turned New York, socially speaking, from a trim and substantial old family mansion to a resounding, glittering, promiscuous monster hotel.

The old family mansion is more than a picturesque background for a story, though it is that too. But it is also a story in itself, or it very easily makes one, with the elaborately composed artificiality of the life that was led there. □

The major work of many writers contemporary with, but younger than, Wharton is conditioned by the First World War and its aftermath. If *The Age of Innocence* is to be considered major, its obliviousness and imperviousness to the war may need more justification than this review provides. Whether New York ever was entirely as Wharton presents it, in the reviewer's words 'a trim and substantial old family mansion', is also debatable. Was it not always a developing city necessarily riven by conflicting energies, for example in Melville's 'Bartleby, The Scrivener' (1853) and in James's 'The Jolly Corner' (1903)?

The review continues:

■ Ellen is exquisite, and she and Archer are both of them much too intelligent to underrate the virtue and the dignity of the forces opposed to them; the old order, in its way, is perfectly just and reasonable, its standards are honourable; two intelligent beings can only in the end respect them. And so the historic setting of the story has made the story – made it by being just what it is, strong and fine, ripely matured and absolutely sure of itself.

That is the plan of the book, and Mrs. Wharton covers it in a manner that hardly leaves an opening for criticism. It is admirably packed; the action is clear against its background, and at the same time the background, the good family party with its perfect manners, is never a mere decoration, it takes its proper place as an essential matter in the story. It does so, at any rate, very soon; for just at first Mrs. Wharton does not quite meet the besetting difficulty of these historic studies. If you are to present what is called a "picture of the times," how are you to keep the centre of interest in your drama? The interest, if you are not very careful, falls back into the romantic or the ironic evocation of the past, and the drama is overshadowed. Necessarily Mrs. Wharton's evocation is ironic – one *must* be ironic about the seventies, they are already too far and not yet far enough to be treated otherwise – and the balance of the tone, that amusing old New York on one side, this difficult drama on the other, is insecure for a time. But it rights itself, and the slight confusion is soon forgotten, and everything goes firmly and lightly, and altogether Mrs. Wharton has accomplished one of the best pieces of her work so far.

As for her picture of the times, how is any of us over here to criticize it, beyond saying that it is full of vivacity and of character and of colour, and that there is not a point in it which *seems* to be false? (A few small anachronisms of fact are of no consequence in such things; but we interject that even the most advanced young people could not have been reading books by Vernon Lee or Huysmans or M. Paul Bourget in the early seventies.) □

Here the reviewer's comment about the insecurity of Wharton's balance of tone is arresting, and we may want to make more of it. The reviewer argues that Wharton '*must* be ironic', but why this compulsion if, as the reviewer insists, old New York is 'perfectly just and reasonable, its standards . . . honourable', its qualities 'strong and fine, [and] ripely matured'? If Wharton genuinely believes this of old New York, on behalf of what need she be ironic at its expense? The irony can only be insecure and superficial, since she has no values to offer other than the ones apparently ironised.

Our second English review[9] is not so persuaded by the values of Wharton's New York:

■ For many English readers this delightful novel will be a revelation of the depths which can be sounded by international ignorance. Gentlemen of unbounded leisure and a taste for commercial probity which amounts to a disease, ladies combining the angel and the bore in a measure beyond the dreams even of Thackeray, troops of obsequious and efficient white domestics! Not such are the inhabitants whom most of us have mentally assigned to New York – at any stage of that city's existence. But Mrs. Wharton abundantly demonstrates that this state of things obtained only in a very limited circle, to a degree inconceivable by older and more corrupt civilizations. A happy circle it cannot well be called, since to assert that happiness may be compatible with dullness is to state a contradiction in terms; by rights it should not be attractive any more than happy, but the author contrives to make it so, partly no doubt through the easy laughter called forth by its patently ludicrous standards, but partly also from admiration for the finer element contained in them. □

What 'the finer element' is remains unspecified. We have no way of knowing, therefore, how Wharton's New York recovers from the reviewer's charges that it was 'very limited' and replete with 'dullness' and 'ludicrous standards'.

K[atherine] M[ansfield][10] initially praises Wharton's balance of irony and romance: 'To keep these two balanced by all manner of delicate adjustments is so much a matter for her skilful hand that it seems more like play than work'. Soon, however, her impatience with the novel surfaces:

■ But what about us? What about her readers? Does Mrs. Wharton expect us to grow warm in a gallery where the temperature is so sparklingly cool? We are looking at portraits – are we not? These are human beings arranged for exhibition purposes, framed, glazed and hung in the perfect light. They pale, they grow paler, they flush, they raise their "clearest eyes," they hold out their arms to each other, "extended, but not rigid," and the voice is the voice of the portrait:

"'What's the use – when you will go back?' he broke out, a great hopeless *How on earth can I keep you?* crying out to her beneath his words."

Is it – in this world – vulgar to ask for more? To ask that the feeling shall be greater than the cause that excites it, to beg to be allowed to share the moment of exposition (is not that the very moment that all our writing leads to?), to entreat a little wildness, a dark place or two in the soul?

We appreciate fully Mrs. Wharton's skill and delicate workmanship; she has the situation in hand from the first page to the last; we realize how savage must sound our cry of protest, and yet we cannot help but make it; that after all we are not above suspicion – even the "finest" of us! □

Vernon L. Parrington, Jr.,[11] takes Mansfield's challenge further, beginning with an excellent assessment of Wharton and her latest novel:

■ The note of distinction is as natural to Edith Wharton as it is rare in our present day literature. She belongs to the "quality," and the grand manner is hers by right of birth. She is as finished as a Sheraton sideboard, and with her poise, grace, high standards, and perfect breeding, she suggests as inevitably old wine and slender decanters. The severe ethical code which Puritanism has bequeathed to her, and the keen intellect which has made her a critical analyst, increase her native distinction; and the irony that plays lambently over her commentary, adds piquancy to her art. She belongs to an earlier age, before a strident generation had come to deny the excellence of standards. No situation which she has conceived in her novels is so ironical as the situation in which she herself is placed; shaken out of an unquestioned acceptance of the aristocratic world to which she belongs, she turns her keen analysis upon her environment, and satirizes what in her heart she loves most.

The Age of Innocence is perfect Whartonian. It is historical satire done with immaculate art, but though she laughs at the deification of "form" by the van der Luydens of Skuytercliff, and the tyranny of their rigid social taboos, she loves them too well to suffer them to be forgotten by a careless generation. She has painted them at full length, to hang upon our walls, where they lend historical dignity to the background of the present and utter a silent reproof to our scrambling vulgarities. New York society of the eighteen seventies, with its little clan of first families that gently simmers in its own dullness – it would be inelegant to say stews – provides a theme that exactly suits Mrs. Wharton's talent. She delights in the make-believe of the clan, in "the Pharisaic voice of a society wholly absorbed in barricading itself against the unpleasant," and she half regrets an age whose innocence "seals the mind against imagination and the heart against experience." She herself, of course, will not defend herself against reality by a decorous denial, but she likes too well many things in that world to be harsh or angry with it. □

She 'satirizes what in her heart she loves most'. This paradox, if true, surely explains Wharton's inability to reach out to a world wider than the one she apparently mocks. Warming to his thesis, Parrington continues:

■ There are no scenes, no vulgar jealousies or accusations, nothing to offend the finest sensibility. A few frank phrases sound almost startling in their context of reticent pretense, but they do not really startle. The book unwinds slowly, somewhat meagerly, with much analysis and little vivacity of conversation. In an environment of dull and selfish respectability, how could there be vivacity; with no ideas, no spontaneity, no intellectual sincerity, it is idle to expect vivacity. The formal routine and hinting gossip wrap themselves like a boa constrictor about the characters and squeeze the naturalness out of them. Nevertheless the story never lags and is never dull. The skill with which dulness is made interesting is a triumph of art.

But when one has said that the craftsmanship is a very great success, why not go further and add that it doesn't make the slightest difference whether one reads the book or not, unless one is a literary epicure who lives for the savor of things. What do the van der Luydens matter to us; or what did they or their kind matter a generation ago? Why waste such skill upon such insignificant material? There were vibrant realities in the New York of the seventies, Commodore Vanderbilt, for example, or even Jay Gould or Jim Fiske. If Mrs. Wharton had only chosen to throw such figures upon her canvas, brutal, cynical, dominating, what a document of American history – but the suggestion is foolish. Mrs. Wharton could not do it. Her distinction is her limitation. She loathes the world of Jim Fiske too much to understand it. She is too well bred to be a snob, but she escapes it only by sheer intelligence. The background of her mind, the furniture of her habits, are packed with potential snobbery, and it is only by scrupulous care that it is held in leash. She is unconsciously shut in behind plate glass, where butlers serve formal dinners, and white shoulders go up at the mere suggestion of everyday gingham. She belongs in spite of herself to the caste which she satirizes, and she cannot make herself at home in households where the mother washes the dishes and the father tends the furnace. If she had lived less easily, if she had been forced to skimp and save and plan, she would have been a greater and richer artist, more significant because more native, more continental. But unfortunately her doors open only to the smart set; the windows from which she surveys life open only to the east, to London, Paris, Rome. She is one of our cosmopolitans, flitting lightly about and at ease with all who bear titles. And this the stay-at-home American secretly resents. What are titles to him, and for that matter, what are the vulgar rich of New York? Let the newspapers exploit them, for that becomes their vulgarity. But for Mrs. Wharton to spend her talents upon rich nobodies is no less than sheer waste. □

Parrington's assertion that Wharton's material does not matter, either in its own time or later, needs to be answered by anyone making a claim for the novel. That there were 'vibrant realities in the New York of the seventies' and that these are ignored by Wharton is surely irrefutable. Parrington concludes:

■ With her ripe culture, her clear and clean intelligence, her classical spirit, her severe standards and austere ethics, Mrs. Wharton is our outstanding literary aristocrat. She has done notable things, but she has paid a great price in aloofness from her own America. There is more hope for our literature in the honest crudities of the younger naturalists, than in her classic irony; they at least are trying to understand America as it is. "You'll never amount to anything, any of you, till you roll up your sleeves and get right down into the muck," commented the one plebeian in the book to Newland Archer, who "mentally shrugged his shoulders and turned the conversation to books." Mrs. Wharton too often mentally shrugs her shoulders over America. That she should ever roll up her sleeves and get down into the muck is unthinkable. □

By the time we get to the last sentence, we may judge that Parrington has said enough in its justification, even though it is not an absolute requirement that a novelist should 'get down into the muck'. Similar charges to Parrington's have been levelled against Henry James, especially against his last novels. Referring only to *The Ambassadors* (1903), one would respond with its exploration of the nature of meaning as it dramatises the interrelationships of Americans and Europeans in an emerging twentieth century, when American energy is beginning to rewrite all the rules. What of equivalent weight could one say on Wharton's behalf?

CHAPTER SIX

The Age of Innocence: The Critical Response

YVOR WINTERS' response to *The Age of Innocence*[1] is part of his consideration of Henry James. As Winters sees it, the inevitable result of James's defective knowledge of American life and manners was that he 'sought to study the ethical judgement of his time and nation in the purest essence to which he could distil it'. Turning to Wharton, Winters argues that:

■ In such a book as *The Age of Innocence*, Mrs Wharton shows us a group of characters whose actions are governed according to the same ethical history and principles which I have mentioned in connection with James. But the characters are living in a society cognate and coterminous with those principles; the society with its customs and usages is the external form of the principles. Now the customs and usages may become unduly externalized, and when they appear so to become, Mrs Wharton satirizes them; but in the main they represent the concrete aspect of the abstract principles of behaviour. Thus when Newland Archer and the Countess Olenska are on the point of eloping, one of the strongest incentives to their withdrawal is the fact that they will be forced into a mode of life of a bohemian and disorderly sort which must inevitably degrade their love in their own eyes; and this incentive is essentially serious, for the usages which they are unwilling to abandon are the embodiments of serious principles; whereas the usages which they are unwilling to adopt represent a weak falling away from those principles. In this way Mrs Wharton gives a greater precision to her moral issues than James is able to achieve, for James endeavours, as I have said, to isolate from the manners which might have given it concreteness a moral sense which is already isolated by history from the ideas which gave rise to it. □

There is obviously a more complicated case to be made for James than is made here, and Winters goes on to make some of it. One line of argument would be to say that Wharton's 'greater precision' with 'her moral issues' derives from greater simplicity; for example, in the way she contrasts New York and Europe in *The Age of Innocence*. In *The Ambassadors* (1903) James is altogether more subtle with Woollet and Paris. Nor is precision always Wharton's strength. What are the 'abominations' of Europe referred to by Ellen Olenska in chapter 24? What are the 'serious principles' of New York Winters adduces, and where are they shown by Wharton to be life-enhancing?

Writing at the same time as Winters, Edmund Wilson[2] rather relegates the novel in that he sees it as Wharton's 'valedictory':

■ The theme is closely related to those of *The House of Mirth* and *Ethan Frome*: the frustration of a potential pair of lovers by social or domestic obstructions. But setting it back in the generation of her parents, she is able to contemplate it now without quite the same rancour, to soften it with a poetic mist of distance. And yet even here the old impulse of protest still makes itself felt as the main motive. . . . one still feels an active resentment against the pusillanimity of the provincial group and also, as in other of her books, a special complaint against the timid American male who has let the lady down.

Up through *The Age of Innocence*, and recurring at all points of her range from *The House of Mirth* to *Ethan Frome*, the typical masculine figure in Edith Wharton's fiction is a man set apart from his neighbours by education, intellect, and feeling, but lacking the force or the courage either to impose himself or to get away. She generalizes about this type in the form in which she knew it best in her autobiographical volume: 'They combined a cultivated taste with marked social gifts', she says; but 'their weakness was that, save in a few cases, they made little use of their ability': they were content to 'live in dilettantish leisure', rendering none of 'the public services that a more enlightened social system would have exacted of them'. But she had described a very common phenomenon of the America of after the Civil War. □

Lawrence Selden and Ralph Marvell in the two novels already discussed, together with Newland Archer in *The Age of Innocence*, exemplify this phenomenon, and perhaps it was as common as Wharton and Wilson claim. Wharton's account of these characters, in other words, might be justified by history. Even so, when we get to *The Age of Innocence*, we might conclude that Wharton is becoming complacently repetitive in her characterisation of her leading men, especially as at least two others (Stephen Glennard in *The Touchstone* (1900) and George Darrow in *The Reef* (1912)) also fit the bill. Suppose any one of these men had embodied some real force. The supposition is surely not unwarrantable, but if Wharton had realised it her formulas about New York could not have been so simply maintained. As things stand, her 'active resentment against the pusillanimity of the provincial group' might seem, contrary to Wilson, an authorial self-indulgence, an easy having-it-both-ways; resenting a group for the lack of the energies she has predetermined it should not have. The man who cannot rise to the woman's occasion has been castrated by the author before he enters the novel.

V. S. Pritchett[3] presents a more complicated case than Wilson's:

■ Again and again we find that novelists who have attacked the conventions because they stultify the spirit, who attack the group for its cruelty to individuals, will end by pointing the virtues of submission. Mrs Wharton may have hated old New York, but she hated the new New York even more. She disliked the prison of silent hypocrisy, but she drew in her skirts when candour came in. Especially after her long life *en grande luxe* in Europe. What indignation denounces creeps back in the name of sentiment. *The Age of Innocence* shows a man giving in, loyally marrying the conventional girl he does not love, throwing over the Europeanised woman who is his natural equal. It is the surrender to the established bourgeois standard. No great harm comes of it; only dullness and disappointment. The sweet young girl he was engaged to was slyer than he thought. She became like her mother-in-law to whose face 'a lifelong mastery over trifles had given factitious authority'. Perhaps, after all, her husband reflects, that old New York which would not 'know' a divorced woman, was rather charming and quite right. Better renunciation than a hole-in-corner affair. □

'Mrs Wharton may have hated old New York, but she hated the new New York even more. . . . What indignation denounces creeps back in the name of sentiment.' Do not these pronouncements get to the heart of the matter? They indicate a Wharton marooned between the old and the new, her hostility to the new preventing significant development after she had so expertly impaled and dissected the old.

Blake Nevius[4] replaces Pritchett's 'sentiment' by what might be a more acceptable 'nostalgia':

■ In *The Age of Innocence* (1920) Mrs. Wharton's recoil from the postwar world is felt mainly by indirection, in her choice of setting. Although it is clear that like her hero, Newland Archer, who "cherished his old New York even when he smiled at it," she could reconcile two points of view, the indictment outweighs the defense. In her protest against the deliberately nurtured innocence of old New York she continued in *The Age of Innocence*, as she had done before in *The Reef* and *Ethan Frome*, to rehearse her own complaint against the failures of education and opportunity that had hampered her growth as a human being and as an artist. But underlying her protest was the nostalgia evoked by the setting and manners familiar to her childhood, a nostalgia that was to grow with the years until it effaced what bitterness remained. □

Change was looming for the New York Wharton depicted, but:

■ the mercantile aristocracy in the 'seventies was for the most part impregnable in its complacency. Julius Beaufort, the beefy financier of *The Age of Innocence*, is a disturbing portent, but his financial disgrace only strengthens Washington Square in its self-esteem. Ellen Olenska, who represents another kind of threat to the tribal security, is vanquished when society closes about the Newland Archers like a Roman wall. What one notices about this little world is that it is hermetically sealed against contamination. The question that arises with respect to such novels as *The Fruit of the Tree*, *A Son at the Front*, and *Hudson River Bracketed* – to what extent was Edith Wharton competent to deal with social and political issues beyond her limited perspective? – is as irrelevant in this instance as it would be for Jane Austen. Nothing in her treatment is more truly representative than its exclusions. We may listen in vain for echoes from the outside world. The crude, boisterous spectacle of post-war expansion, featured by the corruptions of the Grant regime, the rapid extension of the frontier, and the problems posed by labor, immigration and urbanization, fails to penetrate the consciousness of Old New York or to modify in any way its timeless ritual. Never before had Edith Wharton succeeded so well in adapting her subject to her limitations while at the same time allowing full scope for her talents. □

In response to the first half of this passage we might ask why it is that challenges to Wharton's New York tend to be disreputable. R. W. B. Lewis[5] reveals that the model for Beaufort was the Jewish-born millionaire August Belmont. While Beaufort is not identified as a Jew in *The Age of Innocence*, Rosedale in *The House of Mirth* is, and, if we do not allege anti-Semitism against Wharton, there remains the suggestion that she wants Jewish qualities to count against these two characters. Her New York, in other words, can be evoked with sentiment or nostalgia, because nothing better, or even as good, was in her view to replace it. Nor was Jane Austen 'hermetically sealed against contamination, [or the outside world]' as Nevius alleges. We have soldiers pursuing the Bennett sisters in *Pride and Prejudice*, careers in the navy in *Persuasion* and *Mansfield Park* and, also in the last, a spent Sir Thomas Bertram returning from attending to his financial interests in the West Indies. In Austen, too, there are greater internal tensions. The valetudinarianism of Emma Woodhouse's father is driving her mad. May Welland is untroubled by her father's similar malady.

Acknowledging Katherine Mansfield's review, Nevius concludes:

■ The touch of "wildness" may be lacking, but there is no failure of sensibility in the novel. The intimate passages between Newland Archer and Ellen Olenska are as deeply moving as those between Ethan Frome and Mattie Silver, whose dilemma is so curiously repeated under far different circumstances. The frustration of the lovers is expressed with great skill by two main devices. Their affair begins and ends in the glare of publicity, from the moment Archer sees his countess at the opera to the moment he discovers that old New York regards them as lovers. The opening chapter of the novel is superbly conceived from both the novelist's and the social historian's viewpoint. The theater in the 'seventies was just in the process of becoming what it is so clearly today, a social arena in which private dramas could be effectively highlighted. The scene at the opera not only introduces the main characters, together with those secondary characters who will serve as commentators – Sillerton Jackson, the undisputed authority on "family," and Lawrence Lefferts, the arbiter of "form" – but it makes Ellen Olenska a public issue; it establishes her in a position from which she cannot retreat and in which she is subject to the maximum scrutiny. The consciousness of this fact, shared by the lovers, makes their every subsequent encounter a pathetically frustrating one.

The second device I would call attention to is Edith Wharton's insistence on the chaste, almost palpable barrier which divides the lovers from the start and which they maintain, even when they are alone, by the thought of their obligations. Time and again – in Ellen's drawing room, in the carriage coming away from the ferry landing, during the clandestine meeting in the art museum and, finally, during the farewell dinner for Ellen – they reach out to each other across aching distances. At Newport, following a long separation, Archer has a chance to see Ellen again when his hostess asks him to fetch her from the pier. He spots her from a distance and stands watching her awhile. Then he turns and walks back to the house. It is a rehearsal of the gesture he will make, some twenty years later, in the epilogue. At such moments one may measure the force of Edith Wharton's sudden anguished revelation to Charles du Bos, in the year that witnessed the climax of her domestic troubles: "Ah, the poverty, the miserable poverty, of any love that lies outside of marriage, of any love that is not a living together, a sharing of all!"[6] □

Louis Auchincloss[7] also finds nostalgia in the novel. He quotes a passage from Wharton's *A Backward Glance* (1934):

■ When I was young it used to seem to me that the group in which I grew up was like an empty vessel into which no new wine would ever be poured. Now I see that one of its uses lay in preserving a few drops of an old vintage too rare to be savoured by a youthful palate. □

According to Auchincloss:

■ It was in this mood of apology that she wrote *The Age of Innocence*, the finest of her novels. It is bathed in the same rich mood of nostalgia that permeates the chapters on her own childhood in *A Backward Glance*, a mood in which she tries to recapture a little girl's vision of the 'mild blur of rosy and white-whiskered gentlemen, of ladies with bare sloping shoulders rising flower-like from voluminous skirts, peeped at from the stair-top while wraps were removed in the hall below'. Time, however, had not blunted her sharp judgement of the personalities of that world. She still saw them as passive and confined. The only vigour shown by the male characters of *The Age of Innocence* is in their domination of the female. □

Auchincloss's reference to 'a little girl's vision' evokes the method of James's *What Maisie Knew* (1897), thereby suggesting ways in which 'sharp judgement' in *The Age of Innocence* could have been given some needed complication, and its readers invited to be more than passive. Unmindful of such possibilities, Auchincloss continues:

■ But against the smallness and vapidity of its inhabitants the physical background of New York and Newport is painted with a richness of colour and detail that delights the imagination. It is this constant contrast that makes the uniqueness of the novel. The old Academy of Music, with its shabby red and gold boxes, its carefully brushed, white-waistcoated, buttonhole-flowered gentlemen; the Julius Beauforts' conservatory, where camellias and tree ferns arch their foliage over seats of black and gold bamboo; May Archer's living room, with its little plush tables covered with silver toys and efflorescent photograph frames, the small bright lawns and bright sea of Newport, succeed each other like coloured slides to recall the dictum of Edmund Wilson that Mrs Wharton was not only the pioneer but the poet of interior decoration. □

It is an odd claim to make for a novel, especially when it is judged to be the author's finest, that its background material is more interesting than its characters. Nor is the phrase, 'the poet of interior decoration' irresistibly enlightening. Indeed much of what Auchincloss praises in *The Age of Innocence* invites again Virginia Woolf's criticism of the English Edwardian novelists which was quoted in this Guide's previous chapter.

Not that Auchincloss has nothing to say about the characters:

■ Archer's emancipation ultimately carries him too far, for in the end he is ready to ditch his wife, tear himself up by the roots, and flee to Europe in search of Ellen, and May can hold him only by the time-honoured expedient of announcing her pregnancy. He is thus trapped for life in a New York routine, the satisfactions of which have been permanently soured. Yet neither he nor Ellen nor their creator regard the sacrifice as a sterile one. Had he followed Ellen to Europe, *The Age of Innocence* might have become *Anna Karenina*, and Ellen might have ended as badly as Tolstoy's heroine. The only way she and Archer can convert their love into a thing of beauty is by renunciation. And the twist of the plot is that the value of renunciation has been taught them not, after all, by the wise old civilization of Europe, but by the very society of brownstone New York that they have both so resented. Ellen tells Archer:

'It was you who made me understand that under the dullness there are things so fine and sensitive and delicate that even those I most cared for in my other life look cheap in comparison. I don't know how to explain myself, but it seems as if I'd never before understood with how much that is hard and shabby and base the most exquisite pleasure may be paid.' □

Here Auchincloss gets to the heart of the novel's moral message. This being recognised, it is absurd to imply that *The Age of Innocence* ever had a possibility of becoming another *Anna Karenina*, and that somehow it is better that Ellen does not end 'as badly as Tolstoy's heroine'. How can what happens to Anna justify Ellen; or Tolstoy's novel (did Tolstoy fail with Anna?) justify Wharton's? Auchincloss would have done better to have asked what the 'things so fine and sensitive and delicate', referred to by Ellen, are. Is it possible for any reader to know, or are the words mere verbal gestures by Ellen and Wharton herself?

Auchincloss's final view of Wharton is that:

■ Being herself an exception, or at least a refugee (for she had little of the rebel in her), she could never quite conceal a faint condescension for the victims of old New York. The thing that she keeps stressing about the Archers and Wellands and Jacksons and Mingotts is that, however dear and good and honourable they may be, they are not really alive. They have missed, like Newland Archer, the flower of life. But, having missed it – and one feels sure that Edith Wharton believed that most people, everywhere, did miss it – they conducted their lives with a commendable dignity and style. What more, she seems to ask, could one really expect of them? Archer states his credo, which was probably the author's, when he thinks back on his life with May:

Their long years together had shown him that it did not so much matter if marriage was a dull duty, as long as it kept the dignity of a duty: lapsing from that, it became a mere battle of ugly appetites. Looking about him, he honoured his own past, and mourned for it. After all, there was good in the old ways. □

Another good account of the novel on its own terms, but also another failure of criticism. Are we to acquiesce in the view that most people, except presumably people like Wharton herself, miss the flower of life? To do so is to accept that the sentimentalising Archer is representative of most people. Notice too, in the quotation from the final chapter of the novel, the opposition between 'dull duty', however dignified, and 'ugly appetites'. This simplification, which undoubtedly has Wharton's support, suggests we either settle for Archer's way of life or in some way degrade ourselves. Throughout her writing Wharton is uneasy with appetites, especially sexual appetites. They disturb the imperious conservatism which guards her taste from everything she considers 'ugly'. So in chapter 14 of *Summer* (1917), Charity Royall's sexual experience is presented as sucking her down 'into some bottomless abyss'.

Geoffrey Walton[8] also finds in *The Age of Innocence* 'a pervasive nostalgia for the past'. As usual with him, his response is admirably judicious:

■ It has all the ingredients of a historical bestseller, a richly detailed period setting, an emotional situation that the modern reader can flatter himself, or more important, herself would work out more happily at the present day and, combined with the appeal to critical superiority, a pervasive nostalgia for the past. It is, with all its faults, manifestly the product of a distinguished creative mind, if in a consciously relaxed mood, and it does not suffer from the wholly untypical rawness and nerviness of feeling, the uncertainty of tone and attitude that characterize *A Son at the Front*, which was being planned at the same time. The Puritanical element in the New York tradition comes out in *The Age of Innocence* much more strongly than in any part of *The Custom of the Country* and, remembering that Edith Wharton there uses the name Marvell, one is reminded in the later novel of 'The Definition of Love'. There is, of course, no ground for supposing that she consciously took her theme from the poem, but the relationship between Newland Archer and Ellen Olenska has an air of being

. . . begotten by Despair
Upon Impossibility

Everything in the situation is against them, the whole weight of social and moral tradition. Nevertheless, as with the situation in *The Reef*, one finds it pathetic – and sometimes absurd – rather than tragic, and the elaborate moral situation and the epilogue rather heavily sentimental. The social conflict, of the individual against the group, is comparable of Lily Bart with the later New York Society, but it is muted and muffled by the mass of period upholstery. It is not merely that the age enthroned 'Taste', that far-off divinity of whom 'Form' was the more visible representative and viceregent; the whole story on both sides is especially fully visualized in terms of clothes and interior decoration, and documented with accounts of manners, customs and social history. As in the case of the fully historical *Valley of Decision*, Edith Wharton is, to put it simply, more concerned to recreate a past age than to say something she thinks important about life. There is a lack of emotional pressure and ironic tension; elegant as the writing undoubtedly is, it lacks the hard precision of the best earlier books. After all, the stimulus to such writing was not there in the chosen subject matter, except on one or two occasions. ☐

'Pathetic . . . rather than tragic' with an epilogue 'rather heavily sentimental'; 'more concerned to recreate a past age than to say something she thinks important about life' – these judgements surely capture the limitations of *The Age of Innocence*. They are developed in Walton's conclusion:

■ Nevertheless, the final solution can only be taken as a sentimental endorsement of the tribal code. Archer settles down as a model husband – he and May "compromise" by ignoring awkward realities to the end. In the epilogue he reemerges as a public-spirited citizen who has worked with Theodore Roosevelt, but he refuses the chance of a reunion with Ellen when it comes thirty years later. Though Archer has become a more active representative of old New York than Selden or Marvell, one is asked to reverence the persistence of tradition rather than admire its flexibility. The possible pointer toward the later chapters of *The Buccaneers* is not sufficiently followed up to make it truly significant. Edith Wharton apparently endorses both Old New York and Ellen Olenska's and Archer's renunciation of each other which indeed in its idealism, also belongs to old New York; Ellen Olenska is not completely foreign after all. This is a rather sugary version of the kind of conflict that leads to Lily Bart's tragedy. To compare it with the brilliantly comic interplay of values and foibles that James creates in *The Europeans*, where the Baroness after doing so much to aerate the atmosphere of New England lets herself down with a fib, is to realize how leisurely and lacking in vitality *The Age of Innocence* is as a whole. One cannot help also realizing, however, that in its nostalgic escapism, which she admits to in *A Backward Glance*, it is also personal to the author in other ways. One recalls, in connection with Ellen Olenska's attitude, Mrs. Wharton's exclamation quoted by Percy Lubbock, "Ah, the poverty, the miserable poverty, of any love that lies outside of marriage, of any love that is not a living together, a sharing of all!"[9] These words, dating from about 1912, the year of her separation, and about two years after the end of her affair with Morton Fullerton, might have been spoken in the novel and one feels that, in creating Ellen Olenska and giving her human vitality and definition in a world of wax works, Edith Wharton may have been projecting an idealized vision of herself into the Society of her youth, where one knows she was in fact a rather colorless participant. Now that we know how far Mrs. Wharton in fact differed from Ellen Olenska, we see both the pathos and the irony of such an idealization. □

R.W.B. Lewis[10] sees the novel as 'a strenuous act of revivification' of Wharton's youthful past in New York. It suits his purpose to read *The Age of Innocence* biographically, identifying the originals of several of the characters and commenting that:

■ Edith Wharton was not only remembering the numerous individuals who thronged her parents' drawing room or whom she encountered at dinner parties and the great balls, but she was also bringing them back to life and into her own life. *The Age of Innocence* in this regard is a strenuous act of revivification. In no other of Edith Wharton's novels were the names of the characters so audibly close to those of their originals.

There is, in short, a procession of lively and recognizable ghosts. The Reverend Dr. Washburn of Calvary, the father of Pussy Jones's friend Emelyn (still briskly alive, incidentally, in New York), walks again in the briefly seen clergyman the Reverend Dr. Ashmore. Egerton Winthrop reappears in the gossipy, snobbish *and* intelligent Sillerton Jackson, as does William Travers, the entertaining socialite father of Matilda Gay. Lucretia Jones peers out at us from behind the "firm placid features" of Archer's mother-in-law, Mrs. Welland.

Edith Wharton was slyly evasive about one or two of these identifications. When Minnie Jones thought to detect the Jewish-born millionaire August Belmont in the name and figure of the mysterious immigrant financier Julius Beaufort, Edith was quick to deny it – no doubt because Beaufort also incarnated a portion of her reprehensible cousin George Alfred Jones, who had, like Beaufort, embezzled money to support his mistress. But there could be no denying Mrs. Mason Jones – Edith's formidable, benevolent Aunt Mary – in her guise as the lordly and obese Mrs. Manson Mingott, established in the bulging home she had built on upper Fifth Avenue, surrounded by quarries, saloons, wooden greenhouses, and goats grazing in rocky fields. . . .

It is from the vital context of these re-creations that the two central characters draw their fullness of being. For in *The Age of Innocence*, Edith Wharton divided her own past self between Newland Archer and Ellen Olenska. In Archer, she brought back the restive and grop-ing member of the old society she had once been, and as she traced Archer's career she suggested how sedate and yet how unfulfilled she might have become had she failed to break free of that curiously attractive social prison. It may even be that she changed Archer's first name, just before publication, from Langdon to Newland to bring it closer to her own middle name, Newbold. In Countess Olenska, Edith Wharton offered a partial sketch of the intense and nonconformist self, "the young hawk" as someone had called her, that had escaped – though only into a miserably unhappy marriage (the coarsely unfaith-ful Baron Olenski, from what little we know of him, is poor Teddy Wharton stripped of all his redeeming features). In the scenes between Newland and the countess, Edith Wharton was performing, as it were, a retrospective act of self-confrontation.

The most vivid and also the most richly significant scene in this regard is the penultimate one, the dinner party given by Archer's wife, May, on the occasion of Ellen Olenska's departure for Europe. The patrician van der Luydens are there and Sillerton Jackson, and representatives of the Welland and Mingott clans. It is all an elaborate ritual, masking what is in effect the ejection of the disturbing Ellen Olenska from New York society: "the tribal rally," Archer suddenly realizes, "around a kinswoman about to be eliminated from the tribe."

Edith Wharton, always addicted to anthropology (one may recall the ritualistic poem on the death of Theodore Roosevelt), was here making most skillful use of her readings in *The Golden Bough* and other works. In doing so, she was not only appraising her former New York world in tribal terms, but was also dramatizing her own gradual alien-ation and withdrawal from that world as an act of casting off by a society that could neither understand nor contain her. Archer, survey-ing the placid, well-fed guests bent over their canvasback ducks, sees them suddenly as "a band of dumb conspirators, and himself and the pale woman on his right as the center of their conspiracy." Continuing in her own voice, Edith Wharton remarks:

> It was the old New York way of taking life "without effusion of blood": the way of people who dreaded scandal more than disease, who placed decency above courage, and who considered that nothing was more ill-bred than "scenes," except the behavior of those who gave rise to them.

In the epilogue, via Ellen Olenska's later life, Edith Wharton described what had in fact become of herself: permanently expatriated and living in the Faubourg St. Germain section of Paris; separated once and for all from her husband; making the rounds of theaters and galleries; consorting with the aristocracy in the old *hôtels*.

And in that ending, the various times link up with one another. Following the main action set in the late 1870s, near the time of Edith's social debut, the epilogue takes place thirty years later, in 1907: that is, the moment when Edith first settled in Paris. Archer, musing on a bench outside Ellen's Paris building and gazing up at the windows of her apartment, reminds himself (Edith Wharton is careful to note) that he is only fifty-seven years old – Edith Wharton's exact age in 1919 when she wrote the larger part of the novel.

Archer and Olenska, their relationship broken by the bland, implacable force of New York society, will never see each other again. But in the world of her imaginings, Edith Wharton, by the act of writing the novel in just the way she did write it, brought together the phases of her life and her nature. Her successive New York and Europeanized selves – their relation, as she had felt, sundered by the Great War – were, for an indeterminate moment in 1919 and 1920, in harmony. □

All of this is interesting, but it does nothing to answer Walton's point that in *The Age of Innocence* Wharton is 'more concerned to recreate a past than to say something she thinks important about life'.

Cynthia Griffin Wolff[11] offers the best response to Walton's judgement, though she does not refer to the earlier critic. One of her starting points is 'a notion of maturity' developed in Erik Erikson's *Identity, Youth and Crisis*, New York 1968. Supported by this book, she opens her response to *The Age of Innocence* by declaring that:

■ Wharton, a self-conscious product of the old New York she recreates, had finally come to realize that the children of that time and place must forever bear its mark, cherish its values, and suffer in some degree its inadequacies. Growth, then, must proceed from an understanding of one's background – a coming to terms with one's past, not a flight from it. □

The very phrasing of this declaration (especially the repetition of 'must') suggests that Wolff wants immediately to be rid of any alternative positions. Suppose, for example, one changed the last words of the final sentence so that it read: 'a coming to terms with one's past, and then, if necessary, leaving it behind'? Would not the change expose Wolff's terminology as tendentious? In offering 'flight' as the only option, she is simplifying the terms of the debate even before it has properly begun.

Her reading is as prescriptively deterministic as *The Age of Innocence* itself. Within this limitation she offers a persuasive account, especially of Archer. Wharton:

■ traces Archer's struggle to mature, to become in some continuous and authentic way – himself. She lays before us the present and the possible in such a way that the middle-aged man who concludes the novel seems an admirable and significant outgrowth of the untried youth at the beginning. □

As Wolff sees it:

■ Having no occupation sufficient to his energies, Newland has turned them to fantasy: 'He was at heart a dilettante, and thinking over a pleasure to come often gave him a subtler satisfaction than its realization. This was especially the case when the pleasure was a delicate one.'

There is a dangerous vitality in this inner life; his considerable passion, finding no satisfactory outlet, has been sublimated into extraordinary palpable fantasies (old New York gave men like Newland little else to do with their passions).

Unknown to Newland, however, the fantasies that have been nourished by the rich passional needs channelled into them slip quietly back into his perceptions of the actual world, distorting these perceptions and deluding his expectations. □

Wolff's prescriptive determinism is all too evident in the parenthetical assertion about old New York. How could she know whether or not it is true? Where in the novel does she find 'a dangerous vitality in this inner life' and 'rich passional needs'? Such energies are surely the last things Wharton wants to cope with, and it might be argued that she identifies Archer as a 'dilettante', precisely to keep them out of her novel.

But at least Wolff is attempting to make positive claims for the world Wharton depicts. Implicitly she knows that unless these claims can be justified, readers will find little more than the evocation of a period in *The Age of Innocence*. In one of her most significant passages she tells us:

■ The young Newland Archer evaluates his world harshly and superficially. He sees its innocence as a stifling and destructive element – "the innocence that sears the mind against imagination and the heart against experience" – and it weighs insignificantly against Ellen's world of intrigue. Yet there is much in the novel that suggests intricate harmony where Archer perceives only emptiness and silence. There are silences, to be sure; but they are rich with communication – a kind of totality of understanding that is possible precisely *because* the world of old New York is small and limited. It is a world where one can understand, without being told, that Mrs. Beaufort's presence at the opera on the night of her ball indicates "her possession of a staff of servants competent to organize every detail of the entertainment in her absence", a world where Archer strolling abroad in the evening can ascertain that Beaufort must be about on an errand of "clandestine nature" because "it was not an Opera night, and no one was giving a party". This depth of understanding concerns grave things as well as trivial. The very first action Archer takes in the novel is that of joining May at the opera to show his support of her and the family in behalf of Ellen. It is a kind, emotionally generous gesture, and May understands it without a word's being uttered: "As he entered the box his eyes met Miss Welland's, and he saw that she had instantly understood his motive, though the family dignity which both considered so high a virtue would not permit her to tell him so . . . the fact that he and she understood each other without a word seemed to the young man to bring them nearer than any explanation would have done." And so, in many ways, it does.

The novel is filled with instances of May's intuitive flashes of deep understanding. Occasionally these are verbalized, but usually they are not. Her penetration into Archer's growing attachment for Ellen, for instance, is more often revealed in a failure to include him in the family's discussions or in a question that discovers him in a lie. Their relationship is filled with a profound silence, but the very limitations of the code that governs their marriage fill the silence with meaning. The most remarkable instance of this mute dialogue occurs one evening when Archer tells May he must go to Washington and May enjoins him to "be sure to go and see Ellen."

It was the only word that passed between them on the subject; but in the code in which they had both been trained it meant: "Of course you understand that I know all that people have been say- ing about Ellen, and heartily sympathize with my family in their effort to get her to return to her husband. I also know that, for some reason you have not chosen to tell me, you have advised her against this course, which all the older men of the family, as well as our grandmother, agree in approving; and that it is owing to your encouragement that Ellen defies us all, and exposes herself to the kind of criticism of which Mr. Sillerton Jackson probably gave you, this evening, the hint that has made you so irritable. . . . Hints have indeed not been wanting but since you appear unwilling to take them from others, I offer you this one myself, in the only form in which well-bred people of our kind can communicate unpleasant things to each other: by letting you understand that I know you mean to see Ellen when you are in Washington, and are perhaps going there expressly for that purpose; and that, since you are sure to see her, I wish you to do so with my full and explicit approval – and to take the opportunity of letting her know what the course of conduct you have encouraged her in is likely to lead to".

It is true, as Ellen has observed, that Old New Yorkers don't like to talk about "unpleasant" things. But what a wealth of shared knowledge their reticences permit!

Newland perceives May's moments of understanding as mere flickers of light in an otherwise un-illumined darkness. The evocation of her as a young Diana is, in Archer's mind, a reductive vision of empty, unknowing, unsoiled virginity. He can deal with her primitive complexity no more than he can deal with the consequences of Ellen's experiences with Old World culture. He supposes that her "faculty of unawareness was what gave her eyes their transparency, and her face the look of representing a type rather than a person; as if she might have been chosen to pose for a civic virtue or a Greek goddess. The blood that ran so close to her fair skin might have been a preserving fluid rather than a ravaging element; yet her look of indestructible youthfulness made her seem neither hard nor dull, but only primitive and pure". He doesn't hear or understand even her spoken disclaimer: "'You mustn't think that a girl knows as little as her parents imagine. One hears and one notices – one hides one's feelings and ideas'". □

Throughout her chapter on *The Age of Innocence* Wolff assumes that Archer is being placed by Wharton, and that we are therefore invited to have a larger view than his of the novel's events.

Her assumption is true to the extent that the younger Archer has not arrived at Wharton's final, compromising sentimentality. Till then, however, Archer's criticisms of New York are also Wharton's, and the author herself surely agrees with the observation about 'innocence' quoted at the beginning of the above passage. Whether the codes of old New York are, as Wolff claims, 'rich with communication', enabling 'flashes of deep understanding' is for all readers to judge. At the end of the first paragraph in the extract above, however, Wolff omits significant phrases from the lines she chooses to quote. After 'tell him so', Wharton writes: 'The persons of their world lived in an atmosphere of faint implication and pale delicacies'. Would 'flashes of deep understanding' be possible in such an atmosphere?

May does surprise Archer by her manipulative tenacity, but, this aside, she remains another ingredient of the novel about which he and Wharton concur. In the novel's final chapter she is presented by both as:

■ generous, faithful, unwearied; but so lacking in imagination, so incapable of growth, that the world of her youth had fallen into pieces and rebuilt itself without her ever being conscious of the change. . . . she went contentedly to her place in the Archer vault in St Mark's, where Mrs Archer already lay safe from the terrifying 'trend' which her daughter-in-law had never even become aware of. □

How we wish May had not been so complacently created by Wharton, and how feminist critics would have been outraged had this account of a female character been offered by a male novelist. In the long passage from the novel quoted above by Wolff, nothing is left for readers to imagine and discover about May. Wolff offers it as an example of the 'wealth' of May's and Archer's 'shared knowledge', but poverty of authorial investment in May might be another conclusion to draw from Wharton's obtrusive insistence.

Critics who come after Wolff have little, if anything to add to our understanding of *The Age of Innocence*. Elizabeth Ammons[12] for example, ignores any possibility that Wharton simplifies May in order to make the character fit into a facile thesis about New York in the 1870s. When Ammons says 'patriarchy' all critical reading apparently ceases. In her view the preference of New York for May over Ellen:

■ . . . reiterates Wharton's by-now familiar charge against the American patriarchy. She argues that it is a system deliberately designed to arrest female human nature.

May, we are told, has been "carefully trained not to possess . . . the experience, the versatility, the freedom of judgment" one needs in order to deal with adult life; she is "that terrifying product of the social system . . . the young girl who knew nothing and expected everything". She is still in the nursery. Like her mother, who has an "invincible innocence," she typifies the American woman described by the heroine of 'New Year's Day,' a story Edith Wharton wrote about the 1870's and included in her collection of four historical sketches, *Old New York* (1924): "Lizzie Hazeldean had long since come to regard most women of her age as children in the art of life . . . charming creatures who passed from the nursery to marriage as if lifted from one rose-lined cradle into another." In *The Age of Innocence* other people must look out for May Welland's well-being and do her thinking for her. She is a precious human burden, the highest expression of the leisure-class's "nursery parody of life" and symbolic of its freedom from normal economic imperatives. America's answer to Chinese footbinding, the child-woman May perfectly embodies her class's ideal of helpless femininity. She is a lovely human doll whose uselessness aggrandizes her owner's social standing, giving him the "glow of proprietorship" at the same time that her Diana-like virginity arouses "the passion of masculine vanity" for conquest and mastery. □

Surely it is the function of critics to ask questions of characterisation and not simply to summarise it. Similarly, in her account of Ellen, Ammons' purpose needs to be less blinkered:

■ War forces people to think about basic things, and one reality that Edith Wharton obviously thought about was fear. It is the subject of *The Age of Innocence*. Newland Archer and his fellow old New Yorkers are so afraid of Ellen Olenska, a sophisticated, sexually exciting woman, that they end up literally banishing her from New York. To be sure, their fear is not of the same quality that Edith Wharton, during the war, had seen daily – the acute terror of extermination; what the war could and did do to people's lives was very different from the neurotic apprehensions of sheltered old New Yorkers in the period Wharton baptized the Age of Innocence, the American 1870s. At the same time, however, the sexual fear that Ellen Olenska arouses in Newland Archer and his fellows is both deep and serious for, in the opinion of the people threatened, she places in jeopardy the very security of "civilization." Her presence upsets old New York's most basic principles of order and authority; and Wharton repeatedly uses anthropological terms and images in *The Age of Innocence* – elaborating for us "rituals" and "rites," referring to families as "tribes" or "clans," labeling Mrs. Manson Mingott the "grand Matriarch" of her line and comparing the Van der Luydens to tribal judges – to emphasize the way in which this book, lovely as it is, amounts to a sort of laboratory study of the fundamental, primitive attitudes that mold patriarchal aversion to the mature female. □

The problem with this reading is its failure to recognise Wharton's moral endorsement of the outcome of Archer's and Ellen's relationship. How can Wharton be truly critical of Archer's 'sexual fear', if she disapproves of (and could not creatively have faced) what his sexual courage might have brought about? Moreover, it surely would be unlikely in reality that the entirety of 'Newland Archer and his fellows' would have been so scared of Ellen, even if she were as sexually alive as Ammons implies. In fact she is thoroughly conscience-stricken and insistently compliant, therefore, with her author's anaemic moral scheme.

Judith Fryer[13] states that:

■ it is difficult to see *The Age of Innocence* as a novel of reconciliation – or as a successful novel of reconciliation. Rather, it is the pivotal novel in the Wharton canon, the imaginative work in which the moral claims of the family and of the individual are held in perfect tension. . . . Newland Archer might see 'good in the old ways' and 'good in the new order too'. Wharton, however, saw the repression of the self in the old ways and fragmentation of the self in the new ways; the best she could do to achieve a reconciliation, or a resolution, was to tack back and forth between her own two created lives.

In this she was like her contemporary Virginia Woolf, who, likewise responding to the cataclysmic events of the early twentieth century, saw two structures in *Mrs Dalloway* – one of war and the other of roses. □

What we get from Fryer is a re-statement of what the novel obviously says, combined with wayward gesturing. An example of the latter is the reference to *Mrs Dalloway* (1925). Since one of the motives of Woolf's novel is to render obsolete the kind of writing Wharton is offering in *The Age of Innocence*, Fryer is forcing likeness in the face of fundamental differences. It is Woolf's technique, not Wharton's, which can render 'fragmentation of the self'.

Gloria C. Erlich[14] offers another summary of the novel:

■ On the verge of committing himself to what he sees as the standard destiny of a New York gentleman, Archer witnesses at the performance of *Faust* a drama of the human spirit challenging limitations, daring penalties for the privilege of enlarged experience. The legendary Faust risks damnation to look on the face of Helen. Perversely inspired by this, Newland Archer turns out to be the ultimate anti-Faust, a veritable Prufrock in disguise. He will try to break out of his limitations by reaching for what seems to be his Helen of Troy (Ellen), but he is quickly brought to heel by his own weakness and by the conjoined forces of the tribe. Indeed, the mere sight of provocative Ellen seated next to his virginal fiancée in the family opera box prompts our anti-Faust to banish temptation, to foreclose his options by announcing his engagement prematurely that very evening. His way of daring conventions (precipitate announcement, hastened wedding) serves only to put himself irreversibly within the protection of the conventions. Responsive to all that Ellen represents (vitality, sensual sophistication, "European" or bohemian values), he flies to the refuge of tradition, which he interprets as rigidly as possible. Thinking he was protecting May from contamination, he was actually protecting himself from the risks of passion.

The aria from *Faust* that he hears at this moment, "M'ama . . . non m'ama," speaks to Newland's doubts about marrying May Welland and to his ambivalence about committing himself to a thoroughly prescribed and predictable life. But finally, "m'ama" – he banishes these doubts by hastening to seal the marriage. However, by investing in the figure of the now-lost Ellen all that is desirable in woman, he can see May only as Ellen's opposite – invincibly virginal, even boyish, and thoroughly immune to culture.

Cherishing his image of the banished Ellen, he never allows himself to love May; he fails to bring out or develop the latent woman in her. One could think of May as a victim, a sleeping beauty whom Newland Archer declines to awaken because he is too attached to the image of her opposite. Archer is a splitter of internal images – if Ellen signifies all that is richly female and sexually desirable, May becomes to him a static icon of permanent inviolability, a Diana-figure which he visualizes as an adolescent boy. With such polarized imagery, he places desire outside the social pale and embraces renunciation. In order to retain psychic fidelity to his beloved Ellen, he renders his marriage as perfunctory, as dessicated, as possible. And when, after May's death, Newland has an opportunity to renew his relationship to Ellen, who lives a single life in Paris, he abstains even from visiting her. He cannot test his internalized Ellen against reality.

Newland's psychological conservatism is like that of Edith

Wharton who, amidst all the ferment of Paris in the early twenties, chose to live in the staid Faubourg Saint-Germain and to associate, not with the people of the future such as Proust, Gertrude Stein, and Natalie Barney, but with the most conservative avatars of outmoded gentility. As Shari Benstock observes, "She dared not risk exposure to a rebellious and often risqué modernity; she needed the protection of just those social and intellectual traditions on which Proust and other moderns cast such a jaundiced eye."[15]

The aria from *Faust* addresses the paradox of marriage as Edith Wharton experienced it. For her, marriage and fidelity to the social code meant entrapment – not securing love but *foreclosing the possibility of it*. Her fiction plays endless variations on the theme of marital entrapment – enduring it, making the best of it, the social cost of evading it. Only rarely did she depict the freedom of joyfully escaping it.

Observing this conjunction of Faustian desire for unlimited experience and timid rejection of even the most available human pleasures, we marvel at the forces that bound the healthy, sensuous young Edith Wharton into a life of self-denial and, except for a brief interlude, celibacy. □

'Archer turns out to be the ultimate anti-Faust' is an impressively sounding pronouncement, but is it not an attempt to inflate the material Wharton offers? If someone was as bad at tennis as Archer is at rebellion, would we describe him as an anti-Pete Sampras? Like previous critics, Erlich tries to separate Archer from Wharton when significant separation does not exist. Wharton herself, as much as Archer, fails 'to bring out or develop the latent woman in [May]', and Erlich points to the identification of the author and Archer in her observation that 'Newland's psychological conservatism is like that of Edith Wharton'. She then retreats from the novel into biography. What she says is interesting, but the question as to how significantly Wharton's notion of marriage was dramatised and explored in the fiction is avoided.

Carol J. Singley[16] has recourse to elaborate packaging:

■ The novel is set in the 1870s, when the New York society that had evolved slowly over two centuries was under siege by newly moneyed classes. The response to this crisis was to draw the circle tighter, becoming more exclusive and ritualized. Wharton's description of old New Yorkers as a threatened tribe is apt. At the time she wrote the novel, Americans and Europeans were pursuing an unprecedented interest in primitive cultures, and anthropology was rapidly developing as a discipline. Wharton herself visited Morocco in 1917, recording her impressions of this exotic, uncharted land in *In Morocco* which appeared in the same year as *The Age of Innocence*. Jackson Lears interprets the fascination with primitive cultures as an antimodernist impulse, arising from a crisis of cultural authority and backlash against logical order. The primal past reinstated sacred mysteries long since demolished by Darwinism and provided escape from the hectic and seemingly directionless pace of early twentieth-century life.[17]

Indeed, Wharton uses tribal language to suggest that instinct, not reason, rules old New York; and she writes *The Age of Innocence* – just as she writes *In Morocco* – as a guidebook to that primitive culture.

To understand the pressure of old New York's values on Newland Archer – and, in particular, the group's decision to marshal forces and send Ellen Olenska back to Europe – I turn to René Girard's analysis of sacrificial practices. Girard theorizes that the ancient ritual of sacrifice is the means by which a group controls and contains the disruption that threatens it from within: "the purpose of the sacrifice is to restore harmony to the community, to reinforce the social fabric".[18] These communal, ritual practices constitute a religion that helps the society come to terms with its own inadequacies; in more modern societies the same function is served by a system of justice. Wharton reflects both operations in describing New York society as a tribe and the decision making of the leading family, the van der Luydens, as a tribunal.

As Girard notes, the victims of such sacrifice are not chosen randomly. Rather, they are "exterior or marginal individuals, incapable of establishing or sharing the social bonds that link the rest of the inhabitants. Their status as foreigners . . . prevents these future victims from fully integrating themselves into the community".[19] Certain rules govern sacrifice: the victim cannot be in the position to avenge the violence done to her by the community, and the more critical the social crisis, the more "precious" the victim must be.[20] Ellen Olenska, May Welland's cousin and the respected Mrs. Manson Mingott's niece, is an ideal victim. She returns home from Europe at a time when the clan needs to shore up its boundaries. She is also faintly exotic – her life on the continent, her notorious marriage and scandalous departure from it, her Sunday soirees with people whom her family and friends mistrust, even the unorthodox cut of her gown set her apart from others. Archer's attraction to Ellen further jeopardizes group unity, since New York regulates romance and passion as strictly as it does dinner parties. In a series of well-orchestrated but unacknowledged manoeuvres,

Ellen is expelled from the community. She becomes the means by which old New York reaffirms its traditions and seals cracks in its social fortress. Her removal from society becomes not only desirable but necessary for group survival. Revenge, Girard tells us, often passes for justice,[21] thus New York thinks itself justified in expelling Ellen. □

The material from Lears and Girard is interesting in itself, but what does Singley's reference to it add to the comments that have been made on *The Age of Innocence* for over seventy years? To describe the New York society we meet in the novel as a 'primitive culture' is a desperate stretching of terminology, while the parallels with 'sacrificial practices' are only another way of re-stating the novel's story. What is Girard himself saying about scapegoating that several of Shakespeare's plays have not already revealed?

Singley continues:

■ May, whose face suggests "a type rather than a person", is associated with Artemis, the Greek goddess of the hunt. Her role as Artemis suggests her power over her husband: she is master of the hunt and thus of "Archery." According to Ovid's *Metamorphoses*, the virgin Diana (the Roman equivalent of the Greek Artemis) seeks vengeance against Actaeon for watching her bathe naked in a sparkling fountain – that is, for seeing her true nature. Diana turns him into a stag who is then attacked by his own hounds. Archer is a modern-day Actaeon who finally sees May as she is: a conventional woman with no imagination or capacity for change. Wharton somewhat satirically refers to Archer as her victim when May marshals the forces of his own "hounds", – his family – to send Ellen back to Europe. May is also a model of "Civic Virtue" and notable for her unchanging pristine quality; but her virtue is "only primitive and pure" like the savage society she upholds. Ellen, on the other hand, represents the qualities of virtue found in Plato's philosophy. She upholds truth at any cost; May dissembles, announcing an unconfirmed pregnancy in order to ensure Archer's faithfulness. Archer eventually discovers that May's "frankness and innocence were only an artificial product"; even her premarital offer to give Archer up is a calculated gesture based on her guess that his affair is already over (she suspects another woman, not Ellen). May is generous because she believes she has nothing to lose.

Wharton associates Ellen with the Greek goddess Aphrodite, who reigns over all aspects of sexual love and beauty. In the Greek pantheon, Aphrodite was a divine force who humanized but also transcended sexuality. She stirred both mortals and immortals with desire, and she combined high emotion with sophistication and intelligence. Aphrodite is a liminal figure who easily crosses the boundaries of existing structures: Paul Friedrich notes her ability to "bridge physical reality and metaphysical belief".[22]

Aphrodite's complexity is evident in Ellen Olenska's dual role as lover and philosopher in *The Age of Innocence*. Both Ellen and Aphrodite are of ambiguous origins, both make marriages with unlikely men, and both are identified with roses. Archer sends Ellen yellow roses after visiting her. Crimson and amber are the colors Ellen wears at the van der Luyden's party and at her farewell dinner – symbols of passion and decadence by Victorian standards, but also the colors most often associated with Aphrodite.[23] Significantly, Aphrodite, the model of womanly strength and power who gives birth to Eros or Cupid, is the goddess discussed in the *Symposium*. As Aphrodite, Ellen incorporates both erotic *and* higher conceptions of love.

Archer is irresistibly drawn to Ellen not only because of her physical beauty and originality but because of her commitment to levels of truth that he cannot find in May or her world. In contrast to May, who represents the status quo, Ellen is dynamic: she both sparks his romantic desire and initiates his spiritual education. In this respect, she resembles Socrates in the *Symposium*. Socrates is the object of Alcibiades' passionate infatuation as well as a philosopher-teacher. He calls for a life lived according to reason and encourages ascent from the love of a single individual to the love of beauty and goodness as values in and of themselves. Ellen embodies romantic, Hellenic desire – her name, after all, is (H)ellen – but she is also capable of leading Archer into rational reflection about the higher meaning of love. □

If only Archer did come across the naked May as Actaeon comes across the naked Diana! To suggest, or wish for, as much in *The Age of Innocence* is to recognise its impossibility, and to appreciate again Singley's unwarrantable forcing of a parallel. Diana has Actaeon torn limb from limb by his own hounds. Archer, by this measurement, is never the victim of anything that can truly be called 'savage'. As for Ellen, does it help to liken her to both Aphrodite and Socrates? Can she be regarded as a philosopher in any sense that would not make all philosophers despair? Singley gets onto some firmer ground as she moves towards her conclusion:

■ Ellen and Archer's affair is doomed both because of the strength of tribal traditions and because of Ellen's insistence on Platonic rather than romantic ideals. However, Ellen's renunciation of passion seems more Puritan than Platonic. She departs from Platonism in not seeing that the fulfilment of desire is compatible with higher ideals. The failure is Wharton's as much as Ellen's, reflecting the author's long-standing belief in sexual guilt and payment for pleasure. □

Does not Singley, with this last sentence, throw all her packaging into the waste-bin? It confirms a Wharton whose fiction is recurrently moralistic in a very conservative sense. Such a Wharton could hardly manage a significant imaginative investment in Aphrodite.

NOTES

INTRODUCTION

1 *A Backward Glance* (1934), chapter 1, part 3. Further references to *A Backward Glance* (*ABG*) will be given after the quotation.

2 This quotation is from the autobiographical fragment 'Life and I', which was never completed nor published. It is now published in *Edith Wharton: Novellas and Other Writings*, New York, 1990, pp.1071–96. In her notes to this edition Cynthia Griffin Wolff states that Wharton 'may have begun [the fragment] before . . . February 21, 1923'. All quotations from 'Life and I' (*LI*) are from this edition. The one just selected appears on pp.1080–81. Further references will be given after the quotation.

3 'Life and I' (p.1090) describes this particular maternal deed as a 'folly'.

4 See *The Wings of the Dove*, Book IX, chapter 4.

5 R.W.B. Lewis and Nancy Lewis, eds., *The Letters of Edith Wharton*, London and New York, 1988, p.332.

6 Sandra M. Gilbert and Susan Gubar, *The Madwoman in the Attic: The Woman Writer and the Nineteenth Century Literary Imagination*, New Haven and London, 1979, pp.452–3.

CHAPTER ONE

1 *Edith Wharton: A Biography*, London and New York, 1975, pp.150–51.

2 *The Letters of Edith Wharton*, London and New York 1988, pp.54–5.

3 See Wharton's 'George Eliot' (a review of Leslie Stephen's *George Eliot*), *Bookman*, London, 15 May 1902, pp.247–51; reprinted in Stuart Hutchinson, ed., *George Eliot: Critical Assessments*, 2, Robertsbridge, 1996, pp.53–9.

4 *A Backward Glance*, London and New York, 1934, p.207.

5 Leon Edel, ed., *Henry James Letters*, 4,

Cambridge Mass. and London, 1984.

6 'Mrs Wharton's Latest Novel', *Independent*, 59, 20 July 1905, pp.150–51.

7 'A Notable Novel', *Outlook*, 81, 21 October 1905, pp.404–6.

8 The relevant pages of Fenimore Cooper's *Notions of the Americans* (1828) are widely anthologised, for example in *The Norton Anthology of American Literature*, fourth edition, 1, pp.937–49.

9 'The House of Mirth', *Spectator* [England], 95, 28 October 1905, p.657.

10 'Recent Fiction', *Dial*, 40, 1 January 1906, pp.15–16.

11 '*The House of Mirth*, and Other Novels', *Nation*, 81, 30 November 1905, pp.447–8.

12 'Notes on New Novels', *Atlantic Monthly*, 97, January 1906, pp.52–3.

13 'A Group of Novels', *Critic*, 47, December 1905, pp.509–10.

14 '*The House of Mirth*', *Bookman* [England], 29, December 1905, pp.130–31.

15 'Fiction: *The House of Mirth*', 1 December 1905, p.421.

CHAPTER TWO

1 'The Novels of Edith Wharton', *Quarterly Review*, 222, January 1915, pp.182–201; rpt in Irving Howe, ed., *Edith Wharton: A Collection of Critical Essays*, Englewood Cliffs, N.J., 1962, pp.43–61.

2 *Times*, 26 March 1898; rpt in Leon Edel, ed., *The American Essays of Henry James*, New York, 1958, pp.202–3.

3 'Justice to Edith Wharton', *New Republic*, 95, 29 June 1938, pp.209–13; rpt in *The Wound and the Bow*, Boston, 1941.

4 'Edith Wharton', *On Native Grounds*, New York, 1942; rpt in Irving Howe, ed., *Edith Wharton: A Collection of Critical Essays*, Englewood Cliffs, N.J., 1962, pp.89–102.

5 '*The House of Mirth* Revisited', *Harper's Bazaar*, 81, December 1947, pp.126–7, 181–6; rpt in Irving Howe, ed., *Edith Wharton: A Collection of Critical Essays*, Englewood Cliffs, N.J., 1962, pp.103–118.

6 *Edith Wharton: A Study of Her Fiction*, Berkeley and Los Angeles, 1953, pp. 53–62.

7 'Introduction', *The House of Mirth*, New York, 1962; rpt in Irving Howe, ed., *Edith Wharton: A Collection of Critical Essays*, Englewood Cliffs, N.J., 1962, pp. 119–29.

8 *Edith Wharton: A Critical Interpretation*, London and Toronto, 1970, 1982, pp. 49–67.

9 *Bookman*, London, 15 May 1902, pp. 247–51; rpt in Stuart Hutchinson, ed., *George Eliot: Critical Assessments*, 2, Robertsbridge, 1996, pp. 53–9.

10 *Edith Wharton: A Biography*, London and New York, 1975, p. 155.

11 *A Feast of Words: The Triumph of Edith Wharton*, New York, 1977, pp. 109–38.

12 *Edith Wharton's Argument with America*, Athens, Georgia, 1980, pp. 25–43.

13 *The Theory of the Leisure Class*, New York, 1965, p. 60.

14 'Debasing Exchange: Edith Wharton's *The House of Mirth*', *PMLA*, 100, October 1985, pp. 783–92; rpt in Harold Bloom, ed., *Modern Critical Views: Edith Wharton*, New York, Philadelphia, 1986, pp. 123–37.

15 'The Death of the Lady (Novelist): Wharton's *House of Mirth*', *Representations*, 9, Winter 1985, pp. 133–49; rpt in Harold Bloom, ed., *Modern Critical Views: Edith Wharton*, New York, Philadelphia, 1986, pp. 139–54.

16 'The Naturalism of Edith Wharton's *The House of Mirth*', *Twentieth Century Literature*, 41, Summer 1995, pp. 241–8.

17 Edith Wharton's *Letters From the Underworld: Fictions of Women and Writing*, Chapel Hill and London, 1991, pp. 19–49.

18 *The Sexual Education of Edith Wharton*, Berkeley, Los Angeles, Oxford, 1992, pp. ix, 58–64.

19 *Edith Wharton: Matters of Mind and Spirit*, Cambridge, 1995, pp. 67–88.

20 'From *Daniel Deronda* to *The House of Mirth*', *Essays in Criticism*, 47, October 1997, pp. 315–31.

21 For Wharton on Keats and 'Ode on a Grecian Urn' see R. W. B. Lewis and Nancy Lewis, eds., *The Letters of Edith Wharton*, London and New York, 1988, p. 203 and p. 411. On the latter page she names Keats as 'the greatest of all [poets]'.

22 The painting is reproduced in Nicholas Penny, ed., *Reynolds* (Royal Academy of Arts Catalogue, 1986), plate 103, commentary pp. 275–6.

CHAPTER THREE

1 R. W. B. Lewis and Nancy Lewis, eds., *The Letters of Edith Wharton*, London and New York, 1988, p. 146.

2 'The Custom of the Country', *Nation*, 96, 15 May 1913, p. 494.

3 New York *Sun*, 18 October 1913, p. 8.

4 'Mrs Wharton's Novel: *The Custom of the Country*: A Book Which Will Excite Much Discussion', *New York Times Review of Books*, 19 October 1913, p. 557.

5 'Mrs Wharton's Manner', *Nation*, 97, 30 October 1913, pp. 404–5.

6 'The Book of the Month', *North American Review*, 199, February 1914, pp. 294–9.

7 'Fiction', *Athenaeum*, 4490, 15 November 1913, p. 554.

8 'Novels', *Saturday Review*, 116, 22 November 1913, pp. 658–9.

9 *Bookman*, [England] 45, March 1914, p. 330.

10 'The Younger Generation', *Times Literary Supplement*, 2 April 1914, pp. 157–8.

CHAPTER FOUR

1 'The Novels of Edith Wharton', *Quarterly Review*, 222, January 1915, pp. 182–201; rpt in Irving Howe, ed., *Edith Wharton: A Collection of Critical Essays*, Englewood Cliffs, N.J., 1962, pp. 43–61.

2 'Henry James's Heiress: The Importance of Edith Wharton', *Scrutiny*, 7, December 1938, pp. 261–76; rpt in Irving Howe, ed., *Edith Wharton: A*

Collection of Critical Essays, Englewood Cliffs, N.J., 1962, pp. 73–88.

3 'Justice to Edith Wharton', *New Republic*, 95, 29 June 1938, pp. 209–13; rpt in *The Wound and the Bow*, Boston, 1941.

4 *Edith Wharton: A Critical Interpretation*, London and Toronto, 1970, 1982, pp. 114–36.

5 *Edith Wharton: A Biography*, London and New York, 1975, pp. 349–50.

6 'Edith Wharton and her New Yorks', *Partisan Review*, 18, July–August 1951, pp. 411–19; rpt in Irving Howe, ed., *Edith Wharton: A Collection of Critical Essays*, Englewood Cliffs, N.J., 1962, pp. 32–42.

7 Leon Edel, ed., *Henry James Letters*, 4, Cambridge, Mass. and London, 1984, p. 622.

8 *A Feast of Words: The Triumph of Edith Wharton*, New York, 1977, pp. 231–59.

9 'The Woman Who Hated Women', *New York Times Book Review*, 16 November 1986, pp. 11–12.

10 *Edith Wharton's Argument with America*, Athens, Georgia, 1980, pp. 99–124.

11 *Edith Wharton's Letters From the Underworld: Fictions of Women and Writing*, Chapel Hill and London, 1991, pp. 129–72.

12 'New Wives for Old: Divorce and Leisure Class Marriage in Edith Wharton's *The Custom of the Country*', *American Literature*, 68, December 1996, pp. 765–97.

CHAPTER FIVE

1 *Edith Wharton: A Biography*, London and New York, 1975, pp. 422–33.

2 R. W. B. Lewis and Nancy Lewis, eds., *The Letters of Edith Wharton*, London and New York, 1988, p. 433.

3 Katherine Perry, 'Were the Seventies Sinless?', *Publisher's Weekly*, 98, 16 October 1920, pp. 1195–6.

4 'As Mrs Wharton Sees Us', *New York Times Book Review*, 17 October 1920, pp. 1, ii.

5 Leonard Woolf, ed., *Virginia Woolf:*

Collected Essays, 1, London, 1966, pp. 319–37.

6 *Nation*, 111, 3 November 1920, pp. 510–11.

7 'Our America', *New York Saturday Evening Post*, 6 November 1920, p. 3.

8 'The Age of Innocence', *Times Literary Supplement*, 25 November 1920, p. 775.

9 'The Innocence of New York', *Saturday Review*, 130, 4 December 1920, p. 458.

10 'Family Portraits', *Athenaeum*, 4728, 10 December 1920, pp. 810–11.

11 'Our Literary Aristocrat', *Pacific Review*, 2, June 1921, pp. 157–60.

CHAPTER SIX

1 'Maule's Well, or Henry James and the Relation of Morals to Manners', *Maule's Curse*, New York, 1938; rpt in *Defense of Reason*, New York, 1960, pp. 300–43.

2 'Justice to Edith Wharton', *New Republic*, 95, 29 June 1938, pp. 209–13; rpt in *The Wound and the Bow*, Boston, 1941.

3 'Books in General', *New Statesman and Nation*, 25 April 1953, pp. 489–90.

4 *Edith Wharton: A Study of Her Fiction*, Berkeley and Los Angeles, 1953, pp. 177–89.

5 *Edith Wharton: A Biography*, London and New York, 1975, p. 431.

6 Percy Lubbock, *Portrait of Edith Wharton*, New York, 1947, p. 100.

7 'Foreword' to *The Age of Innocence*, New American Library, New York, 1962, pp. v–xi.

8 *Edith Wharton: A Critical Interpretation*, London and Toronto, 1970, 1982, pp. 137–46.

9 Lubbock, *Portrait of Edith Wharton*, p. 100.

10 *Edith Wharton: A Biography*, pp. 425–36.

11 *A Feast of Words: The Triumph of Edith Wharton*, New York, 1977, pp. 310–334.

12. *Edith Wharton's Argument with America*, Athens, Georgia, 1980, pp. 143–53.

13 'Purity and Power in *The Age of*

Innocence', *American Literary Realism 1870–1910*, 17, Autumn 1984, pp. 153–68; rpt in Harold Bloom, ed., *Modern Critical Views: Edith Wharton*, New York, Philadelphia, 1986, pp. 99–115.

14 *The Sexual Education of Edith Wharton*, Berkeley, Los Angeles, Oxford, 1992, pp. 132–4.

15 Shari Benstock, *Women of the Left Bank: Paris, 1900–1940*, Austin, Texas, 1986, p. 40.

16 *Edith Wharton: Matters of Mind and Spirit*, Cambridge, 1995, pp. 164–83.

17 Jackson Lears, *No Place of Grace: Antimodernism and the Transformation of American Culture, 1880–1920*, New York, 1981, pp. 142–3.

18 René Girard, *Violence and the Sacred*, Baltimore, 1972, p. 8.

19 Girard, p. 12.

20 Girard, p. 18.

21 Girard, p. 24

22 Paul Friedrich, *The Meaning of Aphrodite*, Chicago, 1978, p. 134.

23 Friedrich, pp. 75, 78–9.

CRITICAL AND BIOGRAPHICAL WORKS CITED IN THIS GUIDE

Elizabeth Ammons, *Edith Wharton's Argument with America*, Athens, Georgia, 1980.

Louis Auchincloss, 'Edith Wharton and her New Yorks', *Partisan Review*, 18, July–August, 1951, pp. 411–19; rpt in Irving Howe, ed., *Edith Wharton: A Collection of Critical Essays*, Englewood Cliffs, N.J., 1962, pp. 32–42.

'Foreword' to *The Age of Innocence*, New American Library, New York, 1962, pp. v–xi.

Wai-Chee Dimock, 'Debasing Exchange: Edith Wharton's *The House of Mirth*, *PMLA*, 100, October 1985, pp. 783–92; rpt in Harold Bloom, ed., *Modern Critical Views: Edith Wharton*, New York, Philadelphia, 1986, pp. 123–37.

Leon Edel, ed., *Henry James Letters*, 4, Cambridge, Mass. and London, 1984.

Gloria C. Erlich, *The Sexual Education of Edith Wharton*, Berkeley, Los Angeles, Oxford, 1992.

Judith Fryer, 'Purity and Power in *The Age of Innocence*', *American Literary Realism 1870–1910*, 17, Autumn 1984, pp. 153–68; rpt in Harold Bloom, ed., *Modern Critical Views: Edith Wharton*, New York, Philadelphia, 1986, pp. 99–115.

Sandra M. Gilbert and Susan Gubar, *The Madwoman in the Attic: The Woman Writer and the Nineteenth Century Literary Imagination*, New Haven and London, 1979.

Irving Howe, 'Introduction', *The House of Mirth*, New York, 1962; rpt in Irving Howe, ed., *Edith Wharton: A Collection of Critical Essays*, Englewood Cliffs, N.J., 1962, pp. 119–29.

Stuart Hutchinson, 'From *Daniel Deronda* to *The House of Mirth*', *Essays in Criticism*, 47, October 1997, pp. 315–31.

Alfred Kazin, 'Edith Wharton', *On Native Grounds*, New York, 1942; rpt in Irving Howe, ed., *Edith Wharton: A Collection of Critical Essays*, Englewood Cliffs, N.J., 1962, pp. 89–102.

Q. D. Leavis, 'Henry James's Heiress: The Importance of Edith Wharton', *Scrutiny*, 7, December 1938, pp. 261–76; rpt in Irving Howe, ed., *Edith Wharton: A Collection of Critical Essays*, Englewood Cliffs, N.J., 1962, pp. 73–88.

R. W. B. Lewis, *Edith Wharton: A Biography*, London and New York, 1975.

R. W. B. Lewis and Nancy Lewis, eds., *The Letters of Edith Wharton*, London and New York, 1988.

Percy Lubbock, 'The Novels of Edith Wharton', *Quarterly Review*, 222, January 1915, pp. 182–201; rpt in Irving Howe, ed., *Edith Wharton: A Collection of Critical Essays*, Englewood Cliffs, N.J., 1962, pp. 43–61.

—— *Portrait of Edith Wharton*, New York, 1947.

Deborah Ann MacComb, 'New Wives for Old: Divorce and Leisure Class

Marriage in Edith Wharton's *The Custom of the Country'*, *American Literature*, 68, December 1996, pp. 765–97.

Janet Malcolm, 'The Woman Who Hated Women', *New York Times Book Review*, 16 November 1986, pp. 11–12.

Blake Nevius, *Edith Wharton: A Study of Her Fiction*, Berkeley and Los Angeles, 1953.

Vernon L. Parrington, Jr., 'Our Literary Aristocrat', *Pacific Review*, 2, June 1921, pp. 157–60.

Donald Pizer, 'The Naturalism of Edith Wharton's *The House of Mirth'*, *Twentieth Century Literature*, 41, Summer 1995, pp. 241–8.

V. S. Pritchett, 'Books in General', *New Statesman and Nation*, 25 April 1953, pp. 489–90.

Elaine Showalter, 'The Death of the Lady (Novelist): Wharton's *House of Mirth'*, *Representations*, 9, Winter 1985, pp. 133–49; rpt in Harold Bloom, ed., *Modern Critical Views: Edith Wharton*, New York and Philadelphia, 1986, pp. 139–54.

Carol J. Singley, *Edith Wharton: Matters of Mind and Spirit*, Cambridge, 1995.

Diana Trilling, '*The House of Mirth* Revisited', *Harper's Bazaar*, 81, December 1947, pp. 126–7, 181–6; rpt in Irving Howe, ed., *Edith Wharton: A Collection of Critical Essays*, Englewood Cliffs, N.J., 1962, pp. 103–118.

Candace Waid, *Edith Wharton's Letters From the Underworld: Fictions of Women and Writing*, Chapel Hill and London, 1991.

Geoffrey Walton, *Edith Wharton: A Critical Interpretation*, London and Toronto, 1970, 1982.

Edith Wharton, 'George Eliot', *Bookman*, London, 15 May 1902, pp. 247–51; rpt in Stuart Hutchinson, ed., *George Eliot: Critical Assessments*, 2, Robertsbridge, 1996, pp. 53–9.

—— *A Backward Glance*, New York and London, 1934.

Edmund Wilson, 'Justice to Edith Wharton', *New Republic*, 95, 29 June 1938, pp. 209–13; rpt in *The Wound and the Bow*, Boston, 1941.

Yvor Winters, 'Maule's Well, or Henry James and the Relation of Morals to Manners', *Maule's Curse*, New York, 1938; rpt in *In Defense of Reason*, New York, 1960, pp. 300–43.

Cynthia Griffin Wolff, *A Feast of Words: The Triumph of Edith Wharton*, New York, 1977.

Readers seeking further bibliographical information on Wharton should consult Kristin O. Lauer and Margaret P. Murray, eds., *Edith Wharton: An Annotated Bibliography*, New York and London, 1990.

FURTHER READING

Louis Auchincloss, *Edith Wharton: A Woman in Her Time*, New York, 1971.

Nancy Topping Bazin, 'The Destruction of Lily Bart: Capitalism, Christianity, and Male Chauvinism', *Denver Quarterly*, 17, 1983, pp. 97–108.

Robin Beaty, 'Lilies That Fester': Sentimentality in *The House of Mirth*', *College Literature*, 16, 1987, pp. 263–75.

Millicent Bell, *Edith Wharton and Henry James: The Story of Their Friendship*, New York, 1965.

Alfred and Annette Zilversmit Bendixen, eds., *Edith Wharton: New Critical Essays*, New York, 1992.

Shari Benstock, *No Gifts From Chance: A Biography of Edith Wharton*, New York and London, 1994.

Clare Colquitt, 'Succumbing to the Literary Style: Arrested Desire in the *House of Mirth*', *Women's Studies*, 20, November 1991, pp. 154–62.

Curtis Dahl, 'Edith Wharton's *The House of Mirth*: Sermon on a Text', *Modern Fiction Studies*, 21, 1975, pp. 572–6.

Roslyn Dixon, 'Reflecting Vision in *The House of Mirth*', *Twentieth Century Literature*, 33, Summer 1987, pp. 211–22.

Gloria C. Erlich, *The Sexual Education of Edith Wharton*, Berkeley, 1992.

Judith Fetterley, 'The Temptation to Be a Beautiful Object: Double Standard and Double Bind in *The House of Mirth*', *Studies in American Fiction*, 5, 1977, pp. 199–211.

Judith Fryer, *Felicitous Space: The Imaginative Structures of Edith Wharton and Willa Cather*, Chapel Hill, 1986.

Susan Goodman, *Edith Wharton's Women: Friends and Rivals*, Hanover, N.H., 1990.

Carolyn Karcher, 'Male Vision and Female Revision in James's *The Wings of the Dove* and Wharton's *The House of Mirth*', *Women's Studies*, 10, 1984, pp. 227–44.

Joan Lidoff, 'Another Sleeping Beauty: Narcissism in *The House of Mirth*', *American Quarterly*, 32, 1980, pp. 519–39.

Lyall Powers, ed., *Henry James and Edith Wharton: Letters, 1900–1915*, New York, 1990.

Alan Price, 'The Composition of Edith Wharton's *The Age of Innocence*', *Yale University Library Gazette*, 55, July 1980, pp. 22–30.

James A. Robinson, 'Psychological Determinism in *The Age of Innocence*', *Markham Review*, 5, 1975, pp. 1–5.

Carol Wershoven, *The Female Intruder in the Novels of Edith Wharton*, Rutherford, N.J., 1982.

ACKNOWLEDGEMENTS

The editor and publishers wish to thank the following for their permission to reprint copyright material: *PMLA* (for material from 'Debasing Exchange: Edith Wharton's *The House of Mirth*'); Cambridge University Press (for material from *Edith Wharton: Matters of Mind and Spirit*).

Every effort has been made to contact the holders of any copyrights applying to the material quoted in this book. The publishers would be grateful if any such copyright holders whom they have not been able to contact, would write to them.

Stuart Hutchinson is a Senior Lecturer in English and American Literature at the University of Kent at Canterbury. He has written books on Henry James, Mark Twain and nineteenth century American literature, and edited essays on Twain and George Eliot. He is especially interested in a comparative approach to English and American literature and teaches a postgraduate course on George Eliot, Henry James and Edith Wharton. He has also edited the Icon *Critical Guide* to *Tom Sawyer* and *Huckleberry Finn*.

INDEX

THE ICON *CRITICAL GUIDES* SERIES

NEW TITLES FOR SPRING 1999

George Eliot
Middlemarch
The Mill on the Floss
Adam Bede
Edited by Lucie Armitt
ISBN 1 84046 040 7

Nathaniel Hawthorne
The Scarlet Letter
Edited by Elmer Andrews
ISBN 1 84046 041 5

Shakespeare
Hamlet
Edited by Andrew Spong
ISBN 1 84046 038 5

Elizabeth Gaskell
Mary Barton
North and South
Edited by Alison Chapman
ISBN 1 84046 037 7

T.S. Eliot
The Waste Land
Edited by Nick Selby
ISBN 1 84046 039 3

William Faulkner
The Sound and the Fury
As I Lay Dying
Edited by Nicolas Tredell
ISBN 1 84046 036 9